JUST DRIVE

Life in the Bus Lane

DEKE N. BLUE

JUST ZAKANNA PRODUCTIONS

Dedicated to my mother and father, whose loving guidance and support taught me that dreams realized are the product of skill, painstaking dedication and applied self-confidence. Also to my beloved wife, whose constant, sweet and calming presence is the gift I cherish most. This is also written for transit operators worldwide, a family I'm very proud to be part of.

Blog Readers on "Deke's" Writing

"Go to the pine if you want to learn about the pine," advised Matsuo Bashō, the great master of haiku. So, step on board, pay your fare, and let Deke N. Blue guide you into the metaphorical woods of the driver's life. The rain-slick streets, the Herculean duties, the banal and the weird – experience all of it, in the tradition of Studs Terkel, the daily life of the Deke. Read this book and see things from "the driver side," the unsung shepherd who brings us home.
— James B. Pepe, Writing Instructor

I started following From the Driver Side when my son started driving a city bus, and I was curious. It didn't take long to become a fan of Deke's writing. Through his writing I can enter my son's world and learn what he faces every day behind the wheel of a bus. Deke's style encompasses humanity, compassion and humor. His challenging my strong sense of justice reeled me in and keeps me coming back for more.
— Ellen Bryan, FTDS Reader

"Deke N. Blue's blog covers the vast terrain of being a transit bus driver, with insight and humor that comes from keeping the wheels rolling through the highs and the lows."
— Robert, author of BusTropical.org

"This story is my story, and it matters."
— Thomas Palmer

"About time someone tells it like it really is! Not a nice cushy job like most people seem to think."
— Sarah Jane Furlong

A Writer Who Drives a Bus for a Living

My office has six wheels and an incredible view. It's a 20-ton rolling mass of steel and glass. It has no conscience, but I do. As a bus operator in Portland, Oregon the past several years, I've learned how to safely guide this beast through our picturesque and historic city. Shortly after training, I decided to describe what I see, feel and hear on the job.

My blog, *From the Driver Side* is meant to give you a better understanding from "the seat." There's a common myth that "it's easy to drive around all day." Perhaps that is so if you own a luxury car and don't ferry a vast cross section of people around town. When you drive a city bus, you're entrusted with the safety of everyone within and around the vehicle. Learning how to avoid accidents is a skill we're constantly honing. Our personal safety is often threatened as well, as evidenced by increasing assaults on transit workers. *From the Driver Side* has concentrated on how it feels to do this job. As a friend of mine told me one night after a particularly tough run, some days are good, others challenge you to the core. Most of my writing poured out just after finishing a shift.

It's not a job for everyone. For every 50 people who apply, only one is hired. Of the 20 people in each training class, only about 15 make it through probation. It's usually about 10-12 who achieve vesting and retirement. Those who make it that far are often riddled with health problems, and death is sadly common soon after retirement. It is tough on body and soul. Yet surprisingly, most of us enjoy the challenge.

For all the daunting concerns bus operators face daily, there are also rewarding moments. People are surprising, and humanity offers a glimpse of hope from time to time. Bus operators are not machines. We're deeply caring, sometimes irreverent, often maligned and misunderstood. Many are heavily involved in our communities, schools and churches. We take pride in being vital cogs in the economic wheel, and we show up to work in the worst imaginable weather conditions when most of the city is shut down.

This book is a tribute to thousands of transit workers worldwide, especially my beloved local Amalgamated Transit Union (ATU) Local 757 brothers and sisters. Their wisdom and experience are invaluable to me. I have the deepest respect for all who have seen life from the seat. Hopefully these words will help you gain an understanding for what we do.

As my friend Tom Horton likes to say, we are "shepherds of public safety sacrificing daily for the common good." Every day we return the bus safely to the yard, set the parking brake and kill the engine, we've conquered many challenges. You may not recognize when a bus operator saves your life, but that's okay. It's just another day's work for us.

Before I Became a Bus Operator

The train was packed at rush hour in Portland's downtown shopping district. Standing in the crowded elbow-to-elbow aisle, the train jostled me directly into the ire of a fellow passenger, who was seated.

"You'd better get that thing outta my face," she yelled at me. I looked around, wondering who had offended her. She pointed at me. "Yeah you, Mr. Big Belly."

I'm actually a slender fellow, but genetics endowed me with a basketball belly. I hadn't felt any contact with that part of my anatomy, so I quickly checked to make sure the barn door was closed. Like any man, I sometimes forget to zip up, and I mortified to think my equipment was peeking out at this woman. Finding everything okay, I told her I was sorry.

"You sorry all right," she snorted.

Any rational person would have left it there. My apology evidently wasn't enough. This conversation was being viewed intently by my eight-year-old son, who was separated from me by about seven feet and several other riders. His grandfather kept a hand on him, because I could see the boy's face beginning to redden. He's always been a very protective lad, and this woman was picking a fight with his dad.

"Oh yeah," she continued, "I can see you're embarrassed. Uh huh. You need to keep that big belly outta my face."

"Ma'am," I countered, "I already apologized, even though we never touched."

"That thing's still in my face," she growled.

"Sorry, but I'm kinda pinned in."

This still wasn't enough. She began to berate me, seeming to enjoy my reddening face. By then, my little protector had seen enough.

"You leave my Daddy alone, mean old lady!" he shouted at her. Tears of anger stood in his eyes, his jaw was clenched and so were his fists. He was battle-ready. I made eye contact with my father-in-law, whose grip tightened on my fearless little super hero.

"Oh," she said, sitting up and enjoying herself, "I see your little boy fighting his daddy's battles, huh? Well you hush up and mind your own business little dude!"

Now my fellow passengers took notice of the middle-aged bully, who sat while elderly people stood. Rudeness is rarely ignored here, and people were quickly tiring of her game.

"Hey," one chimed in, "leave him alone. He said he was sorry, why don't you just stop?"

"And why don't you mind your own business, ugly sweater boy?" This woman enjoyed ripping into anyone who dared engage her. A chorus of others objected, but it seemed to fuel her zest.

As she turned to harass me again, my son exploded from his grandfather's grasp. He bridged the distance, fist raised, in three steps. He would have punched her square in the face, had I not caught him in mid-air.

My poor boy was sobbing with fury. He cursed the woman for attacking his father.

"He's a nice man, you old meanie!" he shouted.

Seeing my sweet son so upset, others on the train began chastising the woman who had started this mess. Rather than have my struggling son duke it out with her, we exited the next stop. As we left, she was still going at it.

"OOH, he mad, that little boy! Look at him go!" She laughed and pointed, which only made him wrestle even harder. He actually squirmed out of my arms and started back into the train, but I caught him and pulled him back.

Before the train began to move, he raced to the window where she sat and banged his fists against it. I grabbed him and picked him up, turning so he couldn't see her any more. It took a few minutes to calm him down. I was touched he felt protective of me, but sad that he was upset. Holding him tight, I reassured him we were okay. Gradually, he calmed down and relaxed in my arms, quietly sobbing into my shoulder.

Later that evening, after the boys were in bed and my wife and I sat relaxing with her parents, I wondered what makes people so combative. We were comfortable, relaxed and festive as we enjoyed the cold December evening. Perhaps, I thought, my tormentor had a rougher life than we could imagine. Maybe she was abused by a loved one. Had a close relative died over the holidays? As I remembered her worn clothing, I wondered if she even had a home waiting for her. Suddenly I felt guilty for feeling angry. While I abhor anyone taunting my children, I'd likely never see her again.

Pride can goad us into feeling entitled to retaliate when insulted. Yet I remembered the lesson of turning the other cheek, rather than returning unto others what is dealt us. I prayed that she finds happiness in what seemed to be a tortured soul.

Now I drive a bus and see a wide variety of my fellow citizens every day. Whenever there's a passenger issue, part of me remembers that incident a decade ago, and I look for peace hidden within the turmoil.

YEAR ONE

THE 'NEWBIE'

– 2013 –

🚌 **DEKE'S NOTE:** *Oh how bright-eyed and fresh I was, once upon this time! To begin, I offer a rare look at operator training. Then you'll read the first year of my posts, as I was trying to dry the spots behind my ears while learning things only experience can teach. The job was new, it was exciting, and it was fun to write about. At first, I often referred to riders as "customers," rather than what they truly are: passengers on a public conveyance. If you're a bus operator, you'll catch telltale tidbits of my naivete. If not, you'll note the surprises awaiting me and how I reacted.*

The Trainee

I rode the bus long before driving one. To school, to work and home. Waiting in the frigid winter weather with fellow passengers, it was easy to complain about the service. Then I met a friendly operator who explained many of the transit basics, and I began to understand things from his perspective.

Big Jim was beyond kind — he was a prince in uniform. Even though he suffered knee pain and had mobility issues, he was quick to smile and help me feel at ease. At the time, I was between jobs, attending college in hopes of training for a job in the medical profession. Beyond broke, even the few bucks needed for fare stretched our family's resources. While I didn't ask, Jim began refusing my fare a few days each week. He explained he knew how tough times were, and he respected my resolve. Then he surprised me by suggesting I become a bus operator. Jim patiently answered each of my questions about the profession, no matter how ignorant. Before long, we had established a friendship and enjoyed each other's company 30 minutes every weekday.

What could be easier than driving a bus? My Dad began teaching me how to drive a car when I was barely old enough to reach the pedals. Having driven tractor trailer rigs for a short time, I figured this job must be *easy*.

The hiring process itself was challenging. There were background checks, drug screens, psychological profile exams, and panel interviews. The questions were pointed and serious, and I had to prove I had not only good driving sense, but the ability to deal with a wide range of personalities. Contrary to public belief, transit employees are carefully screened. They don't let just *anybody* drive a bus.

Once I had been extended an offer, it seemed the hard part was over. Actually, the initial period was the least stressful. Training began promptly at 6:00 a.m. the following Monday. This meant I had to be up by 4:30 a.m. to shower, eat and be out the door to ensure I arrived on time. Being even one second late could spell termination. After enduring the hiring process, I was determined to persevere.

Expecting a boot camp-type experience, my classmates and I nervously greeted the trainer that first morning. Although we weren't yet acquainted, after a few days together we realized it would be a very trying four weeks. We quickly became a close-knit group, and several enduring friendships were born.

The first day, we were matched with our trainers and had our first opportunity "in the seat." We were expected to catch on fast, and watched keenly for any weakness that could disqualify us. Learning under a finely-focused microscope, it was challenging yet exhilarating. We had to learn a point-by-point inspection of the vehicles and the varying controls of each bus model. After learning how to steer around corners, we were instructed on backing. If you think you're good at parallel parking a car, try doing it in a 40-foot bus! Luckily, our initial "obstacles" were merely traffic cones. Each step of the way, our trainers patiently instructed us on how to make each task easier. By the end of the week, we were actually driving on city streets and becoming accustomed to the vehicles.

Days became weeks and soon we had to pass the tests in order to earn our Commercial Driver's License. This involved memorizing the pre-trip inspection, passing the state written exam, and proving our skills behind the wheel. Then came an even more-intense part: Line Training. Each student is placed with in-service operators on different bus routes. Students drive the routes, learning how to deal with passengers while their trainers help fine-tune their skills. It's often a very-trying experience. Line Trainers usually have many years of experience, and mine were exceptional. I'll always remember many of their lessons, and I still learn from them.

After six weeks of intensive training, scrutiny and testing, we chose "mini runs" for our first signup. We spent another week with our trainers, who helped us learn the routes we'd be driving while offering valuable advice. They reassured us that everyone has "the jitters" as beginners, but we'd learn on our own and time would pass quickly.

Then came our first day as operators. There were no trainers or fellow trainees on the bus. It was time to put knowledge learned to practical use. My first day I was nervous, yet confident. That all flew out the window when I rolled up to a stop to see an intending passenger face-down in a seizure. The poor lady's face was bouncing off the sidewalk, and I winced. A quick call for help brought the paramedics to the scene, and I continued in service. The first day was definitely the hardest, but I learned a lot in those six hours. Days became weeks, and regular training classes helped hone my skills. It wasn't long before I felt more comfortable, but daily incidents kept me from becoming over-confident. Fellow operators taught me great lessons those first few months, and my classmates offered a sounding-board for the frustrating experiences we shared.

Whenever I hear Joe Public telling us we "need more training," I shake my head. Bus operators are *constantly* in training. Not only do we receive regular recertification instruction, but each day behind the wheel increases our knowledge. Practical knowledge is learned while working, and the lessons happens behind the wheel, and the lessons of trainers or fellow operators help guide us through challenging situations. Operating a bus a few thousand miles each month, we are some of the safest drivers on the road at any given moment.

My training period was only a handful of years ago, but it seems more distant. Now I'm a Line Trainer. Much of what I share is a combination of my own experience and that of my co-workers. Road supervisors and station agents have also taught me many useful techniques.

The most important thing I've learned however, is that whenever I think, "Hey I've got this," Murphy's Law steps in and slaps me upside the head with a reality check. It's not a job for conceited people. It's rare I don't learn something new every day. One of my students recently taught me some winter driving tips he learned as a tractor-trailer operator. I've also learned how to improve my public relations skills from my passengers. Training is vital and it happens every day. The trick is to recognize, file, and recall as necessary. It also helps to write it all down, especially when you happen to be a writer who drives a bus.

The next chapter is where From the Driver Side began. I hope you enjoy the ride.

Reasons for Blogging

I began this blog to simply describe my life as a bus operator. Since there are many others more knowledgeable about this profession, I am not truly qualified to discuss union negotiations, long-term debt, the General Manager's job performance, etc. Instead, From the Driver's Side will peer into what it's like to actually do this job, the frustrations we feel on the road, the lighter (and darker) side of customer interaction, and observations "from the seat."

My goal is to inform, but also to entertain and add some thought-provoking insights into bus operation. I hope to keep it interesting and entertaining; why else does a writer write than to be read? I do hope that if you enjoy this blog, that you will tell others about it, whatever their vocation.

I have had a love affair with driving since I was 10. That was a light year ago, and in the interim I've probably driven close to a million miles. From illegally zipping down dirt roads to cruising Main Street as a 14-year-old, to hauling lettuce cross-country in a Freightliner, to ferrying people from one part of town to another in a city bus in Portland, Oregon. In the 40-plus years since I first pressed an accelerator, the most important thing Dad taught me is to expect the 'other guy' to do the stupidest thing possible, and have a plan to avoid a collision. Whether you drive a bus or a Mini Cooper, this is a valuable lesson to remember.

Many are oblivious to the most basic points of safe driving. How many of you judge your following distance of the car in front of you, or check your mirrors regularly? Can you tell at any given time what color that car in your blind spot is? Or do you see that bicyclist making his way from sidewalk to street and back again? That bus ahead of you has just dropped off some passengers, has the "Yield" sign flashing along with a turn signal. What should you do? Let her move. Oregon state law requires you to allow a transit vehicle displaying the "Yield" signal to merge back into traffic.

These things don't seem to register to many. From my vantage point, the estimate is about two in 10 are actually aware of their surroundings, and one of those is a bus operator. We're that driver you curse for taking a few seconds too long to complete the maneuver you might recklessly do quicker, if only you could zip past that… damn…bus!

If everyone would stop and think for a moment about why that driver ahead of you is taking a little more time than it "should," you might realize a few things. That bus turning left in front of you is burning up the green arrow, why doesn't it move faster? A bus is 40 feet long, and it normally takes (at 5-10 mph) about four to five seconds to clear an intersection. It is also 10-and-a-half-feet wide, and its length generates tail-swing so the driver needs to watch her mirrors very carefully to ensure you aren't passing illegally. It takes two or three lanes to safely turn a bus. Watch one turn in front of you next time. Perhaps you'll realize the driver is simply cautious. Any bus driver who makes a turn too quickly is risking trouble.

Many of the buses in our fleet are 20-plus years old, and normally do 0-30mph in about a week. Try as we might, we are no match for the mighty BMW, and it takes what might seem an inordinate amount of time to reach the speed limit. Once there, we won't maintain that speed for long, especially if there is an incline of more than three percent.

Our mechanics work miracles on these old six-wheelers, but their magic is limited. Therefore, remaining behind a bus until it stops (which it most certainly will) is the recommended method. However, if you're driving a BMW or a Mercedes or a Volvo, I've found you consider yourselves *considerably* more important than the 50 people on my bus. Is that why you blast past and cut me off just before stopping for a red light, just so I can slam on the brakes to avoid hitting your preciously-waxed *obnoxiousmobile*? When you do this, the sudden braking causes one of my passengers to bang her head on the stanchion bar in front of her, thus causing her pain and me paperwork, with possible repercussions from my manager.

Evidently, you are more productive to the local economy than those on my bus. You're unaware, or don't care, I could possibly lose my job for not predicting and reacting to these foolish maneuvers quick enough to avoid a collision.

When you flash by me with your inevitable middle-finger salute, I hope somebody else has the *cajones* to tell you off because I can't. I'm too busy. Chances are there's a Volvo right behind you with a Mercedes chaser.

Summer's Here!

🚌 **DEKE'S NOTE:** *My first summer as a bus operator was beckoning, and most of my runs involved older buses without air conditioning. Regardless, I was enjoying it.*

We had a taste of it, briefly for a few weeks. Summer weather, that is. Highs in the mid 80s, sunshine galore, a regular Vitamin-D overdose! Then our normal Northwest springtime weather returned, plunging us back down into the 50s and 60s with rain showers and the occasional "sun break."

As a desert rat who moved to the Northwest a decade ago, I had no idea what they meant by sun breaks. Our southwestern vocabulary just didn't include such a term. The only time we got a measurable "break" was when the sun set. The weathermen down there were usually so bored they made up little stories to accompany their predictable forecasts of constant sun and numbing heat. This radio newsman used "Ready for Freddy the Weather Frog" to spice up his sunny rambles, often asking the ribbit-master his opinion on the chance of any rain. Freddy was usually silent on the subject. Probably dead from heat stroke. One of my favorite TV weathermen reserved Friday nights for his patented weekend celebration of "reaching into the weather wrangler's party pocket," when he would retrieve a handful of styrofoam popcorn and toss it into the air with a comically dry "whoopee."

I find the return to a more typical weather pattern refreshing. My current afternoon route is assigned the oldest buses in the fleet, which have the old-fashioned type of air conditioning: windows down, vents open and drive as fast as you (legally) can. Since my initial uniforms were obtained during the winter months, they consist of two pairs of dark blue pants, two long-sleeved shirts and one polo. No shorts. Constant laundering is required. Panic ensues when the weathermen brag of upcoming sunny / warm days.

You see, my body is no longer accustomed to heat. I get toasty when the temperature rises above 85 and downright unhappy with anything hotter. I only visit my desert relatives in the winter or early spring, and I am finally comfortable without a jacket into the low 50s. In order to prepare for summer on a bus, I need more short sleeves, shorts and an ice water bottle. On our first day in Oregon, a nice August evening greeted us: about 63 degrees, a slight breeze, clear sky. We shivered in our desert attire of jeans and a jacket over long-sleeved shirts. Now my sons wear shorts the entire year. Only when it snows heavily and the mercury threatens sub-20s do they search for something warmer.

On the bright side, I have learned something about signing runs for the summer. I avoid the older buses in the evening, preferring them for my morning run while reserving the best air-conditioned buses for afternoon shifts.

I have enjoyed the regular passengers on my afternoon route, and I will miss them this summer. I feel empathy for them because they will sweat in the old buses while I drive those with decent AC. I will miss our conversations and their laughter as I grumble at inconsiderate motorists. It is nice to make friends in this job, and even nicer that my regulars feel comfortable enough to "friend" me online.

James Taylor's playful song, *Summer's Here* rings within me as I drive, but as it gets hotter you might hear me whistling more along the lines of Jimmy Buffet's *Margaritaville*. It's tempting to add that frozen concoction to my ice jug (to help me hang on), but my employer tends to frown upon that. Oh well, there's always the weekend.

Memorial Day – My First Holiday Run

🚌 **DEKE'S NOTE:** *Holiday work offers extra pay, and for a newbie making grub-level wages, they're vital additions to paychecks lacking that net-pay comma. To a rookie however, that extra time in the seat is a rude awakening.*

I worked a split for the holiday, and today finds me tired and a tad irritable. More seasoned drivers might think I'm a sissy, and they're probably right. But now I have an even higher regard for them, and I can accept their judgment. I've only done this for a short while, just a blink of an eye for some drivers. Evidently my body isn't quite yet accustomed to long stretches behind the wheel.

My youngest son doesn't understand how I can be tired after six hours in the seat. After all, he argues, he is in school for *seven!* What is difficult about driving a bus? First, I am not 15 with a hyperactive metabolism. Second, if I were *only* driving around town for fun, it wouldn't be as difficult. This job, however, involves a need for physical and mental endurance gained over time. As we age, this adjustment period lengthens considerably.

The position of Bus Operator consists of many duties people are not typically aware of. We arrive for work, 20-30 minutes prior to our report time. We sign in, punch transfers, read any route deviations/ detours and mentally prepare for the route. Then we walk out to our bus and do a walk-around inspection of the vehicle, checking tires, brakes, body condition, lights, wipers, bike racks, all windows and windshields, mirror adjustment and all parts of the interior. We check the doors for proper opening/closing, and make sure there are no sharp corners or other dangers that could cause injury. After a brake test and logging in to our computer system, we operate the lift to ensure it works properly. If the bus passes inspection, we then "deadhead" to the beginning of our route. During this trip, there are often customers waiting for their bus and they often mistake us for being in service. When we do not pick them up, they use very colorful language and hand gestures to indicate their displeasure.

Once our route begins, not only are we looking for intending passengers, but we are vigilantly watching pedestrians (especially "texters"), other vehicles, bicyclists, skateboarders, animals off-leash or of the wild variety, and anything else that might cross our path. If you watch a bus driver, you will see him/her turn in the seat to see around barriers that block our vision. Forward, left, right, backwards... twisting and turning to ensure the 20-ton beast (that's 40,000 pounds *empty*) doesn't come into contact with anything or anybody. My neck muscles have grown because they are constantly in motion, helping our eyes see what others may not. If you stare ahead more than five seconds without moving your eyes and head, your peripheral vision is drastically reduced. We are constantly in motion. It is similar to the actions of infants, who move so much even trained athletes don't have the endurance to mimic them.

Next consider the steering wheel. Our hands are constantly maneuvering it. The slightest turn of the wheel can mean trouble if our mind and body aren't constantly in tune. To a teen who has yet learned to drive a car, this is an entirely foreign concept. While their bodies are lean and taut, coordinated and quick, their brains haven't learned all that goes into competent driving. A professional driver's eyes, ears and body are all working together to operate the vehicle while also monitoring those within. Our feet operate accelerator, brake and turn signals in a finely-tuned rhythm. In fact, we even use our feet when we need to use the microphone for an announcement.

While operating, we cannot play music to occupy our thoughts as we wind through rush hour traffic. We concentrate on the immediate job at hand. We're employed to safely transport people (and their service animals) from Points A to Z. Customers ask questions, and I have to simultaneously watch traffic and mentally document what I see while attempting to come up with a reasonably accurate answer.

By the end of yesterday's 10 hours, I was physically and emotionally drained. In between shifts, I barely had time to get back to the garage from my road relief 20 miles distant, eat some lunch and squeeze in a 20-minute nap before I was off to my next adventure. My afternoon shift was more demanding than the route I drove in the morning. Thankfully, I safely completed the run.

As I set the parking brake and shut down my bus, I breathed a grateful sigh of relief. But I still wasn't done. Once I had turned in my pouch and put away my gloves, water bottle and seat cushion, I checked for interoffice mail and chatted with fellow drivers. Twenty minutes later, I was able to get into my car, turn on some soothing Bonnie Raitt, and cruise on home. This was exactly 14 hours after I had departed. Luckily, my driving didn't stress out any bus operators who were still on the job. At least I *hope* not.

The next time you hear people sneering at us, please remind them we work hard to keep them safe; regardless of whether they ride the bus.

🚶 RAW (READERS ALWAYS WRITE)

Al M, an established transit blogger who regularly shares my posts (http://rantingsofatrimetbusdriver.blogspot.com/), discovered FTDS around this time. After this post, he wrote "Wow. Who are you?" My response was to maintain the pseudonym. "Only the Shadow knows," I replied, in tribute to the old radio program from the early 20th century.

Why write as the Deke? Because what the transit agency doesn't know can't hurt me. I think.

The Tone of this Blog

🚌 **DEKE'S NOTE:** *When I began this blog, it was basically an explosion of many thoughts and feelings. Like Stephen King once said, if you want to write, "just start writing." Most of my posts were first-draft, written in short, feverish bursts after a hard day's work.*

Wow... thanks to a fellow blogger, my readership has expanded. Actually, it has *exploded* over the past few days! I thank Al Margulies for this, and in that tone I'd like to make a statement about this blog.

It has been said that I sound like a "newbie," one who hasn't been working long enough to become disenchanted. Yes I am, but the flavor of my blog is intentional. *From the Driver's Side* was created to describe this misunderstood profession, from newbie forward. There is some time on a run for contemplative thought, giving birth to possible bloggery. This humble posting business is merely a bit of fun. Those who have more experience and knowledge are teaching me through their own writing. There is no reason to embarrass myself trying to write what others more ably discuss. I defer to my fellows with more seniority, and I respect them.

I am not a pawn of management. I have lived long enough to know that sometimes a statue might *look* good even though it could be made of something that violates the olfactory sense. An experienced driver told me recently, *"This is the best job I've ever had, but the worst company I've ever worked for."* It gave me pause to hear this, but after a few more years I'll have my own opinion.

If I sound like a wide-eyed flower child here, at this point I am guilty. However, I will present how it feels from *my* point of view, to drive a bus and interact with my customers. Maybe someday I'll feel qualified to branch out. For now, I just want to keep all six wheels on the road.

Onward and Outward

Friday was bittersweet. I finished driving my two mini runs, and it was the end of the Spring Signup. The first one was not hard to walk away from, but the afternoon run was full of nice folks I didn't want to leave.

Becky surprised me with a box of chocolates. Dear, sweet Lady Jane, who has ridden my bus every afternoon (save for one or two days) for the past three months, gave me a young but tall tomato plant! Consider the time and effort put into these gifts for their bus operator, especially the tomato plant. Lady Jane brought it to work with her via two different buses in the morning, kept it at her desk until she left at 5 p.m., and presented it to me when I picked her up. For over 12 hours she babied that plant just so she could give it to me in appreciation for "the rides." I was truly touched.

I've been working with people my entire life. I was a journalist, and I loved interviewing people of different backgrounds. They taught me a lot about the value of being humble and honest. Several other careers found me dealing with a wide variety of folks. Nothing, however, prepared me for this daily interaction with such a diverse group of people. Driving a bus is the easy part. Knowing how to speak with a person for the first time requires sociological finesse. As people ride your bus, you can pretty much determine how they will react to jokes, basic chit-chat, or gentle teasing. Of course, it is easy to make mistakes. But when you find that one person who just "clicks" with you, it is hard to leave them behind when your signup ends.

To Becky and Lady Jane, thanks for keeping our trips light-hearted, fun and interesting. It is I who should have brought *you* gifts, not the other way around. Hopefully my next runs will produce some new friendly acquaintances, but I will always fondly remember you both!

A Philosophical Discussion

A passenger recently boarded my bus and, after a few pleasantries, immediately began a tirade on "lazy men." Being a bit grumpy, I wasn't eager to engage her in conversation. Just as I began to tune her out and started whistling the old Phil Collins tune "I Don't Care Any More," she put me on the spot.

"Do you mind if I ask you a philosophical question?" she asked.

"That depends," I replied, checking my mirrors before proceeding through an intersection. She seemed irritated that I didn't make eye contact, but my task at hand was more important.

"On what?" she asked.

"On whether you're prepared for my answer. I do not discuss religion or politics on my bus."

"Oh, it's nothing like that," she said reassuringly.

"Okay then, fire away." I wasn't sure how long she was riding, but I was two-thirds through my run. I reckoned I could try to have some fun.

Instead of asking a question however, she began a speech on how men are "inherently lazy" while women are not. While her vocabulary suggested some intelligence, she was obviously more impressed with herself than I was. After a few minutes of this sordid soliloquy, it became apparent that she truly enjoyed the sound of her own voice. Sensing her smug sense of superiority tugged at my orneriness, I decided to interrupt.

"What is your question, exactly?" I briefly glanced at her in the passenger mirror. She grimaced, like one who bumps into another who has just farted.

"Well," she stammered, "do you think that as a whole, and I don't mean everybody but on the average... not taking into account their socioeconomic background..."

I yawned. "Is this going somewhere, or are you trying to make another speech?"

"Yes," she said tartly, "and I was just getting there before you interrupted."

"Well then, if you want my opinion, ask a direct question and I'll give you a direct answer. Otherwise, you're a distraction." She sighed, and I took extra time boarding three new passengers, hoping she would get to the point before I retired.

After I had left the stop and the bus was humming along, I started whistling again in hopes she would accost another with her boorish dialogue. This time I began whistling George Thorogood's *"You Talk Too Much."* I think she missed this hint, because she dramatically cleared her throat.

"As I was saying..." she began.

"As opposed to asking?" I retorted.

"I'm getting there," she said crossly.

"OK then, shoot."

"Do you think fat men are inherently lazier than skinny men?"

The question surprised me, but I didn't let that show. *No weakness here, go for the kill*, I thought.

"Depends," I said slowly, as the bus traversed another 300 feet.

"On what?"

"Define *lazy*."

"Well," she stammered, "you know, a man who lets a woman work a job, then come home and cook his dinner, take care of the kids and clean the house. One who acts like a sloth."

"Does this man have a job too?"

"No."

"And he's fat, you say?"

"Yes."

"Does he take care of his kids?"

"We... er, I mean, *he* doesn't have any."

"Define 'fat'. I mean, I'm skinny *and* fat. I work hard and then I take a nap. My wife gets home before me and cooks dinner. Sometimes I cook. My kids clean the kitchen, then I go to bed. Does that make *me* lazy? When our kids were little, I woke up at night, changed and fed them so my wife could get some rest after watching them, cooking and cleaning all day. Does that mean I'm slothful?"

"We're not talking about *you*," she replied stiffly.

"Well," I said, inwardly grinning, "you were originally expounding upon your theory about men, and since I somewhat fit into that category, I needed some clarification as to your definition of those terms."

I could see the end of the line. I could barely suppress my evilest grin. This 'philosophical' passenger was visibly irritated. Hey, I might get a SIP out of this just for being ornery! A quick glance into my mirror showed a few male passengers with expansive waistlines listening with amusement and raised eyebrows. Lady Bigmouth was, for a blessed moment, lost for words. A few seconds later, I pulled into the bus stop.

"End of the line!" I said into the microphone, perhaps a bit too gleefully. "Thank all of you for riding and have a great evening!"

I looked in the mirror to be sure everybody de-boarded. Unfortunately, Lady B was standing just across from me.

"So," she stammered, "you didn't answer my question..."

I just smiled.

Sighing heavily, she started down the steps.

"My advice is to divorce the bum, ma'am. Have a nice evening."

As she cleared the door, I quickly shut it, but I heard her snort as she waddled out of sight: *"Bus drivers. All alike."*

As a general rule, I am kind and respectful to all my passengers. When somebody engages me in conversation, there's no telling where it might go. If they appear dangerous, I'm cautious. But if they appear haughty and act superior, I will have some fun. I am, after all, "just a *bus driver*."

Geezer in a Sun Dress

🚌 **DEKE'S NOTE:** *When you deal with such a wide spectrum of the public, you're bound to see some people who leave you scratching your head. This time my scalp almost bled.*

Just like the arrogant who loves the sound of his own voice, there are those who write just to say that they wrote something. My goal here isn't only to write, but to describe this profession.

Some drivers find a story every day, but they tend to drive the Jerry Springer runs. Now my routes are more like the Mister Rogers type.

I recently encountered a customer many other drivers have come across. An elderly gentleman, with long scraggly hair topped by a rather scarred bald spot, wrinkly skin sagging off spindly arms, bony knees attached to twiggy legs, pushing a walker. He appeared at my bus stop downtown one day, but he was wearing a pink and yellow striped mini skirt and high heels with a matching purse. I am all for being true to yourself, and I don't get uptight at guys holding hands or ladies smooching. People are as they define themselves. But I have to admit this character caught me off guard. After one passenger paid his fare and stepped back, I could see the boarding area again, this intender politely greeted me asking for the lift. I was startled when I saw him.

"Whoa!" I exclaimed a bit too loudly. Usually able to land on my feet even in the most awkward situations, I managed to pull one out of the hat again. I immediately rubbed my back and said, "Man I'm sore today! Hey, how are you? Hold on, let me extend the lift." I purposefully omitted a 'sir' or 'ma'am' because, well, I just didn't know which was appropriate. Plus, I was embarrassed and ashamed of my reaction.

He was pleasant enough, and didn't seem to notice my gaffe. It was a reminder to self, however, to not be surprised at various Portlandia characters. There's no telling how funny looking I must appear to *them*.

HIT COUNTER: 1,000 (June 2013)

Twitterpated

One sweltering afternoon this week, I came upon a lovely lady waiting for my bus. As she boarded, my heart skipped a beat as she winked at me and sat directly across from my perch.

Must be my lucky day. Just be professional, my common sense warned as my middle-aged libido awoke from its nearly-constant slumber.

I stole an occasional glance in my passenger mirror at this beauty. Long, wavy brunette hair framed a face of divine grace. The girl I had dreamed of was sharing my ride! Her very presence made it hard to concentrate. Her scent wafted through the air toward my open window, and I dreamily drank her in.

The graceful way she brushed a strand of her flowing hair away from her forehead, with a hand that could put the most ravishing rose to shame, caused a shudder of desire to course through me. Heaven could not house an equal to this exhilarating feeling I never again wanted to be without.

Unfortunately, a drunken river lizard was up front in the bus as well, regaling me with inane stories of his beer-drenched afternoon on the Clackamas River. Miss Radiance artfully ignored this cretin, meeting each of my stolen glances with an amused smirk. Finally, Bud Light exited the bus.

ALL RI-I-IIGHT! My mind roared silently. Let's see if I can win her heart!

"What's up, hot stuff," I awkwardly stammered, immediately embarrassed by my clumsiness. Surprisingly, it didn't seem to ruin my chances.

"I'm doing good, stud muffin," she replied in a sultry purr. My heart rate increased about 20 beats. Her smile was fuller now, her head tilted in a come-hither pose that sent more shivers up my now-frozen spine.

We talked about the weather, which was beginning to rival Arizona. Then we moved to dinner menus, children and friends as the bus emptied. Our views complemented one another, and where I was liberal she was only mildly conservative. A match made in heaven, I remember thinking.

Our banter had amused a few other passengers, and I was sad when we reached her stop. As I opened the door to let her out, she leaned down and left a sweet, lingering kiss on my cheek. I squeezed her arm as she left.

"Get off my bus, wench," I said in my best Jackie Gleason voice. "Only one person gets to kiss me like that!"

As I closed the door and began to pull away, she smiled, winked and blew me another kiss, which I returned.

My remaining passengers seemed both amused and confused.

"Do you know her?" one gentleman asked.

"I should," I said, smirking. "We've been married almost 19 years now."

This announcement was met with hearty chuckling and a few comments like "what a funny bus driver... I wish more of them were like this... good one, dude!"

Ah, the joys of having my beloved best friend, my cherished and delightful wife, ride with me on what otherwise would have been a boring summer day. We get a kick out of doing this from time to time. I just hope nobody called in to complain about my sexist behavior.

It Hits the Fan

It's getting a bit toasty up here this summer. The week of 90-plus degree temps has us broiling.

My buds in Arizona laugh at this, because 90 is often their low at night. But I've been up here nearly a dozen years. Anything over 85 is uncomfortable to me now. I recently bought uniform shorts to keep me cooler. They are much more comfortable, yet my Portlandish-pale legs are a hazard to other drivers.

Imagine driving around in a 40-foot long metal tube on a hot summer day without the benefit of insulation. You are surrounded by glass, which may filter ultraviolet light but does little to dissipate the heat emanating from our nearest star. I've been lucky to have buses with great AC, but still felt like I was back in the desert. Unlike my passengers, who wisely sit on the shady side of the bus, I am up front where the sun sears me from three directions. It feels like a convection oven on top of a wood stove in that seat sometimes.

One way of battling the heat is to crack open the driver's window, creating a wind tunnel. I was contentedly tooling down the road one day, having found the correct combination of window/fan/AC. As I waited for a traffic signal to change, a huge fly buzzed in through the open window. Great, I thought. With my luck, the little bastard would crawl up my nose, cause me to sneeze and play bumper boogie with Granny Cadillac, who had just cut me off.

I opened the window further and tried to chase the mother buzzer off, or at least toward the back of the bus so my clientele could deal with him. He promptly ignored this ploy and started exploring the windshield. Growling to myself, I tried to shoo him toward the inviting window and the exciting world of cars whizzing by with murderous windshields beckoning.

Harry the Fly would have to exit the way he entered, or buzz out the passenger door at a stop. But when I stopped, he took refuge on my sweaty hand, as if afraid to leave the cozy confines of the Gillig. Not wanting to harbor this terrorist, I shooed him off me. He bounced off the windshield and the little shit promptly hit the fan.

SPLSTTT-PFFTTT.

Fly guts don't taste very good. Harry was now spliced into two dozen or more pieces all over my face, hat, and shirt. Thoroughly grossed out, I grabbed a paper towel and started wiping off the offensive goo. I think his eyes were blasted onto my glasses, as if his last thought was "here's looking at you kid." I couldn't wipe them off until I came to a stop, so I focused my lenses around 10 of his. Of course, of all the times I wanted a stoplight to go red, it wouldn't. No passenger boardings, either. Luckily, I was running early. I rolled into a bus stop, pulled the brake and cleaned up.

Eew and yuck.

Deke Speaks Out

🚌 **DEKE'S NOTE:** *Our union and the transit agency were in the middle of heated contract negotiations, my first as a union member, when an article came out in the local newspaper about the talks. As I read it, I became really angry with the reporter. He seemed to take great pleasure in repeating our general manager's use of the inflammatory phrase "Cadillac benefits." It was very offensive. After refraining from union political issues up to that point, I couldn't stay silent any longer.*

Well it appears Mr. Rose nearly reported a fair story, but I wonder if his political leanings have tarnished his ability to write a balanced account of our union's ongoing contract negotiations with the transit agency.

Having read many of the responses, I'd say there is already some "union busting" going on by the public. Why should we abandon our union leadership? Because of somebody who has no idea of how to safely operate a transit vehicle thinks we're "spoiled?"

Every day, we take a majority of Portland's work force to and from their jobs. We transport people who are too impaired to drive themselves, therefore saving many lives. We subject ourselves to violent attacks on our persons, simply by doing our duty. Transit operators face more chances of getting sick or injured than most (excluding military, cops and firefighters) occupations. This silly notion that we have a "Cadillac" health plan is an insult to anybody who has spent years in the seat of a 20-ton, 30- or 40-foot-long vehicle. It is much more stressful to the body than driving a luxurious SUV straddling two lanes of traffic while you talk on the phone, blithely ignoring many traffic laws and putting the 30-70 people on my bus at risk.

In the desperate-not-to-lose-readership press these days, we often see articles portraying mostly the negative side of our profession. How often do we see articles on 'A Day in the Life' of a driver? Where are the stories about the good things we do for the public on an hourly basis? The ratio of bad to good is pitifully skewed to the negative.

We balance unreasonable operating procedures from upper management with the safety of the public. Transit drivers require a mind that is quick to decide issues that could ultimately affect many lives. The stress we endure affords us the right to expect our health care to be provided at little or no cost. The toll on our bodies is personally expensive. I don't feel guilty that my insurance costs less now than in my previous professions, because my current job has a profoundly negative affect on my long-term health.

As management begs to win public opinion, our union fights for the best possible contract. We rely on the union's negotiating skills to force management to pay its frontline workers top dollar. Why would we abandon it to put ourselves at the agency's mercy while the general manager gets free healthcare for life when he retires?

Have any of you anti-operators ridden a bus, light rail, trolley or tram lately? I'll bet this experience was a positive one. If you haven't exercised your option to use public transportation, then your credibility in this discussion is severely diminished.

Those of you who have used Portland's public transit, do you remember the last positive article in *The Oregonian* about transit operators? This publication seems heavily-weighted toward management rather than taking the traditionally-neutral view expected from journalists and their editors.

There is room for intelligent debate. Unfortunately, one side has an unfair media advantage and relies on propaganda to sway public opinion. From where I sit, ATU 757 is the 'good guy' here, and I am thankful it is negotiating on our behalf.

Without unions, the working man is lost. Those of you who doubt this must forget it was union blood that secured weekends, holidays, overtime pay and countless other rights you still enjoy. Big money interests have been intent on destroying unions and portraying us as 'thugs' for several decades. What positive results could come from the death of unions? Plenty for the powers that be, and a return to the horrific conditions facing workers at the beginning of the Industrial Revolution. While no union is perfect, they are obviously more concerned for workers' rights and conditions than those with whom they negotiate.

If you side with anyone, do it from a position of knowledge and intelligence. If you cannot, please stay out of the discussion because you are part of the problem.

OUCH!

🚌 **DEKE'S NOTE:** *My first on-the-job injury was somewhat an embarrassment. I thought my Mama taught me better!*

It's easier to type now my finger has healed. When you're accustomed to typing as you write, the "hunt & peck" method can be frustrating. I decided to let it heal sufficiently before chronicling this latest adventure.

I will use any means available to remain cool on a hot day. One of our few amenities is a fan, mounted in the left corner directly in front of the operator's seat. They are in various states of disrepair, depending on the age of the bus. This particular demon fan had a defect I didn't discover until it disfigured, or nearly *disfingered*, me.

Each fan has a protective cage around the blades. Some are plastic, but this one was metal. I didn't realize this particular cage was bent on the bottom, just enough for a finger to slip through. On low speed, the metal blades rotate at about a few trillion rpm's. This fan had an annoying habit of nodding downward with each bump, requiring frequent adjustment. I prefer a breeze on my face and chest rather than on my nether regions. I was trying to point it upward, when...

TTHHHZZZZWWWWAAAAPPPPP!!!

In the blink of an eye, my left birdy fingertip became pulp. As would happen when touching a hot stove top, the pain reflex instantly pulled my finger back. Yet in that brief moment, the blood had already erupted, and one quick peek revealed a serious wound. Although the fan blades only managed to damage an area the size of a thumbtack head, they had chewed it into hamburger. There are many tactile nerves located in the fingertips.

Numbing shock lasted just long enough to wrap it in a paper towel. Then the throbbing pain began. It intensified with each heartbeat. I had never felt my heartbeat in my fingers before, but now this damaged digit was loudly trumpeting each thump.

I somehow completed a left turn using my one good hand. I didn't want to sit in the turn lane blocking traffic while I figured out what to do. I pulled up to the nearest bus stop and called Dispatch.

"What's up?" the nice lady asked.

"Uhh, huh huh huh," I began, sounding like Butthead the clueless cartoon character. "I cut my finger on the fan and I'm bleeding all over the driver's seat."

"Oh, that's not good. Are you stopped?"

"I am now."

"How did that happen?" she asked, now sounding concerned.

As briefly as possible, I described the incident. It was embarrassing to admit I had stuck my finger into a place it didn't belong. I didn't think it was safe for me to be ferrying passengers one-handed the rest of the afternoon. It had begun to hurt, and my concentration was severely diminished. I couldn't remember the date of my last tetanus booster.

"I'm sending medical to your location," she assured me. "Just secure your bus and wait there."

A few minutes later, sirens announcing their arrival, the paramedics came to the rescue. Sizing up my finger, I could see they were skeptical.

"How bad is it?" one of them asked.

"See for yourself," I replied, ripping off the paper towel to show off my injury. Only problem was, the blood had dried on the towel by then. Pulling it off renewed the flow of blood and exponentially increased the pain. The paramedic looked at it carefully, prodding the now-agonizing wound with great interest.

"No damage to the bone or anything but tissue," he said. "You got lucky."

He wrapped it in a tight bandage. I thanked them profusely, apologizing for bringing them out there for a mere laceration. They were very kind, but advised me to see a doctor soon.

My passengers were less sympathetic. I returned to the seat, sheepishly holding up my finger. I was careful, though, not to isolate it from the others, as that could have been misconstrued as an obscene gesture. However, the attitude displayed by my passengers would have warranted a *double* bird, I soon found out.

"Nice," a lad of about 20 said. "Now I'm going to miss my connection at the transit center. Can I have a day pass for the inconvenience?"

"How late are we now?" a girl next to him whined.

Not one "how are you?" was offered. I drove the rest of the way to the transit center grimacing in pain and seething in anger. Upon arriving, I thrust a day pass upon the inconsiderate dunce and walked outside to see the supervisor, only to be approached by intending passengers.

"Does this bus go to..." one lady asked. A small crowd formed around her, awaiting my answer.

"Not today," I replied, holding up my heavily-bandaged finger. "I'm sorry but my bus is out-of-service and you'll have to catch a different one."

The supervisor pulled me aside and asked how I was doing. His kind words were greatly appreciated.

"I'm sorry that happened," he said. "Do you want to finish your route, or are you done for the day?"

"Thank you," I replied, truly grateful for his kindness. "But I really think I need to see a doctor. This is a serious wound and it wouldn't be safe for me to continue in-service."

He nodded sympathetically, and herded my passengers to other buses. Most of them just shook their heads at me and rolled their eyes. I had inconvenienced them by being injured, and they were pissed. At this point, I truly didn't care if we stopped all buses and chased the passengers off with bullwhips. I invoked the fleas of a thousand camels to infest their underwear. I was beyond furious with their callous indifference to my injury. However, fools will be fools. I climbed back into the seat and managed to guide the beast safely back to the garage.

The doctor poked and prodded the wound, much to my painful dismay. I finally pulled my hand away from him.

"That hurts enough, you know," I snarled, "*without* your probing."

He sighed and pulled off his now-bloody gloves. The wound wasn't gushing, but was again profusely dripping.

"Nothing there to stitch," he said. "It's pretty torn up. We'll just clean and bandage it, then you'll be on your way."

"Thanks, Doc," I growled.

"Want something for pain?" he asked. He seemed to be mocking me, as if my petty little finger laceration was not worth his time. "Want some Percoset?"

"No thanks Doc," I replied. "I can't drive on narcotics and this lil' chop-job doesn't qualify for the heavy stuff. But I would kill for some Tylenol about now."

Luckily, the nurses were considerably gentler with my finger. They pumped ibuprofen and acetaminophen into me and cleaned the wound. After a few minutes, I was neatly bandaged and the painkillers were working. Somewhat.

My co-workers were kind, mainly ribbing me about putting my finger *there*. It was humiliating, and the report writing took up over an hour of time. Lesson learned: check the fan cage during my pre-trip inspection, preferably *prior* to turning the fan on.

Fast forward 23 days, and I am typing again. The wound was ugly for a couple of weeks, but fresh scar tissue has replaced the unsightly scab. The tip is a bit numb, and still smarts a bit when I bang it on something.

My regular passengers were more sympathetic the following day, and after a few days I was once again a cheerful bus operator.

But Mr. Inconvenience better not ride my bus again for a while. He'll get charged double.

Slow Down!

🚌 **DEKE'S NOTE:** *I just love having kids on my bus. Their general silliness and laughter break up what can be a largely dull, quiet ride. This post reminds me of my dad's timeless lesson: when you drive with passengers, do so with their ultimate comfort in mind.*

Sometimes you'll hear a passenger comment on your driving, but usually not if you're consistently careful and smooth. A few days before the finger mauling, I picked up two sweet kids with special needs, along with their adult companions.

I was cruising along enjoying a beautiful summer day, and the kids were very animated. Having a younger brother with Down's Syndrome, I am accustomed to the antics of kids with cognitive challenges. As I approached a curve in the road, I slowed to below the recommended 15mph. As I reached the apex of the curve, I accelerated into it. Apparently, one of my special passengers stood up immediately prior to this maneuver and lost her balance, but luckily did not fall. Directly behind me, in the cutest "how sweet" little kid's voice, my affected passenger reacted.

"Slow down, *asshole!*"

I choked down spasms of laughter as the adults chastised the girl. In fact, I chuckled the rest of my shift over that one.

As they exited the bus, the adults apologized profusely for the comment and insisted the kids thank me for the ride. I apologized for taking the turn perhaps a mile- or two an hour faster than necessary. I should have added a 'thank you' for the entertainment, but chose not to make light of the situation.

Now as I approach this curve, I say to myself, "Slow down, *asshole!*" And then I smile in remembrance.

Painful Full-Time Blues

🚌 **DEKE'S NOTE:** *Not quite a year into my job, I was promoted to full-time. It's quite a transition, but I just shifted gears and let 'er rip. A part-time operator has fewer challenges. They mostly drive during peak commuting hours. Full-timers deal with the full spectrum of passengers. Learning how to balance safe driving with knowing when or how to referee certain situations is something learned only through experience. This is a glimpse of my continuing education.*

It's been three weeks since I became a full-time bus operator. What an awakening! This post will likely jump around disjointedly, rather than arriving at a predetermined destination. I beg exhaustion as an excuse.

Always a lover of challenge and change, this one is probably one of the toughest of my life. Sitting in that seat for eight-plus hours a day requires extreme endurance. Dealing with a public as diverse as Portlanders can be fascinating one moment and terrifying the next, boring one moment and then highly intense. By the end of a day, my mind is a jumbled mess, my neck and big toe hurt, and most disconcerting of all, I am extremely grumpy.

When transporting the inebriated rider, it is imperative I remember this service is possibly saving lives. If they decide to *drive* rather than *ride*, someone could be injured or killed as a result. It is my duty to transport everybody *safely* to their destination. When I forget this, their behavior irritates me. Lately, drunkards have been constantly testing my patience. One walked into the street in front of my bus because he thought I wasn't going to stop. When I told him that action wasn't his best option, I was lectured on minding my own business.

"Excuse me sir," I growled, "but the difference of you being *in* my bus rather than *splattered all over it* is definitely my *business*."

I gave him the choice of riding or waiting for the next bus, and he became a bit testy. My icily reminding him I was the Captain of the ship he intended to ride annoyed him even more. What did I learn? Don't be a mean bus driver, but also don't let a drunk push you around. He rode quietly, unlike the drunk I had boarded a few minutes earlier. This particular rummy suddenly decided to repeat the word "asshole." Each time, he used a louder, more insistent tone until he was bellowing. Since there were children and sweet old ladies on the bus, I informed him his stop had magically appeared. He was none the wiser, and my bus once again became a peaceful ride. Except for the sweet old lady sitting in the front, who muttered upon his exit, just loud enough for me to hear, "what a fucking jerk, that one."

One thing I detest on the streets are those inhuman, incapable of rational human thought, red light cameras in Beaverton. Last weekend I made a mistake in judgment as I was nearing the end of my run. I pulled up to a stop and the people waiting there were escaping a sudden rain shower. As I pulled away from the stop, the light changed to yellow. I was past already past the crosswalk. My lumbering bus hit the middle of the intersection as the light went red, and POP POP snapped one of those damn cameras.

I had two choices: stop in the middle of the intersection or keep rolling; I didn't stop. My abbreviated tenure as a driver flashed before my eyes. It is a major NO-NO to "run" a red light. This is something we are taught early and often, and we take it seriously. In other parts of town, the city engineers have kindly provided crosswalk timers to inform people just how much time is left before the light changes. Not so on the west side. They're either "Walk" or "Don't Walk" and there is no rhyme or reason when they change. Not to mention they tend to stay red for unnecessarily long stretches. Break time beckons, the belly is aching for nourishment, the butt is begging for a stretch out of the seat. If you allow these distractions to win over common sense, you're a trouble magnet.

I was furious the rest of the trip. My driving record has been flawless for 25 years. Hopefully the traffic techs monitoring the west side take pity on a driver just doing his job.

Anniversaries and Notables

Veterans told me my life would change drastically once I started driving a bus full time. They weren't kidding.

If I'm not working then I'm sleeping, waking up, eating and heading back to the garage. Two days on one route, then something different, back to the original one, and for my Friday (actually on Monday), a split shift. My mind has to reboot each day I get behind the wheel. Some routes are so similar I have to remember which turns to make. By the end of the week, I'm very droopy and ready for some serious pillow time.

It's taken weeks to get accustomed to this twisted schedule. I've been telling myself I need more material for a blog entry, that I refuse to *write just to write*. But it's just a lame excuse, a bit of literary laziness. I promised to chronicle my travels, and for the past several weeks I haven't kept up my end. Save for my self-indulgent mourning of Linda Ronstadt's lost voice, I've been slacking.

I recently earned my one year safe driving bling, which I proudly wear on my sweater collar. While I steadily refuse to wear a name tag, I *earned* this pin. It has been a hard year. There is much to learn about ferrying Portlanders around in a 20-ton vehicle. It is a major commitment and incredibly stressful.

A local radio talk show host who is syndicated nationally, once said bus operators are "overpaid." He has no idea what transit operators do. Prior to taking this job, I didn't think it would be too hard. Hey, all we have to do is *drive a bus*, right? I once drove a big rig, no big deal. Well, driving a semi is easier because the cargo doesn't talk back, stab, bite, punch, or spit on you. All he has to do is flap his lips and breathe sounds into a microphone. His arguments on this subject lack merit and are clearly not based on fact. He can use his bully pulpit without fear of immediate and/or violent feedback. He can simply hang up on an abusive caller. When I am operating a bus, my audience is just a foot away from the driver's seat. They are truly a *live* audience and can be *very* unforgiving.

There are many inconsistencies in the transit profession. Customers expect us to be on schedule. Our agency expects us to drive safely. These conflicting expectations create potentially dangerous bedfellows. If we drive the schedule, safety slides. If we drive safely, schedule suffers. If we fall behind, we lose our recovery time at the end of a run. The loss of a break adds fatigue and stiffness to the mix. Sitting in a bus driver's seat for hours at a stretch is grueling, especially if you didn't get a break on the previous trip.

You know how it feels on a road trip when you drive so long you can barely walk when you stop for gas? Imagine driving your car about 500 miles a day. Then imagine stopping regularly to let passengers in or out. Not only would you be on the road about 12 hours, but you'd feel pretty ornery by the end. I drive a bus an average of 100 miles every day. One of my runs is about 25 miles one way, and I do one round trip and a half. The last leg is a 30-mile deadhead back to the garage. My 100 miles of bus driving easily equals 500 miles driving a car.

Another mind-boggling fact is that we are expected to be *perfect*. One day I counted 92 intersections with traffic lights in one direction on my longest route. I stop and start the bus about 750 times every day. Today 320 people rode my bus. This is anything but easy, Sir. It is damn stressful. On my route I am expected to accurately predict each of 275 traffic light cycles. On average, I will traverse roughly 1,250 intersections every week. Each instance requires me not to run a stale green, yellow or (God forbid) "pink" light. If I do run even just two red lights in a certain period of time, I can lose my job. Do the math: 1,250x4x12=60,000 per year, right? If I run two reds out of 60,000, it's bye-bye job! Even one in just 30,000 means I'm sweating for a couple of years until my slate is clean again. I don't know about you, but to me those are extremely daunting odds to beat for "all the money" I get paid. Makes me almost as nervous as this radio personality would be facing a panel of intellectuals.

About three percent are truly challenging passengers, and some of those are downright dangerous. In training, we learned 90% or more of all arguments begin at the fare box. I recently asked a passenger to please have his fare ready when boarding, as a sign on each bus clearly states. It saves valuable time, I explained. This rider took offense to my request, and began berating me for "rushing" him. Pointing out that he had plenty of time prior to my arrival to gather his fare only fueled his ire. Other passengers tried to calm him, but he berated them too. I asked (as the steam rose from the back of my collar) for some common courtesy. His tirade continued; he used language overly punctuated with obscenity. I finally decided this passenger was a dangerous distraction to my normally mellow ride. I pulled over at the next stop and suggested he have his fare ready to show the next driver. He left, with an extended middle finger as a parting gift.

Another figuring prominently in the Three Percent Club is the guy who insisted I let him out in the middle of an intersection. He wanted to catch a connecting bus. I was in the left-turn lane, preparing to turn onto a very busy street. I was apparently an "asshole" because I wouldn't allow him to dash across three lanes of rush hour traffic.

There are also those who race toward my bus in the traffic lane, waving their arms as if they were cheated out of a functioning brain. When this happens, a bus driver is on high-alert and in super pissed-off mode. He or she is likely to wave you out of the road, and then pass right on by. Management believes we should let these people on, but it's a dangerous precedent. If other riders see you accommodate such foolishness, they're apt to try it themselves. There's an unwritten rule among many operators which states: If you're crazy enough to run toward a rolling 20-ton vehicle, you're too stupid to ride in it.

☥ RAW

Anonymous wrote this note.

Hey D:
    Nice job on the essay.
    I read these (and look forward to seeing them BTW) trying to remind myself that I was once, many moons ago, that new and that fresh to the transit world. Lars is an idiot. Let's talk overpaid. Don't worry about legions of followers. You gain more as you post more... just keep posting. Al had to start somewhere-his followers didn't come from the blogger fairy. Lol. Hell, I'd do it if I had time, but it's more fun to me to voice my opinion like this.

And then Gilberto chimed in:
    There's this poster in my work place, conspicuously placed to remind us....
    "To meet the needs of the public for the highest-quality transit service: Safe, Reliable, Efficient and Courteous" to which I wholeheartedly agree except they (management) fail to realize the delicate balance you so eloquently expressed. I wish I could make copies of your post and put them up in the bulletin board next to the mission statement. This is exactly how I feel, and I've been doing this job now for two years. I'm gonna frame this. This is golden!

A Winter Holiday Arrives

🚌 **DEKE'S NOTE:** *After a tumultuous first year of driving a bus, I was feeling pretty sentimental as Christmas neared.*

Another Christmas upon us, I wish you all a wonderful holiday season... however you celebrate it.

We humans come in all shapes, colors, sizes and flavors. But when you peel back the epidermis, we're biologically identical. Too often we put people into categories, yet when we step back and look at our choices, most of us can make a few changes of our own. I constantly evaluate/upgrade my values and strive to be a better person. Sometimes I fail, and I feel bad. However, I understand that to grow we must learn from our mistakes.

Certain holiday tunes make me a tad misty-eyed. As we grow older, the memories both sweet and sour fill our minds this time of year. The present lasts a heartbeat, while the past grows ever long. Taking the time to let our loved ones know we cherish having them near becomes more important each day.

Thank you for reading my ramblings. I appreciate your being unique individuals, for truly caring about what you say and do, and for forgiving us humble bus drivers our imperfections.

Peace be with you all.

With love,

Deke

Happy Old Year

A year of firsts, come and gone. First full-time work in nearly four years. First year of safe driving (a bus) under my belt. First year of blogging. First nearly-naked man riding my bus. First time sticking my finger into a running fan and still being able to type. Yes, it has been a weird, but good, 2013.

Driving the Extra Board has not left me extra bored. Of the 80 or so runs we have in our district, I've now driven 25. Not a particularly impressive number, but that's only one year's worth. Having the luxury of a day off on Christmas Eve and the grand day itself, I've had plenty of time to reminisce. As usual I wonder how a year could have ticked off so quickly. I'm not nervous at the wheel like I was last December, but even more vigilant. I'm very concerned with safety, striving constantly to improve. I'm learning when to say something and when to zip it shut. My temper is not as hot lately, but I'm still highly annoyed at the blatant disrespect bus drivers are constantly exposed to.

We are held to a higher standard than the average driver, and that's a good thing. When you're negotiating tight city streets in 20-tons of steel and glass, you need to be vigilant. People today are so engrossed in their electronic gadgets they don't pay attention to their own safety. Walking while texting, driving while phoning, riding a bike wearing headphones; these are just a few of the dangers a bus operator has to negotiate. People think of me as "just a bus driver." They don't realize all that entails. Behind the wheel, I'm responsible not only for the safety of my passengers, but also for those *around* my bus.

In one year, I've safely traversed nearly 60,000 traffic signals. The average driver will encounter perhaps a tenth of that. While I'm not exactly sure of my accuracy, I've probably ferried 30,000+ people to their destinations. Only one has fallen while boarding, and she bounced up uninjured, being the young filly she was. One bicyclist foolishly tried to negotiate the narrow space between my bus and the curb, and failed miserably. As a result, I have become even more careful when bicyclists are near. Only a few people have called me "asshole" or worse, and I can live with that because I was only doing my job ensuring their own ignorance didn't kill them.

Mostly, it's been a great first year. From being a tentative and nervous trainee to a full-time operator, I've learned volumes not only about driving, but also human nature. The gentleman who trained me is brilliant, and I recall his words of wisdom on a nearly daily basis. His patience and passion for the job are something I try to emulate. Other trainers are also helpful, and I am deeply grateful for their dedication. My fellow bus operators are amazingly deep wells of information, and they teach me little tricks all the time.

This isn't an easy job, but it's an honorable profession. My hopes for the next year center around management accepting that we are valuable, trusted civil servants who deserve to be treated with respect. Without us, they'd be employed elsewhere. I hope the contract negotiations evolve from insulting to gratifying, and I trust our union will continue to have our backs.

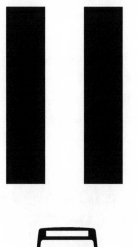

YEAR TWO

BUTT LEATHER

– 2014 –

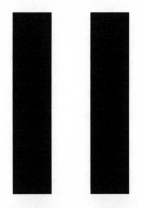

🚍 **DEKE'S NOTE:** *As I began my second year, a few months of full-time driving found me grumpy at times, but I was still enjoying the job. My posts ranged from mundane to fun to angry to sometimes confused. Some posts rambled on and on (edited for brevity here), but showed promise.*

Since it had been several years since I wrote regularly, my tools were rusty. People who know me best can attest to my dislike of poor grammar and spelling. I began editing, striking out 10 words and replacing them with three or four. Then I wrote a post about the mantra I say each day before driving (which I still recite), and the brevity took a brief vacation. In fact, my 10-item mantra took three posts to cover!

I was feeling more comfortable behind the wheel. Interactions with passengers were intriguing. Winter weather set in and I learned about driving in icy conditions. My writing was improving, and I wrote some hard-hitting posts. Finding more creative things to write about, I really began to enjoy the entertaining aspects of the job. I learned more of Portland's history. Driving the extra board generated a wealth of post ideas, and fellow drivers not only started taking notice of my work but also offering suggestions. I created a FaceBook page to keep the Deke's identity a thinly veiled secret and joined some operator groups around the country. Soon I was posting blog entries on about 5-10 different group pages and readership exploded.

The extra board allowed me to drive many different runs, and I quickly learned which ones were not ideally suited to my temperament. As I stretched my literary muscles, posts came pouring out an average of once or twice a week. Fellow operators often told me how much a certain post "nailed" how they felt about the same thing, and my confidence grew. The toughest posts brought more readers, but also more scrutiny and criticism.

A Few Clips

As I pulled into a transit center, I saw a gentleman pushing a large flat screen TV toward the boarding platform. The bus in front of me refused him service, so he proceeded toward my bus. The monstrous set was on a large cabinet, making the entire ensemble about five feet tall and at least as wide, about two feet deep.

"Sorry sir," I managed to say without laughing, "this is not a moving van. That is too big to transport on a city bus. It's not safe." His shoulders sagged. It was NFL playoff weekend, and he seemed desperate to get this purchase to his living room.

One passenger in the back exploded into gleeful laughter. "Never seen that before in all my years riding a bus!" he said. "Dude wanted to bring that big screen TV on! You guys see that?" His laughter was contagious. As I closed the door and prepared to leave the stop, I had to turn my head so the dejected fellow wouldn't see me smiling.

"Hey driver," the passenger shouted as we left, "let that dude on! I wanna watch some football!" I responded with a big smile in my passenger mirror. He told everyone who boarded about it. He was more entertaining than the guy with the TV. We passed the next 10 minutes joking about amenities that would be nice on a city bus. Music would be a great addition. Phone chargers would be nice.

I avoided working Christmas because it's my regular day off. I enjoyed time with the family, cooked a marvelous prime rib with a ham, garlic mashed potatoes and all the extras. Since I'm of the age where New Year's Day is just another flip of the calendar page, I decided to work it. Normally, a holiday like this is a piece of cake, but the line I was driving was busy. It helps if you choose your own holiday work, but I forgot to go to the signup and this run was assigned to me. It was a line I've done many times before, but never have I been so busy on a holiday! Oh well, at least the drunkards were home in bed nursing hangovers, because everyone was pleasant.

Now the calendar is flipped, it's time to take this gargantuan tree down, along with the lights outside. Sigh. I hate this part!

Winter Sunshine

For over a month now I've been an extra-board operator. This means I am available to do any run necessary. Each day is different. I chose this work because it gets a bit tedious driving the same route every day. If a job becomes boring, you can become complacent. I've learned that complacency doesn't beget excellence. I relish a challenge.

I truly enjoy the variety of runs. I've now driven 35 of them. Some are less desirable than others and I tend to get them frequently. Weekdays find me on commuter runs, ferrying the working people to their daily grind. These passengers are mostly courteous, fare-ready professionals. I take them to work in the morning, then have a break until mid-afternoon when I take them home. Students are amusing in the morning because they are grumpy, but they are quite lively in the afternoon.

Weekends tend to be busier than weekdays due to recent atmospheric anomalies. Lately our weather in the Northwest has been simply beautiful, and people want to enjoy it. I keep waiting for the hammer to fall because we normally don't see the sun this time of year. We've had only a third of the rainfall we normally do. Usually in winter, constant rain will sometimes give way to what weathermen here call "sun breaks," but lately we've had so much sun my roses think it's springtime. Buses are busy on sunny weekends. When the rain hits, people tend to hibernate more and bus less. At least the sunshine makes for mostly happy people, which is rare this time of year.

Yesterday presented an interesting exchange. A young man who had just been released from jail boarded my bus. Even though he was a quarter short, I gave him a transfer. Nothing is free in life but if people at least contribute something I give them a break. Times are hard. He was also very polite, which is a bonus. A few minutes later, he informed me he had found a bag somebody left behind with prescription drugs inside. He wanted to keep it and call the person who left it to inform her.

"Let me see," I said slowly, crafting my next sentence carefully. "You were just released from jail, right?"

"Yes, sir," he replied.

"Tell me what happens if you are caught with someone else's prescription narcotics?"

He paused, his expression thoughtful. "I go back to jail," he said. "I don't want that."

"Okay," I said. "First of all, anything left behind on this bus is *my* responsibility, so please give me that bag. I will turn it into Lost and Found. Let me do my job. That passenger gets her medicine back legally, and you remain out of jail. You see, if you keep it, then you are technically breaking the law. If I keep it, I'm simply doing my job. Make sense?"

"Yeah man, cool."

Later I opened the bag to inspect its contents and found a few prescriptions for a person who evidently has epilepsy. I called Dispatch and explained the situation, in case the person who lost it realized the bag was on the bus. I was worried they might desperately need the lost medicine.

We're often presented with situations that require careful thought and deliberation. I hope the person who lost it has already been reunited with their medicine. And, I'm glad the young man realized the possible implications of his proposed actions.

There is some down time on the Extra Board, which helps the aching back and posterior aspect. This gives my mind a chance to think beyond the scope of bus operation. I originally thought I'd have more time to write, but I've spent more time driving than sitting around the bullpen.

People constantly using their cell phones or tablets while walking risk their own safety. While I am very grateful to have a Santa who brought me this fancy Samsung gadget, I don't feel married to it. Folks on the street and on the bus however, are plugged in and tuned out. If you make an announcement, many don't hear it. They get angry because they didn't get the message. Am I supposed to text them from the driver's seat? Those who are not tuned out tend to be more amiable and engaged with their driver and fellow riders. This tends to include people of my generation and older folks. I fondly recall when telephones were on the wall in the kitchen, not permanently attached to our hands. Many people of my generation use a cell phone only when necessary, yet still remain engaged with our surroundings. What a concept.

Yesterday a passenger was telling me about a pedestrian accident he witnessed a few weeks ago. The pedestrian had the green walk signal, but was busily texting away, not paying attention. As he watched her crossing the very busy six-lane road, somebody ran a red light and SMACK! I hope and pray this person survived, but what a price to pay for being hypnotized by an electronic gadget. I remember getting in trouble 20 years ago when I refused to answer a mobile phone while driving a company truck. It was a distraction then, even more so today. It's troubling how electronics have become a danger more than a convenience.

What text message is more important than your life? Many of us are sometimes guilty of texting while walking, but when you cross a street it's vital to watch for that impatient red-light runner. Bus operators live with the fear that somebody will step out in front of our moving 20-ton monster without seeing it. Luckily, we see them and predict their actions. I hope and pray to always be alert enough to make up for those who are not.

The Blizzard of 2014

🚌 **DEKE'S NOTE:** *February brought a brutal winter storm to Portland. Three days of constant heavy snow, immediately followed by a few inches of ice, made travel treacherous for almost a week. Driving conditions aside, this former desert rat was severely tested during the icy episode.*

If I see another snowflake this winter, I'm gonna blowtorch the bastard. After five days of driving in this wretched storm, my body felt like it had gone 10 rounds with Muhammad Ali.

First, the good part. Your local bus operators are well-trained in how to drive a bus under normal conditions. The rest comes from experience. Those who have stepped up into supervisory positions *know* what we're going through out there, and they busted their butts to help us. Many of the "white shirts" were out from early morning to late at night throughout the storm. Trainers with shovels and kitty litter rescued stuck buses. Our union leaders ferried stranded drivers to restrooms, brought coffee and food to them too. Maintenance crews tirelessly chained hundreds of buses, fixed broken chains and repaired other issues on the road. Dispatchers and Station Agents patiently answered questions and guided us through re-routes. As a new driver, I am thankful for all of them. I'm also very appreciative of the many pointers veterans gave me along the way. Without all their help, this marathon stretch would have been 10 times more stressful than it was. When times are hard, we come together.

A great majority of our riders are gracious and transit-savvy. Only a few are whiny. I was thanked many times for safely maneuvering the sloppy streets to get people where they needed to be. Residents along bus lines brought food and hot coffee to stranded drivers. On my breaks, people walking by would stop and thank me for working in such harsh conditions. Many patted me on the shoulder on the way out the door telling me "great job, driver, thank you!" It was inspirational. They were extremely patient, kind, and thoughtful. Only once did I have to remind a rider who was in charge. He quickly backed off and let me do my job in peace. One ornery rider out of a few thousand? I wish people were always so understanding and supportive.

As operators congregated at the garage, we shared stories from the road. One told me about a passenger who left his marijuana stash on board. He was evidently too stoned to remember his pot, but the operator duly bagged and tagged it for Lost and Found. Another driver was alerted by his passengers about a man struggling to get to the bus stop in his manual wheelchair. The driver pulled over, deployed his ramp, ran out into the raging snow and pushed the man into the bus. As soon as he pulled away, the man rang for the very next stop, a block away. Other drivers picked people up between stops because they were desperately slipping and sliding in their haste to catch the bus.

Having never driven a bus in snow and ice, I was on edge all five days. Had I not been vigilant and deliberate, I could have been stuck on the side of the road. For instance, I was turning into a transit center when I noticed a bus sideways at the intersection just past the stop. I stopped and thought how long I might have to wait if I pulled in behind it. I informed the disembarking passengers we were going to Plan B and detoured around this mess. Later, I sat waiting at the bottom of a hill where another bus had been previously stuck, until the light turned green at the top. After a few stressful slips, I fish-tailed that sucker through the intersection and made the left turn without getting stuck. My riders applauded! That was nice. Thinking from the seat helps you avoid tricky situations. This constant state of alertness, however, is exhausting.

There is some bad to go with the good and ugly. One pedestrian tried to push a bus that was attempting to climb an incline at an intersection. Four of us were stuck there for about 90 minutes because we couldn't move. It was blowing snow, the bus was slipping toward a parked car, and this idiot thought he could push 40,000 pounds of glass and steel up a slope. I honked and waved him away, at which he angrily motioned for me to push the bus with my own! As if A) I would do such a stupid thing; and B) it would do any good since the both of us had no chains on our buses?

A local radio station posted a photo of some high school students pushing a bus from behind in a snowstorm. The caption praised the kids for their selfless and commendable behavior. One bus driver observed how utterly stupid it was of them. Picture this: sweet kids trying to help, one or more slips and falls, bus slips backwards and runs over them. Word of advice: stay the hell away from a stuck bus or one you can see trying to free itself from icy bonds. Better yet: *never* touch a bus except from the inside of one.

Idling for 90 minutes was actually a nice break, but it was a waste of resources to have so many unchained buses out of service. After we were freed from our icy prison, we were instructed to go get chained, which took another 90 minutes because there were only two maintenance workers chaining at that location.

Even though a "major snow event" happens only about once every five years, where are the snowplows when needed? I understand the interstate highways take top priority, but the major transit routes should have been plowed after the first 24 hours of the storm, which dumped over a foot of snow in three days. The downtown transit mall quickly became a treacherous, icy mess. Street markers showing which lanes cars could legally traverse were covered, and we were navigating in impossible conditions to begin with, watching other vehicles turning right in front of the bus or honking at us for pulling out into our legal transitway.

Also invisible was upper management. They tell the public our union demands "Cadillac benefits," but where were *they*? While I was out there safeguarding countless human lives while risking my own, I didn't see or hear of the General Manager being out there. Nor was his union hit man anywhere to be seen. If they *were* out there, then good on them. I just didn't feel their pain.

There were only a few collisions, but a couple of drivers were seriously injured due to falls. One question looms large now that it's all history. If we are so vital to the economy that the state made it illegal for us to strike, then why are we fighting for our lives in contract talks? Where is our local support? Why aren't we taking advantage of public opinion which is heavily on our side after the storm? Upper management is whupping us in the court of public opinion by making us look "greedy" while they hide their raises and offend us with ludicrous contract proposals. If you love your bus operators, and by definition that includes all who work with us, please call in and give us commendations. People are quick to call in a complaint, but fail to report all the good we do.

I wear a button that states "I Love my Riders." I certainly do appreciate... most of them. I love my job and the important role it serves in the local economy. We'll see how long the public will remember how we pulled through another winter storm and kept the wheels rolling.

Tidbits and Annoyances

From snow to wind to rain to sun to spring to... rain again. Our basic, normal Portland winter weather. For the first time in 12 years I've been a Nor'westerner, I am sick of the wet. We had a beautiful fall, with not much rain until a few months ago. Cry me a river, you say. Well somebody must have, because the rivers are almost up to my neighborhood. Enough already!

It was raining hard one early, dark morning. It was tough to see people trying to catch my bus. As I was burning some early time, a cop pulled in front of me with lights flashing, got out and held up his index finger. Wondering if I was in trouble, I couldn't think of anything I'd done wrong. Mr. Copper opened his back door, and a lady raced through the pounding deluge to come aboard. I had missed her a few stops back, running for the bus in the soupy darkness. This kind cop picked her up and brought her to my bus so she didn't have to wait 30 minutes for the next one. (Personally, I'd rather wait several hours rather than take a ride in the BACK seat of a cop car any day.) Another first: a police escort for an intending passenger? It was a nice thing to do.

Fancy cars and inconsideration. If one has the money to plunk down for a Mercedes, Land Rover, or Audi, chances are good they don't ever ride a bus. Don't *need* to ride one, sneer at the very *thought* of it. To them, buses are just another annoying obstacle in their way. These people seem to be the rudest drivers on the road. Then you have the 4x4's with rebel flags flying, a bed full of beer cans and misspelled bumper stickers who have to make sure they hit that red light first. Trying to make Richard Petty look like a rookie, they flip their middle finger as they whip around the bus with inches to spare and then slam on the brakes. I'm supposed to let all this slide right off me, but it isn't easy. The rudest of them are sure to get a few quietly-muttered choice words. My solace is to gleefully blast them here *From The Driver Side,* where my words replace an actual extended middle digit.

Be honest, he says. Driving a particularly undesirable route one day, an old dude approached me, saying "I got a question for you, so be honest." First of all, I abhor when people say "be honest," for it implies I'm inherently *dishonest.*

The old guy then asked, "Did you find an illegal apparatus, in other words, a crack pipe, on your bus?"

"No, I did not," I replied.

"Are you sure? Cuz I saw you put something in your coat. Be honest now."

There it was again, telling me to be honest. OK, if I had found this guy's crack pipe, what was I gonna do with it? Smoke it? Give it away? Sell it on CraigsList? I certainly wouldn't put something that another's Hepatitis-ridden mouth has defiled in my own coat pocket! Come on dude, really? I got a bit hot with him.

"I *said* I didn't find anything, which means I did not," I replied. "If you're going to ride this bus, show me your fare. If not, there's the door. I gotta roll, sir."

Calling him "sir" really rankled me, but I remained professional. He left, mumbling something about crack-addicted bus drivers. He's lucky he didn't leave with my size 11 stuck in *his* crack.

Uh oh. Can you tell I'm getting a tad bitter? It's been a year since I started this blog. I need a vacation. I'm sick and tired. People annoy me more often. I haven't had a commendation in ages. I am a nice bus

driver. Lately though, I've found myself angrier than I've ever been...
at management, rude passengers, life in general. Time to meditate
and cleanse my soul of negativity.

The Mantras, Parts I, II and III

🚌 **DEKE'S NOTE**: *From the first day as an operator, I formed my*
"Safety Mantra." I repeat this prior to every run. It has evolved since
then, but I still say it. It's not a superstitious belief, but a daily
reminder of what's important while doing this job.

Prior to starting any run, I faithfully repeat my *mantra*. It prepares
me for the responsibility of keeping everyone SAFE, and focuses
my mind on the task at hand.

Origins. When I first started driving a bus I was paranoid,
bordering on terrified. In order to keep this job, I had to complete a
six-month probation period with no runs, hits or errors. My mantra
was NO this and NO that. NO accidents, NO injuries, NO NO NO.
Then one day I realized how negative it was to preface this with
a myriad of NO's. To avoid negativity following me around like a
former spouse wielding a sharp axe, I modified it. Positively *altered* it.

Now I say, "Be SAFE, be KIND, be CONSIDERATE, be
THOUGHTFUL, be PATIENT, be POLITE, be SMART, be SMOOTH."

The more I say it, the more Forrest Gumpish it sounds. I've
always loved that movie. Gump's simple and positive outlook on
life is praiseworthy. Lately, I've been grouchy and it's a bit harder to
practice. Nothing good is ever easy.

Driving around town, my mind is awash with things to write.
Sadly, only a few thoughts remain when I'm able to jot them down.
Since I recite this every day, it's easier to remember. I will *briefly*
explain the importance of each part.

BE SAFE

Since Day One, safety has been drilled into us. With respect to those who have lost loved ones due to transit-related accidents, yes we *are* highly-trained in safe operation. It's a challenge to constantly provide a safe environment for everyone around such a large vehicle. Today's buses are 30-40 feet long, eight-and-a-half feet wide, and nearly 11 feet tall. They weigh 20 tons. An operator has to be constantly vigilant. There are so many unavoidable distractions, we can't always be perfect, yet we are held to extremely high (sometimes impossible) safety standards. We take safety *very* seriously, and strive to remain focused every second we're behind the wheel. If we're not safe, we hear about it from fellow drivers, supervisors, trainers, other motorists, cops, bicyclists, radio personalities, various inept newspaper reporters, pedestrians, the news media, and the mother-in-law.

Driving safely means to always be aware of everything that is around, immediately as well as 12-15 seconds ahead the vehicle, and behind it. Our speed depends upon conditions, not just the speed limit. If a car cuts a bus off and turns right immediately in front of it, our speed is usually 0-5 mph. This is called *predictive* driving. If the car stops directly ahead, in mid-turn, our speed is 0mph, because our foot has already covered the brake in anticipation of the motorist's worst possible actions. Prior to the Prius pushing its luck, we've noted in split-second fashion the elderly lady pushing a walker into its path, a bicyclist coming up on the left, and predicted the outcome of each disastrous possibility. Our brain registers this before Prudy Prius sees it, and sends an order to the right foot, which covers and depresses the brake pedal. Disaster averted. Plus, we've simultaneously noted several other traffic conditions around our vehicle we must deal with immediately after dealing with the imminent dangers directly ahead. An operator's brain is constantly evaluating visual data and making decisions, all centered around safety. Our bodies are constantly ready to take action as this data is analyzed.

The typical driver of a car or truck is over confident. They think they're the world's best driver, always in a hurry to get nowhere fast. Even if the traffic light ahead is red, they need to be there *first*.

"That bus is in my way, damnit! After all, I'm a great driver, so who's

this simpleton bus operator to tell me to YIELD? Oh good, the bus is stopped, probably dropping off another loser. I can zip around... WAIT, what? How dare they pull out in front of ME? I'll show THEM! Yield this, JERKWAD!"

Newsflash, YuppieFish: That bus driver saw you coming a block away, properly signaled his intentions and legally deployed the YIELD signal. By state law (Oregon Revised Statutes 811.167), vehicles are *required* to allow a transit vehicle to merge back into traffic after servicing a stop. We rarely see police officers citing anybody for failing to obey this law. If cops were more cognizant of vehicular behavior around a bus, they could write citations galore on this violation.

Boarding Issues. People boarding a bus are also a safety concern. They're often staring at their mobile gadget trying to figure out when the bus will get there, even when it's right in front of their nose. I can be servicing a stop, doors open, external speaker blaring, and they're still looking at their device. Of course, they have ear buds in and they can't hear the bus and they have no peripheral vision because they're focused on a tiny screen six inches from their face. A blast of my horn sometimes jerks them to their senses. Then they fumble in their purse or pocket for their pass or fare money and look annoyed when you sigh because they've already burned 45 seconds of your time. If you dare mention the fact it is customary to have the fare or pass ready upon boarding, a conniption fit and quite possibly a complaint lodged against you are predictable results. If they're looking at their phone while boarding, trip and fall, you could be at fault if the bus isn't kneeled down. Begin rolling before they have thought to hold on, a fall inside the bus is possible. Be too quick to close the door when they board, miss a late comer who snuck in on their tails, and you can accidentally close the door in their face or on whatever body part has crossed the threshold.

Of Bicycles, Beware. Even though they're some of the most vulnerable, bicyclists believe they own the road. If they do the stupidest thing imaginable around a bus and get hurt, they often blame the bus driver. Many consider themselves above the law. That yield light applies to *all* vehicles on the road, and yes, a bicycle is considered a *vehicle*. You'd think they might be extremely cautious around a bus, but they seem to think they're invincible (although often invisible) and that they have a protective shield around them. In reality, they're as invincible as an ant about to be stepped on.

A bus has several blind spots. If a bike pulls directly behind me (out of my field of vision) while I'm servicing a stop, then impatiently passes as I'm preparing to re-enter traffic, they fail to recognize the danger. Even though they could wait five seconds, they risk their life for no time advantage whatsoever. Once they pull around the bus after the driver has already done an over-the-shoulder and mirror check, they're in imminent danger as the bus starts to move. I have saved many of them major pain by constantly mirror-checking in heavy bicycle traffic areas. Often, they'll flip me a bird as they leisurely pedal by. They have no idea my pulse has doubled and my adrenalin is off the charts, because they just missed getting squashed. Because I was patient even though they were not, I saved their life.

The professional bike rider is smart. She (I will use the feminine here, because I believe female cyclists are usually safer) will signal a bus driver with every move she makes. As I'm pulling to service a stop and there's a bicyclist ahead of or beside me, I will wait for them to roll past the stop before I pull in. The professional rider waves her thanks.

Safety, period. This subject, once again, could encompass so many areas I hesitate to venture further. Overall, safety is our constant goal. Whenever you hear somebody talking about how that "stupid bus driver" cut them off, ask yourself just how reliable the source is. It may happen from time to time, but you can bet high dollar the "stupid" part usually doesn't apply to the bus operator.

We're intensely-trained professionals. We drive a bus, on average, about 30,000 miles a year. Translated into car miles, imagine driving yours about 200,000 miles a year, stopping every few blocks.

BE KIND

No matter what's going on in my mind while I'm driving, I try to be *kind*. As we all know, everyone can have a bad day, no matter how many people tell us to have a *good* one. Perhaps it's been a good day, but life can often throw them more than they can handle. My first response to a boarding passenger is to simply smile and greet them.

A human being's normal response to a smile is to return it. If someone is having a bad day, sometimes a single act of kindness can cancel their frown. While on my bus, I want passengers as relaxed as possible. A rider's first impression of a bus operator can be a precursor to their own behavior. If they're already annoyed, a grumpy bus driver doesn't help. They need to go someplace, and I am their conduit in time travel. Not only do I want to provide a safe ride, it's important for them to have a pleasant one. Therefore, a smile followed by a *"Good Morning"* or *"Hello"* does a lot to set people at ease.

Of course, there are the rude, sneering teenagers who think it's cool to hold their pass to my face while purposefully looking away. They walk by looking like Grandma just opened the door to their date in her underwear. They refuse to even acknowledge me. They're annoyed if I even *speak* to them. I say hello anyway, a bit louder than usual. I truly love how elderly people put kids in their place when they're rude. "Hey, young man you better treat that driver with respect. I know where your mama lives, boy. Mind your manners."

Then there are those who are distraught. They missed the last bus, or their significant other argued with them before they left home. While I avoid extended conversations with them, I do offer an "I'm sorry that happened, and I hope your day gets better."

People are plugged in and tuned out these days, it's harder to be kind when you feel dismissed. But I sure try. If I can help make one moment just a tad better for them, that makes my day more pleasant.

BE CONSIDERATE, THOUGHTFUL, POLITE

If I see an elderly person at a bus stop, or someone who uses any type of mobility device, I am careful to address them with the utmost respect. As they prepare to use the ramp or lift, I get out of my seat and greet them. Some cannot speak for themselves and have other means of communication, but I always address them directly even if they are accompanied by an assistant. Even if they may not be able to respond to me, they understand what I'm saying.

A friend of mine who was severely physically disabled taught me how demeaning it was when people wouldn't address her, instead speaking to her parents as if she wasn't even there. Physically disabled people are not necessarily mentally impaired.

A person who has visual impairment also warrants careful consideration and thoughtfulness. It is helpful to stop very close to the curb, eliminating the gap, and lowering the bus to curb-level. Having a visually-impaired friend who has a guide dog, I learned from her to inform sight-impaired people how far from the curb you are when they board. When they exit, it is again helpful to describe how far from the curb the bus is, any defections in the sidewalk, and any directions they may request. In training, we were blindfolded and asked to perform simple tasks we sighted folks take for granted. This exercise gave me greater understanding and empathy for those who cannot see. Some people assume the blind can't hear either, when in fact theirs is usually much better than sighted people.

Special attention is paid to pedestrians; when they step off the curb, motorists are legally required to stop and give them the right of way. Waiting several minutes for traffic to stop, they see a bus coming and know the professional driver will let them cross. While a person on a bicycle is not considered a pedestrian, I would rather yield than risk their injury. The danger lies with vehicles who see a stopped bus and think only of zipping past it; these drivers can't see through or around the bus. Pedestrians are in danger if they assume oncoming traffic see them or are prepared to stop at the crosswalk.

We are constantly giving other motorists thoughtful consideration, even though they don't always deserve it. When they're particularly ignorant of their mortality, I give them a beep-beep. Officially, it's a driver's way of saying "HEY look out!" Unofficially, it's another way of saying "You dumbass, you were nearly pretzelized!" Another consideration is for those attempting to parallel park. Once I see the reverse lights come on, I stop well behind them and wait. It's also amusing to watch. Most are terrible at this maneuver.

Being *polite* encompasses many points. When you're tired, this is one of the most challenging. Especially when people are rude to you. Using "sir" or "ma'am" is important. Sometimes you're not sure which to use. Treating people with respect shows you are worthy of theirs. These days, many are wrapped up in their own idea of "morality." One person's definition of "normal" is sure to contradict another's. Yet we all share the same air, space and time. Who am I to judge? I tend to leave that job to a higher power. Whenever my ego is allowed free reign, my "judgements" are usually faulty. That guy with multiple piercings, wild hair and rough look about him is usually the first to come to our defense.

BE PATIENT

When you've been in the seat for a few hours, the guy who boards last and fumbles in his pocket for his fare money is a true test of *patience*. One time I politely asked a guy to please have his fare ready upon boarding. He spent the next five minutes verbally assaulting me. Now, the most I do is sigh. My bladder might be straining against its limit, but an argument only prolongs the agony.

At intersections, patience is vital. Waiting for a light to change, often a car on the cross street will run the red. Perhaps the one following it will too. They're in a hurry to get nowhere fast. They don't see the lady with the guide dog who is about to cross in front of them, and they punch it to get through. Braking isn't an option because there's a Hummer closing in behind to rear end them if they change their mind and slam on the brakes. Cars behind me might honk impatiently, but I've just saved their bacon and my passengers' as well by taking a moment to assess the situation. They can't see the pedestrians who waited too long or didn't notice the light change, leisurely strolling across while they check the latest online recipe for vegemite sandwiches. Bicyclists routinely race by the bus when they see a green, taking for granted it is safe to proceed. That extra scan, the utmost in patience and vigilance, can often save a careless person's life.

At the end of the day, I set the parking brake, and put the transmission in neutral. The bus has returned safely to the yard. My breathing returns to normal, my mind relaxes. Time to go home, eat, love the family, read a bit and go to sleep. Before I know it, the alarm sounds and I'm out driving again. Maybe my body and mind will have recovered from the previous day's work. Perhaps I won't have to use my "Cadillac benefits" today. But as long as you're delivered home safe and sound, my life is about as good as it can be.

Dad taught me how to drive when I was 10. We lived on a ranch that was miles from the edge of nowhere. I noted how he manipulated the clutch and shifted down or up as conditions required. His braking was smooth and under control. Dad was also a pilot, and a very careful one. Always on the lookout for possible landing spots in case he needed one, he was deliberately safe in the air as well as on the ground. I spent many hours in planes with him, often taking the controls under his careful supervision. I think he liked that I was curious and attentive.

My father once taught driving in Chicago to those who had flunked driver's education. When I got behind the wheel for the first time, I felt like I had won a sweepstakes. I've had a love affair with rolling wheels ever since.

Dad's common-sense lessons have proven valuable not only to me, but also to my own children. He taught my wife how to drive before we married. When I entered bus operator training, I was pleasantly surprised to find that most of what Dad taught me echoed in the voices of my trainers. Of course, it's all basic, yet timelessly relevant. Much of what he taught me is timelessly relevant.

The points that stick out like a wasp with a hangover are; A) expect other drivers to do the worst possible thing, and have at least three exit strategies ready to deploy; B) parking lots are the most dangerous places to drive; and C) there's no need to be the first one to arrive at a red light. There are others, but these are the most constant.

This brings about the two final pieces of my daily driving mantra. So far, I've outlined *Be Safe, Be Kind, Be Considerate, Be Thoughtful, Be Patient,* and *Be Polite.* The final two tie it all together; one is physical, the other mental. With me, all things must be in balance. If my physical being is out of kilter, the mental is too. On every run, these final pieces are dependent upon one another.

BE SMART

Operating a bus requires a mental toughness found in people who work in challenging conditions. If a fireman isn't cool under pressure, he can lose his/her life to the flames. One slip for a police officer or firefighter in a tense situation could also mean the loss of others as well. Snap judgments by bus drivers, if not the absolute correct one for that precise moment, can be disastrous. A person need not have the mental ability of Bill Gates or Neil deGrasse Tyson to drive a bus, but you can bet they have a certain savvy not always found in more glamorous occupations.

"You can't legislate intelligence and common sense into people"
– Will Rogers

Operators constantly evaluate a variety of situations. Every second our eyes are scanning streets, sidewalks and hidden corners for possible danger. The average driver mostly just sees the road directly ahead. The bus operator watches *everything* around their vehicle.

When you stare straight ahead for more than two seconds, you lose your peripheral vision. Often, it's those dangers to the side that are most hazardous. A bus driver will scan left over the shoulder, in the mirror, sweep across the front to the passenger mirror, to the right traffic mirror and over the right shoulder before we even *move* the bus. Considering we come to a stop roughly 750 times a shift, that's a lot of looking around. Being smart means evaluating potential risks before they become dangerous situations. We predict the future and take the necessary actions to avoid disaster.

Dealing with the public requires another type of vigilance. While we see all types of humans and their animals, it isn't easy to predict their behavior. A person can smile at you one second and verbally thrash you the next. Even worse, they can curse, spit at, kick, slap or punch you without warning. Humans are unpredictable savages. One misspoken word or the tone of our voice can set off a violent reaction in some. Many drivers have been attacked in the past year, and it's downright scary.

Being aware of our surroundings is paramount to being safe. If I see a driver busily texting away in the car next to me, I look at the position of their wheels, their car's position in the lane, and whether they're paying any attention to anything but their phone. I've avoided collisions by not moving until said adjacent vehicle has cleared the intersection, because they immediately changed lanes and made an un-signaled right turn right in front of me. That's one example of *predictive* driving. Because they were intensely inattentive, they failed to notice my bus right next to them, and made an extremely foolish move which I was prepared for. *Lucky them.*

My buddy's bus was struck by an SUV as they simultaneously made left hand turns in adjacent lanes. He was in the far right turn lane, the other vehicle to his left. Good thing he had his foot covering the brake, because the other driver changed lanes and turned right directly in front of him in an attempt to enter a business. Result of alert bus operator's actions: minor crunch to smaller vehicle, no injuries. The motorist's statement: "I didn't see the bus." Driver's reply: "Well you traversed the entire 40-foot length of my bus before turning, how could you *not* see it?" Selective vision isn't peripheral.

BE SMOOTH

Another of Dad's valuable lessons is to ensure your passengers have a smooth ride. If a passenger is tense and on-edge *because* of your driving, you're doing something wrong. Conversely, if a passenger is already upset, they don't need a bus operator adding to their woes. Some drivers will engage passengers in conversations. Don't take offense if we won't take our eyes off the road to look at your pencil scribblings of an address. Wait until we've stopped, then ask directions. Better yet, ask a fellow passenger. They're often more knowledgeable about connecting routes and schedules than we are. Plus, it is distracting to take our mind off the road to consider your destination. There are apps to help you find your way; let us drive you there.

We drive many different buses, some old, some new, many in between. It's an art getting to know the personality of any bus *before* you pick up any passengers. It's an even bigger challenge to road-relieve another bus operator mid-run and immediately figure out that ride's particular quirks. Each bus brakes, accelerates and handles turns differently. Giving your passengers a smooth ride is imperative, because at any time they can stand, bend over, or slip. If you have to brake suddenly, physics can create passenger injuries even though the action you just took saved another's life.

After signaling a stop request a bit later than she should have, a recent passenger chose to walk to the front of the bus as I braked into a landing. She was thrust forward even though I came at it smoothly. She was not hanging on, and nearly fell. As the bus stopped, she was already in front of the door. I hesitated before opening it, asked if she was okay, and asked her to remember not to step in front of the yellow stop line until the bus was fully stopped. Rather than take responsibility for her not hanging on, she chose to blame me.

"I would have been fine except for your braking," she snapped.

"Well ma'am," I replied, "brakes are what we use to stop. When our forward momentum is reduced, objects within the bus that aren't secure will move forward. Please remember to hold on next time."

Her response wasn't as polite. I learned from that moment that when passengers pull the stop request late, it's best to give them the next stop rather than braking hard in order to accommodate their not being prepared.

When I'm not accelerating, my foot is covering the brake. This is an invaluable lesson taught to me by a wise Line Trainer. It has saved my derrière many a time. A bus operator negotiates thousands of intersections a year. At every one, we cover the brake well before the intersection, scan for safety threats, and only accelerate when we have determined it is safe. This is also a good idea driving through residential neighborhoods. Kids on bikes or playing ball on or near the street, people getting into their cars, and any number of other perilous situations are constant.

There's no need to do the speed "limit" on a narrow street. When you consider how long it takes a bus to stop, having to move your foot from accelerator to brake is a precious waste of time. The time it takes to move that foot adds distance to stopping time. By covering the brake, you can eliminate some reaction time and safely stop without sending Grampa's walker careening into Jane's knees.

That's about it for The Mantra. It's malleable, and I change it as necessary. Kind of like growing my beard. Mrs. Blue doesn't like it. It keeps my face warm in winter. It also negates extra shaving time. I remove it for summer months as a compromise. The grey is taking over though. That's the life of a bus operator.

We age 10 years every time someone cuts us off.

Mantra Revisited

🚌 **DEKE'S NOTE:** *This next post is related to the previous one, so it's presented out of chronological order. About a year after I posted the Mantra series, I added a few points to my daily ritual. It has evolved along with my driving skills.*

My earliest posts were very long. So long in fact, I had to cut my mantra description into three pieces. The first post dealt with only two points of the mantra, and it resembled an article written by a 19th century author being paid by the word. By the time I finished reading the trilogy, my eyes were blinking from exhaustion. Three excruciatingly-long parts to describe a 12-point mantra that takes as many seconds to recite? Guess I was a bit over-eager back then.

Here's an updated version. I've added a few points to the mix. Over the years it's become necessary to amend and improve it.

THE MANTRA: *Be safe, be kind, be courteous, be considerate, be polite, be thoughtful, be patient, be vigilant, be calm, be smart, be smooth... but above all, BE SAFE!*

BE COURTEOUS

When I'm running late and somebody stands at the bus doorway as the light goes green, it's not a good idea to slam the door shut in their face. Bad for business. But when it happens on the transit mall downtown with three buses waiting for me to leave, I really have to struggle with the door handle. I grit my teeth and show a smile that would signal people who know me to hurry up, I have miles to roll. Usually, the answer lies on the reader board they've failed to notice, so I point them to it.

What I *want* to say: "I have no idea when the next 19 bus will be here, I don't drive that route. Do you see 'Schedule Guru' tattooed on my freakin' forehead? Isn't that a smart phone in your hand? Figure this one out on your own."

What I *do* say: "There should be one coming along soon." This is a more courteous, albeit somewhat misleading, way to answer their question. If I knew the schedule of every line and train, I'd be too smart to work here.

This is also where be polite comes in. When you're tired, or as my brother Dan describes it in his blog, in "fourth gear," this is an excruciatingly difficult part to practice. On my Friday night, I have to vigorously restrain myself from rudely answering the inevitable schedule inquiries.

There are times when I can combine parts of my mantra. Tonight, I realized it can be efficient to *be polite, thoughtful,* and *considerate* to be *courteous* in traffic. Part of my route runs on a two-lane highway; one lane of traffic in either direction for several miles. If someone wants to turn left, traffic backs up for blocks. Tonight, I let off some passengers, and as I scanned coming out of the stop, I saw a bus coming the opposite direction stuck in a long line of traffic behind a left-turner. I stopped, blocking traffic behind me so the motorist could turn out of Ollie Operator's way. I was early anyway, and the car had been waiting to turn for over a minute. I could almost see Ollie's fingers tapping impatiently on his wheel. All it cost me was a hairy finger extension at my next stop, but I'm used to that fool bird.

When you won't find me stopping for another motorist is if I'm trying to make it through an intersection that has an annoyingly-long stoplight sequence. They can just sit there and wait, thank you, rather than cut into a line I've been inching forward in for several minutes. Try the next guy, lady... I'm *working* here! Bus schedules are tighter than a transit management's budget at contract negotiation time. You may be on your way home or headed to the grocery, but we're on the clock.

BE VIGILANT

Sometimes it's just so damn hard to remain focused. You have to be a *vigilant* scanner, or you could miss something potentially disastrous. You know how it is when you're at work. Sometimes we have a tendency to daydream, the mind begins to wander and you catch yourself waking up from a mini excursion to nowhereville a few minutes later. If that happens on our job, the results could be deadly. It is imperative to remain vigilant and alert for any danger. When you drive something that weighs 40,000 pounds empty, it's vital to stay in top form. Much better that, than on top *of* somebody.

BE CALM

There are so many stresses we constantly deal with. When we're bombarded with several of them at once, it can wreak havoc. People curse us for being late, even though they can see the line of traffic inching past them before we reach their stop. They will also stare at their phone until we're passing their stop, then yell at you for not stopping on a dime. I'm not going to slam on the brake pedal to compensate for inattentive people.

Folks will say things to irritate you just for fun. Or, they'll get into arguments over the most mundane topics. This is when I take a deep breath, hold it a second or two, then slowly exhale. Not long ago, I'd explode at them. Show them who's boss. But that's a recipe for professional indigestion. I'm supposed to be good at customer service, but mediating civil disputes is Perry Patrolman's job. Now I just let it play out. If they want to duke it out, I suggest they use the nearest exit.

Whew! Hope it resonates with some of you. We have a tough job, but once you find your own way, it becomes easier. The hardest part for me nowadays is dealing with the body aches associated with sitting in a seat for eight or more hours. And they want me to work on my day off? No thanks.

Runnin' on Empty

It's refreshing to be away from work a few days, especially when you deal with everyone else's family more than your own. I've been relaxing a few days in a cabin at the beach. Contemplating this odd universe, you might say. Drinking some brewskies, resting, having fun with my family. After the past few weeks driving a bus, I needed some time off. My patience was thinner than a sand dollar on diet pills.

When you wear a uniform for a living, it's rare to wear your regular clothing. My favorite boots are KEEN's, and my feet ache when they're in my dreadful work shoes all week. One good thing about this gig is my clothing budget has shrunk. Sometimes I'll find a shirt I haven't worn in a while, and it's like visiting an old friend. Most of my clothes are old, because I'm pretty much a jeans and T-shirt guy and they tend to last a long time when you wear a uniform five days a week. I have one suit, worn only for weddings and funerals. I'm an ordinary average guy, as Joe Walsh sings.

The past few days have included long, contemplative walks with my beloved, alone time at a favorite outdoor perch, reading, eating wonderful food, and driving as little as possible. This mini-vacation is something I've needed for a long time. I've counted down the days. Of course, the time *before* drags on, and the time *during* flies quicker than a bus fart. Before I know it, this will all be a memory. In the meantime, I'm making the best of it. I'm ready to finish another fine Portland pale ale by the fire pit before I hit the sack for a rare eight-hour rest.

HIT COUNTER: 6,500 (April 2014)

NO! I Don't Want to Work My RDO!

My Friday is actually Monday. Usually I work long hours on my last day of the week, so when I set the parking brake in the yard, I'm D-O-N-E. Do I really want to work my weekend? Absolutely, irrevocably, most definitely, *not*.

Last week my Friday work was 12 hours. The final nine were in the fleet's oldest bus. My butt flat-out hurt. (It was worn flat, too.) My thighs were numb, I had a raging headache and cramping calves from the lack of ergonomic comfort in the driver's seat. When I limped off the bus, I short-hopped in a manner vaguely resembling walking. Finally in my kitchen, the quickest meal to heat up was devoured. Within 20 minutes, I was in bed, asleep. The time was 7:40 p.m.

Daylight drivers get up early, shower, and put on a fresh uniform. For me, it's worn from before dawn to well after sunset. On my first day off, it is joyous to throw the uniform in the laundry basket and put on my civvies. Hello old concert T-shirt, long time no see! Howdy, my favorite blue jeans, grey athletic socks, revered and decrepit smashed-up hat. And the shoes! My feet sigh with ecstasy as I slip into my comfortable shoes.

There's always a long honey-do list in our house. Because I have teenage boys, that makes me "Honey." The long winter has rendered our yard an overgrown tangle. The grass is up to my knees. The raised beds are sprouting weeds of every variety rather than neat rows of yummy veggies. The roses need pruning, even though they were leafing out a month ago. Our bathroom seriously needs a paint job.

On my last two days off, I finally had the chance to wash, wax and detail our 6-year-old car. It was a mess, but now it looks new again. It was long and grueling, and my body was sore, but at least my butt no longer hurt.

Sorry Boss, Homie won't drive a bus on his days off. Period. For two days a week, I'm my *beloved's* man, not yours. There's plenty of work to be done here, and it keeps home boss happy. She does still like to see me out of uniform from time to time. Plus, she *hates* a flat butt.

Why Do We Do That?

🚌 **DEKE'S NOTE:** *This was my first post to generate over 1,000 hits. It resonated with my readers, who generously shared it. FTDS' readership rose exponentially from here on.*

Many folks believe they are *great* drivers. In fact, each of us might just be the *best* damn driver on the road. Everyone *else* is a moron. Especially that pokey goofball operating the bus just ahead.

Bus drivers are subject to being on the receiving end of excessive road rage. This is probably due to a chronic lack of understanding by the motoring public as to what operating a bus entails. We are held to higher standards. Run two red lights, you're fired. Getting too many complaints, no matter how outrageous or false they may be, results in discipline up to and including termination. The list of no-no's is long and daunting.

Of those who drive for a living, operators of buses and other transport vehicles are easily the most attentive drivers on the road. This is a bold statement, eh? Well let's take a look at those who do the most driving: truckers, bus operators, cops, taxi drivers, delivery drivers. In my life, I've done three of these five jobs. Professional truck drivers are generally safe and careful, because their livelihoods depend on it. Over-the-road truckers mostly travel highways and interstates, yet overall, their inner-city driving is excellent. While I've never been in law enforcement, I've noticed cops are distracted with all the gadgets they manipulate while driving, and this can cause accidents. Taxi drivers are often reckless, yet you'd think it imperative for them to deliver their fares safely. Some delivery drivers who face tight schedules take unnecessary gambles at the most inopportune moments.

The average motorist is concerned with their immediate destination. They may know how to drive reasonably well, but their impatience replaces vigilance. Risky behavior befuddles the mind of a safe driver. A study of the behaviors of risky drivers by the National

Highway Traffic Safety Administration finds people are more apt to exhibit unsafe maneuvers in heavy traffic. I've found this to be very true. Even though I pride myself in relatively safe personal driving, I'm sometimes guilty of making foolish decisions in heavy traffic. When you're headed home after a hectic day at work, the slightest interruption in the smooth flow of your commute can be frustrating.

To many motorists, a bus is merely an irritating obstacle. Yet we're taking thousands of cars off the road. We drive slower than most, because we have to. When you wonder why a bus is performing certain maneuvers that slow you down, remember these explanations.

Why is that bus just sitting there? There are times when a bus operator is ahead of schedule. We're supposed to find a safe place to burn time, but some time points are terribly inconvenient to those behind us.

Imagine hurrying to your bus stop in the pouring rain, an hour before dawn. You should be there a few minutes before it is scheduled to arrive, but as you're almost there the bus cruises past. The driver doesn't see you. Some bus lines run every 10 minutes, but early in the morning they can be 20-30 minutes apart. You just missed the bus, which means the connecting bus you usually catch will leave without you. You're going to be late, and the boss will be very unhappy. For this and other reasons, bus schedules are very important.

We can be late, but not too early. Bus routes have certain areas that are passenger-heavy, and others that are less so. If nobody's at the busy stops, the clock goes from happy-green on-time to angry early-yellow. If we hit a time point more than a minute early, we have to stop and let the time burn off. That allows people to get to their stops ahead before we roll up. This can be inconvenient to traffic behind the bus, especially if the street is narrow and there's not room enough to pull out of the flow and let cars pass by. Bus operators usually can avoid this by burning time before they reach a time point.

Another reason we don't move is when we load someone using a mobility device, it takes time to deploy the ramp, ensure they board safely, and secure their device if asked. Bicyclists take a few seconds to secure their bike on the rack. People who don't have fare ready upon boarding can delay us as well.

That light is green! Why won't the bus GO? Several factors determine when a bus will proceed through an intersection. We cross, on average, about 250-300 signaled intersections per shift. When you're waiting behind a bus, you can't see what we can. It's illegal to block a signaled intersection, so if there's traffic backed up to the far crosswalk, we have to wait for a 40-foot window ahead before moving. There could be a pedestrian crossing the street, or a texter who isn't paying attention who we are either protecting or waiting upon. Cross-traffic vehicles running red lights and blocking the intersection can also prevent us from proceeding. There could be a truck partially blocking our lane ahead, a motorist who isn't being safe, or a Lance Armstrong wannabe darting through a red light. We have to be vigilant, because other drivers usually are not.

Also, if a bus is stopped at a green, remember the pedestrian signal counters. It takes a bus at least four seconds to safely cross an intersection. If we pull from a stop at a traffic signal and the counter is down below five, we don't have time to cross before the light turns red. Why is this important? First and foremost, it's not safe to push through "pink" signals. If we get a ticket, we're in trouble with our transit agency as well as the local courts. If we're convicted of two red light citations, we could lose our job. That is why we don't normally take the chance, and will wait through a full light cycle. A thirty-second light cycle is certainly worth waiting for, when the alternative could mean a loss of life.

Remember, a bus accelerates 0-30mph in about a week. Timing and patience are paramount to driving safely. If you are impatient around a bus, chances are good you will pay dearly, and most can't afford that kind of pain. Operators certainly do not want the anguish and nightmares associated with hurting another. We are slow, deliberate and patient, for everyone's safety.

Why did our driver stop, turn off the bus and run into a convenience store? We have the same bodily functions as everyone else. Some runs are very long. If nature calls and the end of the run isn't for another half-hour, any port in the storm will do. Some schedules do not allow drivers to take a proper break at the end of the line. The transit agency has agreements with businesses on bus routes for us to use their restrooms. I will not sacrifice my kidneys, bladder or colon for a bus schedule. If you're worried about the schedule, take an earlier bus.

I got off the bus and started to cross in front of it. Why did this upset the driver? This one's easy, although you might guess part of the answer. You're probably thinking the driver might not see you before implanting you into the windshield. Well that's partially correct. (Like the song goes, "sometimes you're the windshield, sometimes you're the bug.") Just remember the dimensions of the vehicle you've just exited is 40-feet long. That's about *three* mid-size sedans, *four* Mini Coopers, or *two* Hummers, in length. Standing on the curb at the front bumper of a bus, a pedestrian cannot see what's coming around it, nor can Joey ZipCar see *through* it. Motorists, as we know, *hate* to be stuck behind our gargantuan road hog. They will sit behind it maybe a whopping 4.2 seconds before they decide Junior's soccer practice can't wait another five. They'll whip around the bus quicker than a politician jumps to money. No matter there's a double-yellow line prohibiting such a foolish move. No idea as to what traffic might lie ahead of the bus. No regard for anybody's safety, unaware of the dangers lurking just ahead of their field of vision. *They're simply in a hurry to get nowhere fast.* When you consider the tragedies many gamble upon just getting there, it's a wonder they arrive *anywhere* other than a hospital, or even worse, the morgue. Just get off the bus, wait for it to leave, *then* scan the traffic. You can see better, and more importantly, traffic should be able to see *you* better.

☈ RAW

Anonymous:
  When I was very pregnant and on my way to the doctor's office, the driver said, "This is my first solo trip, please don't go into labor on me!" About two blocks from my stop, I felt the first contraction and inadvertently groaned in pain. He stopped the bus and asked how close we were to the office. I told him about three blocks. He stood up and apologized but informed the rest of the passengers he was taking me directly to the doctor's

office because I was in labor. They cheered him on, and when we arrived, he walked me across the street to the doctor's office. He made sure the RN knew I'd had a contraction on the bus. What a great start to his career! Thanks to all the conscientious people movers out there.

Cinco de Mayo Fiesta

🚌 **DEKE'S NOTE:** *This is just a humble thank you, of sorts, to those who linked up to FTDS early and often, sharing it and nurturing my fragile writer's ego.*

On May 3, 2013, this new driver had an aching desire to write about his fascinating job. With a wealth of information to draw from, the obvious choice was *blog it*.

Now there are 9,660 hits. Not long ago, the readership exploded from a paltry 30-40 hits to over 600 in one day. This is quite inspiring. A writer's job is to write. Sometimes though, there is not enough material to warrant a post. Plus, this job is often so physically exhausting to the point where I can only devote a few hours of writing every other week.

The other day, I was talking to a passenger who had heard of this blog. It was an amazing feeling. He also told me other drivers know about it, but they won't divulge my true identity. Thank you, brothers and sisters. It's hard enough to do this job amidst the fear of Big Brother watching my every move.

There are plenty of blogs out there that make mine look sophomoric in comparison. But I have had little instruction except for college journalism over 30 years ago. I'm just one of you, telling a story as it comes to me. We all have stories within us, few write them down. I've heard many great tales from drivers, and it's a wonder more aren't written.

Bus operators are a rare breed. The diversity range of experiences boggles the mind. Most of us have had several other careers and just happened to land in the transit gig. They are kind, generous souls whose good deeds are ignored by the media in favor of the sensational views of crashed buses and angry "victims." You know how it goes. Airplane pilots and bus operators safely carry millions of passengers every year. Yet this statistic doesn't sell. Don Henley got it right when he wrote: "It's interesting when people die, give us dirty laundry."

No dirty laundry here. The stench bothers me.

Thank you all for reading *my* stories. I hope to keep your interest, and that of others, for as long as possible. The next blog entry hasn't come to me yet, but I'm in no hurry. Right now, it's time for a Corona with lime.

Cops and Rude Postal Employees

A few posts ago, I mentioned how cops are the most distracted drivers on the road. I see them pulling goobers more often than I'd like to see from those responsible for protecting us. Plus, their distraction means they often miss traffic violations that put buses, our passengers and others in danger.

Take, for example, the number of drivers in Oregon who think the blinking red triangle on the back of a bus that reads "YIELD" is only there for looks. Today as I was preparing to pull away from a service stop, three cars plainly ignored the yield signal. Oregon law states: *"A person commits the offense of failure to yield the right-of-way to a transit bus entering traffic if the person does not yield the right of way to a transit bus when: (a) a yield sign is displayed on the back of the transit bus; (b) the person operating a vehicle that is overtaking the transit bus from the rear of the transit bus and; (c) the transit bus, after stopping to either receive or discharge passengers, is signaling an intention to enter the traffic lane occupied by the person [ORS 811.167]."* Not only did the three cars in a row ignore my yield signal, but they sped up, then passed me over a double-yellow line.

This happens several times a shift. But today, a cop who was busy pecking away at his onboard computer actually violated this law! (Oh well, they're quick to come to our rescue when needed, so he was quickly forgiven.) If a police officer were to follow any bus or stake out a bus stop, the citations would quickly multiply.

Motorists are extremely impatient, yet we all are guilty of being annoyed at the sight of a transit vehicle directly ahead. What people fail to realize is they will be able to pass the bus safely if they simply wait. A bus will stop several times in the space of five minutes, and stops are often placed so the bus leaves the flow of traffic to service them, giving vehicles a chance to pass safely. Buses obey speed limits; anybody who is in such a hurry as to drive 5-15mph over the posted limit is courting disaster. They simply arrive at the next red light a few seconds earlier than my bus.

Patience, I stress to myself every time I get behind the wheel. I wish the motoring public would practice the same restraint.

❧

Sometimes, our light rail goes out of service. These trains rely on a constant source of electricity to operate. When this is interrupted, they are out of service until the anomaly is repaired.

As I arrived at a terminus downtown, a light-rail vehicle was stopped in the middle of a traffic lane. As I discussed the plan of action with a uniformed supervisor, a postal truck pulled up. The supe held his hand out as a "stop" signal, because a bus was about to maneuver around the train. The driver started screaming at the supe, who very politely and professionally tried to explain why he stopped the postal vehicle. Talk about *going postal*. This driver epitomized the term "classless," not to mention "clueless."

"I don't give a (bleep) who you are, you are not a (bleeping) cop, and I ONLY take direction from them!" he bellowed.

As the supe calmly tried to explain vital information to this driver, he cursed again and drove off, barely missing my baffled brother. My hat's off to the supe, who took it in stride and went right back to work trying to keep us, and the public, safe in the presence of a difficult situation.

Killin' Time On the Board

For the first time in a month, I sit idle at the garage. Extra bored on the Extra Board, with no work. Actually, it's rather refreshing, but the time sure drags. Easy money like this doesn't come along very often though.

Shined my shoes. Last time they had a fresh coat of black it was cold outside. That was the last time I was on report longer than a few hours. Took a nap. Now I'm watching drivers come and go, the mini runners, the full timers. My brothers and sisters share stories of the road, of people walking onto the bus with burning smokes. Folks boarding with full, open beer cans which spill all over the floor. Drunks peeing in shelters as intending passengers huddle as far away from the offensive offender as possible; they cringe as the drunken ogre sits in his own pee.

It's amazing to hear the wide range of experiences "from the seat." Last year, an operator had a passenger without proper fare. When she wouldn't give him a transfer, he repeatedly punched her and ran off. He recently plea-bargained and basically got a slap on the wrist: probation, fines, letter of apology, and a one-year exclusion. I'm sorry, but I believe he should be in jail, and never allowed to ride transit again. For life. His complaint? He won't be able to ride the bus to get to his job or community service. Poor baby. To her credit, our sister forgave him.

It's my Monday. Spent my weekend doing yard work, and now I'm pretty sore. Sitting here today has its benefits, but it won't last.

HIT COUNTER: 10,000 (May 2014)

Fare Thee Well

To fare, or not to, seems to be the prevailing question these days. The company's stance is curiously ambiguous. The public is impossibly fickle. The drivers are split on the subject.

We are responsible for inspecting the fare of everyone who boards the bus, the company states in its Standard Operating Procedure (SOP). Some drivers carefully inspect each ticket. Others give a once-over and let them pass. White shirts mostly forgive our ambiguity, perhaps because of the rising numbers of assaults against operators the past few years. We are told to be fare "informers" rather than "enforcers."

When somebody pays a partial fare, they usually say they're short a few cents. That's okay by me. Times are hard, and life cruelly twists the economic knife sometimes. Many people put in more than their share, which makes up for those who do not. It all evens out in the end. It's redundant to "inform" passengers of the correct amount; they know the score. Plus, the fare is plainly stated on each bus. Honest people account for most riders. They'll say "I'm 20 cents short today, is that all right?" Once you've reached middle age, it's easier to sort the cons from the honest. A con artist will get no more from me than a sideways glance. An honest person will get a smile and "sure, it's okay" from me. I can be conned. But experience has taught me the majority of the working class is honest; it's the ruling class I distrust.

On a regular run last year, I'd occasionally get this teenager who had the same story each time.

"I forgot my pass, but I'm only riding a few blocks..."

After the first few times, he was as predictable as a Brady Bunch reunion. I took to prodding him as he boarded. Gently. Since he's a kid, he's considered "vulnerable." Pretty tough looking, strong kid, but still considered 'at risk.' I challenged him to A) remember his pass next time; or B) come up with more creative excuses. I like kids, have sired three myself, and I know they love to bend rules to their breaking point. This one simply chose to ride a different bus, rather than accept my challenge. *"Be consistent,"* the SOP insists. *"Ask customers to show their fare every day."* The agency wants us to nag people, even though we see them daily. I've driven regular routes, and the riders faithfully show their passes. It's a tedious everyday annoyance. I've had regulars actually dig through their pockets even though I tell them not to bother. The time it takes to find their pass only extends their ride time, which could make them late to their transfer point.

The next part of Fare SOP is dangerously vague. *"If a customer does not pay the fare, inform the customer of the fare policy: 'I'm sorry, it's unlawful for any person to ride without proof of fare.' Operators may deny boarding to a fare evader if it will not pose a threat to the operator's safety."* Wow. We're not supposed to deny Joe Wormbreath service for being drunk and obnoxious, but Freddy FareEvader gets the boot? But wait! We're supposed to *know* whether Freddy is a danger to society and act accordingly. This assumes we're excellent mind readers. Either way operators choose to proceed, we could be disciplined for making the *wrong* decision. If Freddy seems fairly normal, he might just shrug his shoulders and say, "I know I can't ride for free, my bad" and just get off the bus. Or, he could just as easily produce a hunting knife and prepare *Filet de Chauffeur d'Autobus Gonades* for a horrified audience.

A supervisor summed it up nicely, when asked what is the best course of action in dealing with fare evaders. He suggested saying, "I'm not a fare inspector." This lets them know that if they're caught without a transfer, they're on their own. It also tells them, "Sure, have a ride but don't blame me if you get caught." It takes the heat off us if a belligerent person boards. This works well. If I'm tired and wee bit cranky, I might notice yesterday's ticket flashed in my face. However, I've seen enough mental instability to know it's not worth being assaulted. The most normal-looking person could be Paulie Psycho in disguise.

You don't have the fare to ride my bus? Fine. Just be polite, thankful, and respectful. We'll get along fine, and you'll get where you need to be unless an actual inspector gets on board. Perhaps you'll be cited, or maybe next time you'll pay a little extra. Either way, the wheels on the bus are still gonna roll.

To Serve, Or Bite?

🚌 **DEKE'S NOTE:** *Fido has become more than just a pet, he's a family member. Many people will tell us Fido is their "service animal," even though 90% of them have no idea what actually goes into training one. Transit agencies have to be vague in what constitutes a service animal because the federal government refuses to tighten the rules in the Americans with Disabilities Act (ADA). This puts the onus upon the operator to determine whether to allow an animal to board that isn't in a carrier.*

It's advisable to give people the benefit of the doubt who use service animals. However, such goodwill can sometimes border on the absurd. Before going into details, here's what our Standard Operating Procedures (SOPs) have to say about service animals:

"The animal is considered a service animal or companion animal if the customer says it is; there is no documentation required to board a service animal."

As you can see, it's vague. The word 'ludicrous' comes to mind. Why? Because human nature being what it is, people can manipulate rules to the point where they don't follow them at all. I've seen many dogs brought aboard by people who haven't the slightest clue what training a service animal entails. They're out to buck the system. They just want to take Fido with them, so they'll just say he's a service animal. Boom. Free ride for Fido, no hassle.

Drivers can ask what their animal has been trained to do. But what if they stammer and hem and haw before coming up with a comically lame answer? "Um, he wakes me up when I go to sleep." Or, "he keeps me calm because I'm a nervous person." Really? Perhaps they're telling the truth, but I'll bet the lug nuts on my bus that many are lying.

The Americans with Disabilities Act is very generous to the riding public. Granted, those who truly have disabilities need these protections. But it is very vague as to specific guidelines as to what constitutes an actual service animal. Trained service animals are on-the-job when they ride a bus. Operators do not speak to or touch the dog. The honest folks know exactly what is expected of them and their animal. The dog will lie at the person's feet, always under control, on a leash or harness. The dog will not interact with other riders or animals.

Dogs who are not trained by certified agencies can be trained by their owners, as circumstances dictate. Perhaps they need an animal immediately and can't be put on a waiting list, or maybe they simply can't afford a professionally-trained dog. People who do this on their own are intelligent enough to research what they need to know, and usually do a decent job of training.

My problem is with Fido, the simple pet. He could be a bully, aggressive toward people or other animals. Fido can cause disruptions, urinate on the bus, growl/bark at or even attack people. These are the things a driver has to closely watch for. This takes our attention away from the road, causing a potential hazard. If Fido takes a chunk out of a passenger's leg, am I responsible just because I let him board? Dispatch will send "help" in the form of a supervisor, and/or police/medical if necessary. But then there's the waiting time. We're not supposed to leave the driver's seat, except in the most dire circumstances. We are extremely vulnerable if we do. Fido could be "sicced" on us by a mentally-unstable owner who resents being asked to leave. Or, Fido could attack an actual service animal. A friend of mine who is vision-impaired actually had this happen at a boarding platform. To my knowledge, no action was taken against the aggressor. She was terribly shaken by this, as was her service animal. Luckily, neither she nor the dog was seriously wounded.

Having a brother who is mentally disabled, I agree with rules which are meant to protect people with all types of disabilities. I understand it takes time and money to properly train an animal to serve and guide disabled people. But service animals should have documentation, which specifically describes its training and expertise, on file with the transit agency. Common sense surely dictates this, and the safety of drivers and their passengers should override false cries of discrimination.

Often, our society tends to over-compensate for past errors. Later, it is imperative that we apply common sense when amending legislation. I believe it is time to do this regarding service animals.

Service Animals, Or Animal Service?

🚌 **DEKE'S NOTE:** *Not long after the previous article was posted, our agency modified the language regarding service animals on transit vehicles. It didn't make our lives any easier.*

We are on the front lines of mass transit. Professionals behind the wheel of a 20-ton urban assault vehicle. When management makes a change, it's on us to inform the public and also enact these rules. We take the shots while the decision makers sit back and relax.

Our management recently fine-tuned its policy regarding Service Animals:

"All service animals traveling on (our) vehicle must: Be on a leash or in a container under its owner/handler's control and behave appropriately. Cats, birds, reptiles, amphibians and rodents must be kept within an enclosed carrier or container. Must remain at its owner/handler's feet, or on owner/handler's lap. The animal is not to sit on a vehicle seat. And, must not be aggressive toward people or other animals. The care and supervision of a service animal is solely the responsibility of its owner/handler. Customers traveling with animals are subject to the same general rules that apply to all passengers. Any damage or soiling caused by the animal is the responsibility of the animal's owner/handler. Operators may ask the customer if the animal is a service animal. Operators may refuse service if the animal does not meet the guidelines listed above."

Not much of a change, per se, except they made it easier for passengers to lie about their pets being "service animals." And lie they do, not only about Fido's status, but they also encourage others to follow their lead. "Just say it's a service animal," I heard a girl whisper to a boarding passenger. "Then they *have* to let you ride."

I recently informed a rider that his pet had to be in a carrier. Another passenger immediately began berating the driver for "not knowing the rules." I was trying to tell the lady she could ride but had to keep Fido on her lap. Snobby Sally insisted on their getting off the bus and threatened to complain, citing my "attitude."

This new wording encourages more deception from the riding public. Some people give us grief at every opportunity. Now, everybody's dog can ride on a lie, and they can sit in owner's lap or at their "handler's" feet. *Right.* I've seen people struggling to keep their dogs under control on the sidewalk, then drag them onto my bus and insist it's their service, or *companion* animal.

Just last year, an aggressive dog killed another passenger's smaller dog on a light rail car. If we allow an animal on board which in turn attacks another passenger and/or their mutt, are we then liable? We cannot predict the future, our hands are fairly tied when it comes to enforcement, and we're trained to be non-confrontational. By not allowing frauds on our bus, we can get customer complaints; if we were to allow Snarling Sid on the bus and he takes a chunk out of Snidely Sam's leg, we're in trouble for that too? Something smells bad here, and we're the ones choking on it.

Our federal government needs to fix the ADA rules. Not only should service animals be professionally trained, but they should have documentation to prove it. I love when a *true* service animal boards my bus. They usually have a harness with a proper handle. Once inside, they lie quietly and act as trained. Several times, I've had to ask passengers to make their counterfeit companions lie down and not bother others. By doing so, I'm setting myself up for abuse, snide comments, or worse. Until the government cracks down and forces the issue, people will fraudulently bring Fido on their rambles about town.

Sure, trained service animals are expensive. Yet those who actually have service animals probably agree there need to be tighter guidelines. Until then, I don't feel safe when dishonest people bring their brutes aboard.

Woof.

Only the Good

People are interesting, and I enjoy interacting with our diverse populace. In the bullpen, some operators can be negative and many are mum about their experiences, but others are quite comical in their descriptions and anecdotes.

It is difficult to avoid negative, but I try. Regardless, here's some good things I've seen. Maybe writing this will renew my spirit while also giving you reason to smile.

One of my regulars is Arnie, a gentleman I've grown quite fond of. He always says kind words of encouragement. He has called in commendations, realizing many complain rather than praise. The other day I saw him and thanked him for his last commendation. It has been a while since I've had one, I told him, and it really made me feel good. "Well then," he said with his trademark smile, "I think it's time I call in another one."

Thank you, sir!

The front seating area of a bus is reserved for those who have physical difficulties. Sometimes, people sit there who have no reason to. An older gentleman wearing a World War II cap was sitting in this area one afternoon when I boarded a lady using a mobility device. When none of the 20-something passengers occupying priority seating would move, this gentleman rose and lifted the seats as the lady boarded. The youngsters seemed oblivious to his decency. Finally, a middle-aged man just behind the priority area rose and offered the veteran his seat. I smiled and thanked the man for his kindness. A bit louder than I normally would, in hopes the young dolts would hear. Evidently, my words weren't loud enough to penetrate their earphones.

"It's okay," the vet told me on the way out, "I think the headphones keep their brains from leaking out." He smiled, patted me on the shoulder and skipped out the door like a man 30 years younger.

Cruising downtown one morning, I saw a fellow wearing a Darth Vader costume and a brown kilt, rolling down the sidewalk. He was riding a uni-segway while playing bagpipes. It was an amusing sight. Seems he has his own FaceBook page with over 12,000 likes.

Keepin' Portland Weird, I reckon.

A young couple boarded with their groceries one day. Two of the bags broke, spilling groceries all over ground. Fellow passengers helped the guy pick it all up and get it on the bus; when he got off, the same friendly folks helped transport items off the bus.

While some passengers can be obnoxious, it's nice to see people helping each other. If we had more of this and less of a "me first" attitude, this world would be a lot nicer to live in.

A bus operator recently spotted a toddler on the loose. He stopped his bus and stopped the lad from wandering out into rush hour traffic on a busy street. Bringing him onto the bus, the operator alerted Dispatch and was met a short time later by a supervisor and the police at a transit center. The little guy's father had fallen asleep after his graveyard shift, and the tyke escaped. I salute the operator for his quick thinking, as this story could have easily had a tragic ending. His act was called heroic by many, but this modest operator said he just did what anybody else would have. Thanks brother, for most likely saving that child's life.

꩜

I came upon a line of traffic stopping for no apparent reason one morning. As I scanned the street ahead, I saw movement in front of one of the vehicles. Marching in single file were Mama Goose and her five goslings, followed by Papa. They took their sweet time, but the cars sat patiently until they were safely across. Only in Oregon.

Biking to My Liking

🚌 **DEKE'S NOTE:** *About two years into my career, I was a bit shell-shocked. Although I'd seen many foolish things happen on the road, my rose-colored glasses remained intact. I try to look for the good things in people. While I've been guilty at times of singling out bicyclists for dangerous behaviors, this post reveals the fear which the unsafe among them brings out in a professional driver, while also recognizing the many who are safe riders.*

The recent Naked Bike Ride fired up some long-smoldering thoughts. From what I've read, this protest was originally intended to raise awareness of bicycle safety on public streets. As a bus operator, I've seen bicyclists make some pretty foolish maneuvers. However, while the public has been less supportive of the Naked Bike Ride because of the nudity, it would certainly balk at the possibility of a Naked Bus Operator Day to protest a lack of bike safety.

The other day a bicyclist blew a stop sign to cross a major boulevard. He failed to see my bus barreling toward him at 28 miles per hour. When a large vehicle moves toward you, it is nearly impossible to calculate its speed. You think you have time to cross in front of it, but suddenly you are directly in its path. I don't know the equation to calculate mass in motion, but he was surely tempting fate on a very large scale. This bicyclist either didn't see my bus or ignored it, and was only able to cross the street unscathed because I braked. Hard. I beeped twice as a friendly reminder to WATCH OUT. His response was to show me his single-digit IQ score as he sailed by.

I applaud pedaling a bike rather than polluting our air. Alternative transportation reduces traffic congestion, but it can also pose some dangerous situations for the professional driver. For the most part, bicyclists tend to be safer than motorists. They *must* be. They don't have the armored protection a vehicle does. It's them and their 15-pound cycle versus thousands of armored vehicles. Bikes have no airbags, and the road doesn't offer cushions. Still, there are many who self-righteously believe they own the road. Bus drivers vigilantly protect those oblivious to their own danger. Even so, unless a bicyclist consistently employs safe riding practices, they are more likely to be involved in a collision.

"Cyclists account for 2% of road deaths and injuries," according to a Bicyclist Universe article regarding accidents involving cyclists. Bicycle groups maintain most of these disasters are the fault of the motorist, but many people are probably hurt or killed due to a lack of awareness or basic safety. I see many bicyclists pedaling along safely wearing reflective materials, scanning around them, signaling their intentions, using common sense and following the law. I applaud these riders, because they are easier to see and are predictable. They make my job of driving safely a bit easier. I've also noticed an alarming percentage of bicyclists guilty of unsafe practices.

The rider I described in the second paragraph of this post is part of a group I see several times a week. I saw one guy riding down a mildly-busy bike lane with both his hands (and his eyes) on his phone, texting as he approached a busy intersection. Downtown on the transit mall, bicyclists routinely blow through red lights, passing cars and buses with abandon. Rather than waiting for a traffic light to turn green, they look both ways (sometimes) and just ride through. Several people carrying large bags as they pedal along lurch into traffic lanes when their load shifts. Bicyclists who dart from sidewalk to traffic lane to bike lane are unpredictable. Those who zip between long lines of vehicles stopped in traffic are in danger when traffic begins moving again.

Portland is a bike riding mecca, with more than two million rides over the Hawthorne Bridge each year. There are miles of bike paths, and many streets have special bike lanes. We proudly boast the Springwater Corridor, a 21-mile-long bike/pedestrian path running from Sellwood on the west to Gresham on the east. Our city will soon have an innovative bridge over the Willamette River for transit, bicyclists and pedestrians only.

Bus operators give bicyclists the benefit of doubt more than we're given credit for. When a bicyclist boards my bus, I employ the parking brake, put on the 4-way emergency flashers, shift into neutral, and lower the bus to make it easier for them to place their bike on the rack. While they are securing their bike, I watch them and traffic around my bus. When they are safely aboard, I simultaneously take their fare as I release all these safety features employed for their benefit, while constantly scanning around the bus prior to moving it. Do bikers see this, or is it something they take for granted? As long as I do my part to keep everyone safe — those on the bus as well as those outside of it — I am doing my job. When I am flipped off, you might see me muttering in disbelief, but I only return the hand gesture within my mind.

When riding a bike near a bus, please take extreme caution. Remember that you are more difficult to see, especially if it's dark outside. We appreciate blinking lights, reflective clothing, or anything else that improves your visibility. When a bus is servicing a stop, watch closely for our signals. Right turn signal means we are boarding passengers; 4-way flashers indicate we are boarding people who use mobility devices or bicycles; left turn signals, often accompanying the flashing red YIELD symbol warning we are about to pull from the curb. Be patient, and be visible. If you're passing us as we change from boarding to merging, use extreme caution and be sure you're not in our blind spot. If you can see us looking at you in our mirror, that's good. Chances are excellent we will see you, but it's always better to be patient and wait behind the bus. It normally only takes a few seconds to board passengers, and those few seconds are certainly worth your life.

People are quick to blame the operator for any transit disaster.

However, how often is our safety celebrated, considering we transport over a million riders each week? I'd like to see stats showing a ratio of accident-free rides to injuries. I'm proud of my fellow operators because that ratio is heavily-weighted to the public's benefit. Bus operators everywhere always strive to keep people safe, yet rarely get credit for it.

Your safety is vital. Not only because we value our job, but also because it is every operator's nightmare to see anyone injured in traffic. We are human beings who care about you.

When you're out there pedaling along, remember bus operators are watching out for you. But humans are anything but perfect, so do as much as you can to improve your odds of keeping safe. Hopefully you'll wave at us with an *entire* hand, and appreciate our efforts to share the road with you and everyone else out there on our busy streets.

Brooklyn Horse Rings

Driving a bus gives me the opportunity to see many fascinating Portland neighborhoods. Having only lived here a little more than a decade, it is interesting to find "new" things out there. Walking back to the garage after a delicious lunch at Edelweiss Deli, I came across an interesting sight.

Embedded in a sidewalk dating to 1910, there are steel rings in front of many historic homes in Portland, especially in the Brooklyn neighborhood. They were used by early residents to keep their horses from straying. Prior to the advent of the automobile, horses and horse-drawn buggies were the main mode of transportation, and residents would tether their rides to these rings.

As the sidewalks were repaired these rings were removed as a safety concern. Proud of the city's heritage, Portland residents demanded these rings of history be preserved. In 2005, Woodstock Neighborhood resident Scott Wayne Indiana started a trend of tying toy horses to these rings in an effort to illustrate their originally-intended use. Now there are many of these displays, and often there are offerings left for them... hay, saddles, blankets and such.

The Brooklyn Neighborhood is a fascinating piece of Portland history. I love the architecture there. One home reminds me of the dollhouse I built for my daughter years ago. Many trees are over 100 years old. Combined with the beautiful gardens, Brooklyn's charms make for a picturesque stroll through this part of historic Portland.

Those Blasted Signs!

People are in a hurry to get nowhere fast. Especially at rush hour. Signs? Screw 'em. Buses? Get out of the way! People don't understand that buses must follow traffic laws. If not, we might plow into something or somebody. Patience, an important part of my daily mantra, is something learned. Sure, perhaps the ol' bladder is straining against its elasticity limit, but the prospect of a PA (preventable accident) adding to our troubles demands consistency. Other motorists scorn those who actually obey traffic signs.

Do not block the intersection

"Must not apply to my shiny new Audi, because I'm more important than those poor suckers on that bus! They can wait."

So says the self-absorbed commuter. Seemingly endless lines of traffic prompt foolish behavior once that intersection is clear. Motorists hate to stop if the light is about to change to yellow or red. They inch out in hopes the traffic ahead will move forward in time for them to get through. Never mind that bus at the cross street which had to wait an extra light cycle because earlier motorists ignored the SIGN.

"Hey, what? Why is this bus bearing down on me like a divorce attorney trying to get into the Jerry Springer Show? How dare he honk at me! So what, I'm clogging his precious intersection! Get a life, for crying out loud! Stupid bus drivers, geez!"

No right on red

Busy two-lane streets are perilous enough for cars, but when there's a bus ahead, motorists throw caution out the window with their empty beer can. It takes an average of 20 seconds to board and discharge passengers depending on the number of people involved. Then it takes an extra few seconds to close the doors and scan around the bus for possible danger before moving again. Apparently, this is an unbearable delay for Susie Soccer Mom. Not only is she unable to see the warning sign from behind the bus, she's probably driven this road countless times before. She knows the sign is there. Big deal.

"Come on, STUPID BUS! I have to get to Susie's game so I can abuse the refs, coaches and opposing spectators while simultaneously embarrassing my smartass kid! You're in the way, and I need to turn right."

Susie's solution? She sees a two-second opening in oncoming traffic. The bus operator has deployed his left turn and YIELD signals, preparing to merge. As he looks over his left shoulder, he sees Susie zip around him, across a double-yellow line. She barely clears his front bumper as she begins her illegal right turn. Lucky for her, a cop isn't lying there in wait. Unluckily for the pedestrian using a walker, Susie doesn't see him in time and is now sporting a spurting-red hood ornament with wheels.

Left turn yield to oncoming traffic

Bus operators approach an intersection with our foot covering the brake. A relatively-intelligent driver should be able to judge whether he has time to safely turn left before the bus enters the intersection. However, people in a hurry leave most of their intelligence three car-lengths behind.

"Finally, an opening! That bus is waaaay back there, no problemo. Once this bicycle gets through, I'm gone!"

What Brainless Barney has failed to calculate is the bus is traveling a few miles an hour under the speed limit, which is about 10 mph faster than the bicyclist. By the time the bike approaches, the bus has closed the distance. SCREEEECH! Operator predicts Barney's inability to calculate speed vs. distance and stops just tin time to avoid taking the bed off his '82 Chevy pickup. The only thanks offered is a hairy middle-finger pointed at the now-muttering bus operator. If he could only see life from Buddy Bus Operator's perspective, maybe he would retract that salute.

I rest my case. My blood pressure has risen merely thinking of this subject. Time for a snack, a nap, and repetition of the Daily Mantra. Be safe out there, folks. Your loved ones want you home in one piece; not delivered to your church in a one-way box.

Relieving Myself

🚌 **DEKE'S NOTE:** *I've always been mischievous. Out on the road I have some "play time" in my mind. This is one I made up one day when the runs I was assigned were on the same paddle.*

When you work the extra board, you are given runs in which you must be creative and resourceful. Driving a bus is also a good time for the creative mind to wander. The other day, I experienced both, thanks to an actively-humorous rider. Gonna have some fun with this post, creating a 'what if' scenario.

Customer Service Representative (CSR): Thank you for calling, how may I help you today?

Penny Ultra-Naive (PUN): Hello? Is this the complaint line?

CSR: Yes, ma'am, but you can also...

PUN: I don't want to hear your excuses or get the runaround young lady.

CSR: Mmm hmm, yes ma'am I understand. How...

PUN: Your driver this morning truly disgusted me. I can't believe you hire trash like him!

CSR: I'm sorry to hear you had an issue...

PUN: It's not me who has the problem, for heaven's sake. (audible shudder) He told me he was going to relieve himself! Disgustingly too much information. And if that wasn't bad enough, he...

CSR: Excuse me for interrupting, but did you say your driver relieved himself?

PUN: Yes.

CSR: And where was he when he did this?

PUN: I don't know where he was. I couldn't bear to watch.

CSR: Was he on the bus when he did this?

PUN: He was driving!

CSR: Let me get this straight. Your driver said he was going to relieve himself as he was driving the bus?

PUN: Yes! Isn't that disgusting?

CSR: I wonder how he did that?

PUN: Well, he did have a water bottle. What's worse, after he said that I saw him take a drink out of it!

CSR: Oh dear.

PUN: Are you going to fire that filth, or what?

CSR: We will certainly look into this, ma'am. Let me get some details first. I need to determine the line and train...

PUN: ARE YOU ALL IDIOTS OVER THERE? I said it was a bus, not a train!

CSR: I'm sorry ma'am, I meant which bus were you on?

PUN: A blue one.

(At this point, CSR has to mute her headset because she's started to chuckle. Unfortunately, PUN hears this before it can be fully muted.)

PUN: Why are you laughing at me?

(It takes a few seconds for CSR to recover, leaving an awkward pause on the line.)

CSR: I'm sorry, ma'am. I don't mean to laugh, but I just got carried away. The visual, you know, just struck me as funny.

PUN: I'm deadly serious, young lady. I don't see anything funny about it.

(This time, CSR snorts before muting. She is losing the battle to maintain control.)

CSR: Yes, ma'am. Now let's get to the bottom of this...

PUN hangs up.

By this time, a few of CSR's co-workers have looked over to see why she's laughing.

"I just had this lady call in and complain about a driver 'relieving himself on the bus'!"

"Did you explain to her what that means?" Carrie CoWorker asks. CSR is still rather new to the job.

"I didn't make it that far," she replies. "You gotta hear this call... she was really mad!"

Those of us who have driven a bus know what it means to 'relieve yourself.' Normally, a bus operator will drive part of the paddle, and then another driver will meet them en route and take over. If there isn't a driver waiting at the relief point, we sometimes refer to it as 'relieving myself.' I had to drive two continuous parts of a run last week, and I mentioned to a rider that I'd have to 'relieve myself' at a specific point in the route. The conversation went downhill from there.

Searching for the Right Bus

I get out to the yard, find the bus, wipe it down, start and pre-trip it, and then it hits me.

"Damnit, this isn't the right bus!"

By now I should be deadheading to the line's starting point. Time is running out. Pulling off my back cushion, ice pack with snacks/drinks, backpack, water bottle, and trip pouch, I jump out and find the correct bus. The ritual begins anew. Five minutes later and 15 minutes late, I pull out of the yard. While it's not the best scenario, it beats being called on the road to be informed you took the wrong bus.

Duh, Mr. Blue.

Of course, this is to be expected from Mr. Absent Minded Blue. Once in a fit of youthful morning confusion I spit at the medicine cabinet and threw my toothbrush into the sink.

This is a repeat, but important nonetheless. DO **NOT** WALK, OR RUN, IN FRONT OF A BUS!

A few weeks ago, waiting for the bus in front of me to leave so I could pull up to the stop, this dunce came sprinting across the street directly in front of my bus. A second earlier I had glanced over my left shoulder before moving and found no immediate danger. Then, a sweep in front and to the right side. This kid was fast. As soon as I let my foot off the brake and started to roll, he was right... there. Luckily my foot was still covering the brake and I stopped as soon as my peripheral vision registered this potential disaster. The young man came perilously close to serious injury, and my bus wasn't even the one he wanted!

I pulled up to the stop and opened the door. Intending passengers began to crowd the entry, but I waved them away and yelled at the offender to catch his attention.

"Hey you! Yeah, you. That was a STUPID thing to do!" I shouted.

Driven by the terror of what could have happened, I was furious.

Dumbo stared at me. Sullenly. He lifted his eyes to meet mine, acutely aware that everyone at the stop knew I was addressing him.

"Don't you ever do that again!" I continued. "NO bus is worth your life, and you just escaped serious injury. Good grief that was foolish!"

"I'm sorry," he stammered.

"Not as sorry as you might have been had I not seen you!" I wanted to instruct him on basic safety, but I was just too mad.

Then there are those who exit and cross the street in front of my bus. Why is this not a good idea? Well, these buses are 40 feet long, 10.5 feet wide and 11 feet tall. You can't see through one, nor can you see around it. Not until you've already stepped into oncoming traffic that is. Nor can the motorists see you. What do they usually do? That's right, they pass the bus. No matter there's a double-yellow line prohibiting such an ignorant gamble, they hate to wait behind this lumbering old traffic clogger.

Patience is a lifesaver. Wait for the bus to pull away before venturing into Suicide Alley. Then you can see all the cars behind me and pick the opportune (and safe) time to cross.

Portland is picturesque. One thing I love about my job is the opportunity to see great swaths of it every day. We live in a mystical rain forest. In the span of minutes, we can jump onto a trail and escape city noise, hearing little else but the whisper of wind in the pines, birdsong of countless variety, and our own breathing. All this while traffic buzzes along not far away.

In early summer, the shades of green are too many to count. There are numerous vistas to enjoy. I see something new each day. It's an adventure to live here. Most people are genuine and friendly. Conversations can be quite lively and interesting.

Thanks, Portland. You make my job fun... most of the time.

Talking About Customers

Operators come into contact with thousands of riders a month. Most are new faces, as Extra Board operators drive different routes every day. Some are vaguely familiar; others can be happy reunions or dismal reminders of painful encounters.

There is this one woman who can be found riding any number of lines. She always has a roll-along bag. Petite, middle-aged woman who wears brown/black garb, head covered even in the heat of summer. The only thing she says to the driver is "Ramp, please." Never a "thank you," or even "have a nice day." She sometimes rides for a while, but she's also known to ride just a few stops. Her fare is always current, she never speaks to anybody, rarely causes trouble. I used to see her almost daily, and I would groan when I did. Usually she would board when I was running late, so it would annoy me to run the ramp out for her to board knowing I'd have to do it all over again in a few minutes. Now I want to know her story. I'm curious. A glimpse of her eyes spoke volumes of sadness or anger. She mostly avoids eye contact, so I can't describe her face. I can only hope she has a home and people who love her.

It is common to see people ride the bus to avoid the rain. Portland has a large homeless population, and there's not a lot of shelter for them. I once had an elderly couple who would lug several bags to the very back seats where they would remain for the duration of my run. They were very polite, but quiet. I tried to engage them, but they kept to themselves. When they did speak to me, I thought I detected a hint of Jamaican accent. The lady's eyes bespoke a kindness I was attracted to, but she wouldn't be drawn out.

Then there are those who ride with an annoying twist. They're compelled to tell anyone their life story who isn't plugged in and tuned out. Or they brag about just getting out of jail. Some are on their way to the nearest methadone clinic. Maybe their baby's dad just had sex with their sister's best friend and they are going to castrate the sorry creep. Others are just bent on causing trouble.

They sneak booze on board and drink it only to leave empty bottles and/or vomit behind. Others are racist slobs who spread their hatred toward anyone who looks different than they do.

Most people ride the bus to work or school. They are self-absorbed, and it can annoy me. When a passenger boards my bus, I greet them with a welcoming smile. Many smile and nod in greeting. But if they don't even look at me, I get a bit perturbed. They hold their pass out for me to see, but purposefully turn their head away. It's dismissive, and teenagers are professionals at this. Perhaps they don't realize how rude it is, and I have to hope their parents would chastise them if they saw this behavior. I certainly wouldn't condone this rudeness in my own children.

If you ride my bus, I'll smile at you. Even if I've had a horribly rotten day. It doesn't matter if a recent passenger trampled my soul. I'm happy to have a job I enjoy. You are my passenger, and you are important to me. If you're a Class A jerk, that's okay... I can ignore it because you'll be leaving soon.

Busted Auto Pilot

Working a split shift on two lines that mirror each other for parts of the route can be a bit tricky. Especially when you drive one for five hours and the next for four. The first one tools down Broadway a bit further than the next. On the latter, I forgot I wasn't the former. Missed a vital left turn, didn't immediately realize it. I would have kept on towards the transit center, but Buddy Bubbaloo crept up behind me.

"Hey man," he crowed. "Like, you missed a turn back there." All I knew was somebody pulled the cord and I was cruising into the stop. Another line's stop.

"Oops," I sheepishly replied. "Guess I'm not a 77 any more, am I?"

Luckily it was mid-morning. None of my passengers seemed in a hurry. It only took a series of three right turns to put my bus back on route. It was time to eat some crow. Luckily, my riders were more amused than annoyed with my seemingly-rookie error.

"Folks," I said via the PA, "seems I shoulda gone left back there. I failed to re-program my auto pilot after doing the 77. A slight adjustment here will get us back on route, but I apologize for the momentary lack of reason and any inconvenience it might cause you. I seem to be suffering a slight case of rectal-cranial inversion."

The sudden pause of chatter worried me. But then several chuckles and one outright guffaw eased the pain of my embarrassment. One passenger even had a word of advice as he left the bus.

"I'd see a doctor for that condition as soon as possible."

🚶 RAW

This post brought out several appreciative comments from fellow operators.
The Rampant Lion:
"LOL Yeeeeeehp! Been there, done that! Worst one I did (with the most miraculous outcome) was, after driving Line 35 to Lake Oswego the previous day, got assigned Extra Service and then a late-night fill on Line 40 to Milwaukee. Ooops! Was supposed to turn off the highway to go over the Sellwood Bridge, but forgot to turn the Line 35 autopilot off. Good thing the highway was five lanes wide, cause unless I hung a u-ie right then and there it would have been impossible to turn around until we got all the way to Lake O!"
Anonymous #1
"Every time I screw up a Route I say #1) It's my first day! or #2) I don't know why dispatch had me turn here. I don't see any accident. You just have to have a semi - believable story ready. It's the good/bad carpenter theory. Every carpenter makes mistakes. The good carpenter hides those mistakes better. I make lots of mistakes. I just try to hide my mistakes better!
"The funny thing is...these folks are so hardened to seeing reroutes all the time, most of them likely thought you were on one!"

Anonymous #2:

"My eye-opening story though is just a bit weirder. On the extra board, I get a 30-Estacada run for the very first time. Never even been anywhere east of I-205. I go and ask my fellow "boardies" all the usual things-what to look for, where to turn, etc, etc, blah blah, blah...and this is the day no one feels compelled to help me out! The only advice I get is "Watch your speed heading out there or you'll end up in the river." Swell.

So I leave the yard 20-25 minutes early (as a new x-board operator, I found this often helped keep me out of trouble—I didn't care about time donation as much as keeping myself centered) and head out to Estacada. Figure if I don't see any signs that say "Welcome to Burns" or Idaho I'm doin' ok. Let's make matters worse though by being the very first bus out there of the morning; it's pitch black, with HEAVY fog and road signs? Who needs road signs?! I manage to get myself all the way out there and now I'm trying to figure out where my starting point is. The Route Description says something about Main Street, then up to 6th or something...problem is the streets would go 4th, 3rd, 2nd and then Main. The was no 6th. You go past 4th and it was some other LETTERED street. I had arrived in Estacada 20 minutes early. I circled a two block radius...the SAME two blocks, for 1/2 an hour before I finally gave up. I just couldn't find where I was supposed to go. The Chevron gas station guy (who saw me circle, it had to be six times, wouldn't come out to help). I had called dispatch 20 minutes earlier; still no callback.

"I sat in the middle of the street with my four ways on and my window open for a good five minutes when suddenly I heard a big, booming voice "Do you need help?" My first instinct was to say "Yes Lord, please save me!" I say yes kinda hesitantly because at first I couldn't see who owned the voice (the fog, remember?). Then this tall man with a gentle stature came up and got on the bus and helped route me around, explaining that had I just went three more blocks I would have found that the street numbers start going back up again. He also told me that I needed to turn my interior lights off in order to see intending passengers and if *they didn't flash a light at me as I approached, they didn't want my bus. (He was right there too, though I was a bit worried at first about turning my lights off at 5 am with people on board.) It turned out to eventually be a good trip and I actually made up the lost time by the time I got all the way into Portland. Oh, and dispatch finally called me back as I left Clackamas Town Center inbound (thankfully it wasn't THAT important). Note to self: The next time a more "experienced" operator tells me I didn't need to worry about riding/driving some of these remote routes-WRONG ANSWER."*

Patience + Safety = Longevity

It's amazing how much I learn about driving every day I'm behind the wheel of a city bus.

While I was in training, I thought what my trainers were teaching was old news. Big mistake. People often scoff at the term "professional driver." What they don't know is that no matter how good a driver you think you are, the odds are that you pull bonehead moves every day that could get you, or someone else, seriously injured or killed. Instantly. No do-overs allowed. No extra lives. Just one lapse of judgement and in a few days you'd be laying under flowers or ashes scattered on the wind. Your loved ones will forever be asking "Why?" or "How could this happen?" Sadly, you wouldn't be there to answer.

As a child, I had a very dear friend who was a bright star to me. She was so full of life, I adored her. She laughed at nearly everything, found beauty in the ordinary, danced with the wind and played in the snow. She was extremely intelligent, a fascinating conversationalist, loved by all she touched. A 25-year-old mother of an infant with another on the way, she made such a mistake one beautiful spring day. Stuck behind a large truck on a dirt road, eating its dust, she became impatient. Even though she couldn't see ahead of it, she decided to pass. She was killed instantly as she drove head-on into an approaching vehicle. Her son was critically injured, but survived.

In one instant, my beloved friend made a decision that horribly altered my happiness. She couldn't have imagined how horrible the aftermath would be. She was in a hurry to run an errand that, in the scheme of things, wasn't very important.

She left behind a husband who so loved her the smile rarely left his face when they were together. He was utterly devastated by her death. As a 13-year-old who idolized her, I was traumatized for years. In fact, her passing was so incredibly sad, hundreds mourned her. I still do, several decades later.

The next time you're annoyed there's a bus ahead, please remember we're trained to help keep you safe. We can see a lot more than you can. When you're impatient, remember that you can afford a few seconds, or minutes. Especially when your life could end in the snap of a vertebrae.

Wicked Wretch of the West

I still have a healthy distrust of Mercedes Benz drivers. Sure, some of my friends own them, but they know how to drive. To be fair, I've had several Benzers yield to me lately. My best friend, whose raise this year equals my annual salary, owns one. He can drive it, too. But there's always one who spoils it for the others.

Cruising down a very busy one-way street the other day, I found the one. As I was pulling from a service stop, I put on my turn signal and yield light. Allowing the first two cars past, I then noticed a new Benz SL550 ragtop speeding up to try and beat me to the punch. Benzie had plenty of time to see my signal and lawfully yield.

Evidently, her broom was still in the shop. The Benz must have been a loaner.

Construction had narrowed traffic to one lane, and Benzie didn't want to be stuck behind my bus for an entire city block. Already running behind, I was in no mood to suffer the fool. I had plenty of room to pull out, and I did.

HONK!

"Asshole!" I could hear her scream from her luxurious ego-encrusted seat.

seats. An ass as well, that is still more attractive than the shenanigans practiced by many politicians. In fact, I would bet my ass is infinitely finer than the contract-negotiating motives of our top brass. But enough about my posterior aspect.

Once upon a time in another state of Corporata, I wrote a piece for the employee newsletter. I truly enjoyed my job, and thought it would be helpful to give folks helpful hints on how to do for themselves what I routinely did for them. Having duly submitted my polished draft, I eagerly awaited its publication. When it came out, it had the byline of our department's vice president rather than mine. It was printed, verbatim, exactly as I had written it. The sonofabitch had the gall to claim my work! I raised hell. All the way to a brick wall called Human Resources. Since the plagiarist was in upper management, I was advised to swallow my pride and keep my job. This scumbag, however, would no longer look me in the eye after his dirty deed. And boy lemme tell ya, I stared daggers at him every time we crossed paths.

I'm careful to merely express my opinion in this blog. I know we'll never get to remodel the GM's office, or expect people to suddenly learn how to behave safely. We all believe as life has taught us. Bus drivers are fallible, but we still watch out for people incapable of sensing the danger of their actions.

Want to enjoy Labor Day? Just remember that if not for unions, you wouldn't have this holiday weekend. And if you get too drunk out there, hop on a bus. At least you can count on us to get you there. Safely.

"I love you too," I said softly, an overstated smile on my face.

Normally, people are only stuck behind me briefly, because the nature of bus transportation is simple. We drive, stop, pick up and/or drop off passengers, rinse and repeat. Drivers blessed with common sense tend to realize this. They simply pass us when we pull to the next stop. Easy pleasy. Evidently, Benzie thought she was more important than those on my bus.

Immediately past my next service stop, a utility truck was parked. Jim Hardhat was placing cones around his work area. Traffic in the left lane was backed up. As I scanned my surroundings, I saw the still-agitated Benzie lurking there. Revving her impressive engine.

Mr. Hardhat, seeing the situation I was in, walked up to my window.

"Need some help getting out of here?" he asked, a kind smile on his weathered face.

"Yeah thanks," I replied, "that would be great!"

He proceeded to the car nearest my rear bumper and stepped in front of it, putting out his hand in a STOP gesture. I gleefully realized he'd picked Benzie.

HONK! HONK! HONK!

"Get out of my fucking way you asshole!" Benzie's tongue was growing hairier, I noticed.

Leaving them, I noticed Jim's smile had disappeared. I opened my window and yelled a cheerful "THANK YOU VERY MUCH" in Benzie's general direction. I doubt Benzie heard it, because Jim was lecturing her. With gusto. I tried to hear his words, but I couldn't afford the time to stick around and listen. I could see in my mirror that Jim was giving her hell. From what I could see as I cleared the intersection, he stood there long enough to ensure she missed the green light.

I love it when karma picks an appropriate victim to strike.

Thanks, Mr. Hardhat.

HIT COUNTER: 15,000 (August 2014)

11 Hours Down and Happy Labor Day!

It was once written (by whom nobody seems to be able to pin down -- Hemingway perhaps?), that one should "write drunk, edit sober." Well I'm not drunk, but I have had a shot of bourbon to begin this rare Friday night libation.

Since it is a strict no-no to drink during the work week since you never know when your next shift will be, I wait until I'm safely home Friday night, out of uniform and happily celebratory before I imbibe. It is in the infant stages of inebriation that I write tonight. Except, it's technically Saturday. The end of Friday's service day. So... (*burp*) cheers, and Happy Labor Day weekend!

My driver friends (and carefully-screened passengers) have been treated to the brand-spanking-new business cards I've had printed up to celebrate FTDS blog's 15,000th hit. They are sworn to secrecy. What's my name, you might ask? Deke N. Blue, of course! A pen name is a shield against any possible ramifications from practicing my right to free speech. The transit agency states we have this right, but you never know; they could launch vendettas against employees who dare speak their mind. If you know my true identity, please do not ever reveal it. I am simply Deke. Okay? It is a thinly-veiled alter ego, but still... please protect me.

I like to joke that lacking any mental illness I'm aware of, I've concocted a separate personality for myself. Since I know I've done this, it's not a psychosis. My wife might argue this point, but she's stuck with me. It's fun to write freely about what I see "out there" and whatever else comes to mind. I may, on occasion, spurt out a diatribe aimed at our management. Having one of the most-stressful jobs in the world, I feel entitled to do so when situations require it. Hence, the pen name.

Am I a coward for this dual personality schtick? Hell no! I'm simply a middle-aged fellow who has been burned by corporate America. I've simply learned to cover my ass. An ass, I may add, that is flattening due to long hours in horribly-uncomfortable operator

"Good" Drivers?

We all tend to consider ourselves "good" drivers when we're tooling around in our own wheels. Ask 10 licensed drivers to rate their driving skills and chances are all will give themselves high marks. Ask a bus operator to rate the average driver, and their score drops drastically.

With such a wide, elevated view of the road, we see things the average Jane does not. It becomes second nature to see impending trouble, so we routinely take action to avoid becoming part of the problem. Since we're such huge targets, there's little we can do to avoid another vehicle slamming into us. Yet we often protect the motoring public from its own mistakes. Do we get credit? Rarely. People are loathe to take personal responsibility for their mistakes. It's a product of our "feel good" society. All too often, it's the professional who pays the price.

If someone falls on our bus, it could be a Preventable Accident (PA) if we braked too hard or turned too quickly. Imagine this scenario: a passenger has experienced such a smooth ride they feel comfortable enough to stand prior to the bus arriving at their stop. Suddenly, a car turns directly into the path of the bus. To avoid crushing Billy's Beemer full of high school students, the bus operator brakes. Fast and hard. Paulie Passenger had a coupla beers before riding the bus, misses the stanchion he grabs for and is suddenly thrust forward. He crashes to the floor, head bleeding.

Billy is long-gone down the road, having "saluted" the honking operator, his passengers blissfully oblivious their young lives have been spared. For Paulie and the operator, it's a nightmare. Paramedics arrive and determine Paulie should be transported to hospital. A Road Supervisor arrives and interviews Ollie Operator, who says yes, he saw Billy approaching the stop sign and then glanced at his mirrors and scanned his entire field of vision prior to servicing the bus stop. Billy ran the stop sign and shot out in front of the bus. With another car to his left, the only recourse Ollie had was to brake and avoid slamming into a car full of teenagers.

Sounds pretty cut and dry. Right? Wrong. All it takes is one extra "nay" vote from a member of the accident review board to lay the blame on Ollie. Perhaps he was "driving too fast for conditions," even though he was operating under the speed limit. Maybe he braked "too hard." There are many reasons Ollie could be assessed a PA, even though he made a split-second decision that saved lives.

While in Line Training, one driver had a passenger fall on his bus as he travelled in a straight line, 10mph under the speed limit. Although the stars were aligned for his not getting a PA, he was still nervous. While on probation, we're not protected by the appeals process. In fact, if a probie gets three PA's, he's fired.

The other day as I sat at a traffic light, I counted 11 of 15 people looking at their cell phones as they rolled past. Next time you're tooling down the parkway, think twice about allowing yourself to become distracted. Three times, even. Injuring or even killing somebody is something your soul can't afford.

State of Our Union

🚌 **DEKE'S NOTE:** *While it's my intention to avoid politics here, sometimes circumstances require a deviation. This post annoyed a classmate/friend of mine. I told him it's simply an exercise in freedom of speech. I've studied American history since I was a child, loving the biographies of those who helped shape our earliest ideals. Some label me a liberal, as if it's a dirty word. Others recognize I also have conservative values which help balance my political philosophy.*

While this blog's regular intention is not to discuss politics, it's time for a frank discussion of current issues facing transit operators. This past weekend, our drivers were invited to take part in a "bus roadeo," coordinated by volunteer employees and sponsored by our agency. Our union's executive board passed a motion declaring a boycott, which I support.

An estimated 65 operators and retirees participated. Since there are about 1,000 operators, the boycott seems a success. It was meant to be an ice breaker in the midst of stressful contract negotiations. Under a fair and reasonable contract, this roadeo would be a fun and positive way to showcase our talents. However, our management has not shown us respect considering its union-busting tactics and negative portrayals of us recently.

Since the Reagan administration, corporatists have diligently attempted to dismantle worker protections. These detractors have unleashed harsh rhetoric to support their opinions, encouraging their supporters to believe propaganda painting unions negatively. Since President Reagan fired the striking air traffic controllers in 1981, unions seem targeted for destruction. Corporations as well as public entities have attempted to paint union representatives as thugs, and label union proposals as socialist. Good people have been led to believe unions are distrustful, or bad for business. This causes people to rally against their own best interests. This is a very shrewd, yet effective tactic. Maybe it's something that cannot be changed in one generation. As hard-working Americans, we must stop emulating lemmings or face economic bondage.

In the past few decades, we've seen a war against the middle class. A frightening number of Americans do not understand how the powerful elite have conspired against union workers who paved the way for corporate success the past 100 years. Many valuable benefits were secured by unions. The 40-hour week, overtime pay, sick leave, holidays, worksite safety laws, Social Security, and military leave are some protections won by American unions. Regardless whether you support them, it's very likely you have benefited from their efforts.

According to Business Week, 2013 corporate profits increased five times more than wages. In the past 30 years, the minimum wage has not even kept up with inflation; if it had, it would now be about $22/hour. Corporations outsourced and off-shored millions of jobs once held by hard-working Americans, thrusting many loyal employees into poverty. They supported politicians who helped shift power from the masses to the few. They further solidified power by encouraging wars based on outright lies, which fed billions into the industrial war machine. Simultaneously, their paid-for politicians waged war upon our military veterans by cutting their benefits. Many who voted for the cuts never served in uniform, yet heartily supported sending our troops to war. They also voted to deny benefits to those most affected by the Great Recession, while bailing out the institutions which created it. Considering that for the first time in our history, half of all Congressmen are millionaires, it's no secret whose interests they serve.

Purchased politicians have nearly erased the ability of unions to protect American workers. People are so happy to find any job, they fear reprisal for joining a union. It's like the Big Bad Wolf trying to convince Goldilocks that her sweet Granny is the true villain. Fortunately, Goldilocks grew wise and fought the Wolf's attempts to steal her goodies. Unfortunately, the triumphant woodsman who comes to her rescue has now been reduced to a sickly kid with a dull axe.

Our plight in Portland mirrors that of transit workers across the country. Thirty years ago, the union and our transportation district agreed on a generous, yet necessary pact. In exchange for large raises, employees were guaranteed a fully-funded pension and health insurance paid by the district. For reasons the district hasn't directly answered, the pension wasn't fully funded. Last year, since we had no contract, it began charging us a percentage of insurance premiums.

During the Great Recession, the district found itself in dire straits. While it pushed forward a controversial and expensive new light rail project, bus routes were cut. It also enacted hefty fare increases on the very people hardest hit by the recession. Passengers were frustrated. Many of them saw their jobs sail overseas or simply disappear. Assaults on operators increased while the district hid behind carefully-crafted press releases blaming budget deficits on "Cadillac benefits enjoyed by union employees." Corporate media further demonized unions by repeating this phrase ad nauseum. It even singled out a handful of operators who, simply by working tons of overtime, made over $100,000 a year. Meanwhile, the district secretly gave raises to non-union employees. Union employees however, haven't had cost of living increases in years.

Contract negotiations have stalled. Union employees are

frustrated and cynical. We hope we're able to hold off Mr. Wolf so he bites off only one butt cheek. Many are resigned to having to pay for medical insurance even though the rigors of our job guarantee a decline in our general health. The pension plan was replaced with a 401k, which is no security blanket given the volatility of the stock market. Our retirees, many of whom devoted their entire working lives to this district, face poverty or worse due to rising insurance costs.

Morale is bleak. Opinions about current leadership range from "okay" to "useless." Nobody I've spoken to has 100% confidence we can secure an acceptable contract. Some wonder why our union doesn't break away from non-local entities to give ours the ability to concentrate solely on our own issues. Several union members support a vote of no confidence in the district management. Without the ability to strike, we are negotiating from a position of extreme weakness.

Union officials encourage our members to participate, attend meetings, and speak up. Scheduling conflicts often make it impossible for many to attend. Those who represent us often burn out due to the long hours involved.

While I'm unsure just how the public stands, one man told me at a layover that "this country is a union, something your general manager needs to realize."

There are many eloquent members among us with strong opinions about current issues. Some speak up, others say their input wouldn't make a difference. We've arrived at the point of apathy and chaos. If working people cannot put aside differences, roll up our collective sleeves, and plunge into the fray as a united front, we're doomed.

In our current plight, I cannot simultaneously support my union and participate in a district-sponsored dog-and-pony show. Sure, the roadeo sounds fun. Once this district treats us with respect, I might be more agreeable to participating.

Priority Battles and Honored Antics

There must be zillions of "Honored" citizens in Portland. A reduced fare is available to those over 65 years, or to people with disabilities. Many who claim Honored status could run the length of a bus backward and hop-skip back to the front quicker than I can get out of the seat. Methinks many of them simply don't want to pay the full Adult fare. I believe you should have to prove, if under 65, that you qualify for Honored status.

There are many who either can't read or be bothered by rules. The "Priority Seating" area of buses and trains are "reserved for seniors and people with disabilities." That's a vague statement, so many abuse it.

Let's take for example, a crowded bus meandering toward downtown. In the Priority Seating area are two seniors with bulging shopping carts. The bus is their only means of transportation, and they're crowded by "standees" in the aisles. The right side of the priority area is dominated by a man in a large mobility device, displacing three seats. Squeezed into the two remaining spots are Smelly Shelly the Streetwalker and Limping Larry Loudmouth (her companion, who drones on about his own supposed "disabilities").

Pop hops on board with Lil' Sally in the stroller. He demands one of these seats, after arguing with Ollie Operator whether he should remove Snoozin' Sally from her comfy stroller SUV. In order to comply with transit rules, he's asked to remove Sally and fold up the stroller. Today's strollers have many handy spots to store the 150 items necessary to transport small children, and are inconvenient to fold up. Ollie informs him the next bus is just a few minutes behind (and gaining every second this bozo argues). Perhaps he'd be more comfortable on that one. Ollie's follower is enjoying a relatively empty bus now that Ollie's picking up his/her passengers. Pop continues to argue until one stately gentleman stands and offers his seat to this rude young father, just to get the bus rolling again. After all, Aging Arnold is on his way to an important doctor's visit that took several weeks to schedule.

With that squabble settled, Ollie rolls on. At the very next stop, his buddy Madame Guttersnipe awaits her favorite operator's overloaded ride. Legally sight and hearing impaired, she is also unsteady on her feet. She's also very well-versed in ADA (Americans with Disability Act) laws. She will blatantly tell people to "MOVE" if she determines they occupy a seat reserved for Honored Citizens. Only problem is this time, most have fairly-valid reasons for sitting there. Except for Pops and Smelly Shelly, who refuse to budge.

Operators often have to deal with these delicate situations. If not handled properly, it can result in one or more complaints. Usually, the annoyed one ends up harassing the operator. If passengers cannot resolve the conflict, Ollie's only recourse is to call Dispatch and ask for help. Or, he can pivot in his seat and roar in his impressive lion voice for Priority offenders to make room. Meanwhile, the clock ticks off precious seconds.

Other passengers start badgering Shelly to move. Arnie nervously checks his watch. Franny Follower zips past Ollie's bus. Meanwhile, Madame begins reading Smelly the riot act, because her back is hurting and she needs to sit. Terry Teenybopper in the seat behind Shelly unplugs and re-engages to ask "Sup?" Upon learning of the ordeal, he (surprisingly) offers Madame his seat, who thanks him profusely and accidentally-on-purpose thumps Smelly with her cane (muttering "Sorry, dumbass" as she sits).

Feigning indignation, Shelly yells at Madame. Ollie smirks in spite of his growing headache, because he knows what comes next.

"Stifle," Madame hisses, "or suffer my wrath, you odoriferous waste of oxygen."

Shelly pauses, trying in her drug-induced confusion to decipher Madame's insulting command.

"Hey bish," Shelly complains.

"You don't even know the definition of bitch, let alone properly pronounce the word. Now back off or you'll be sporting a rectal-cranial inversion brought about by my handy mobility device." Madame waves her cane in Shelly's angrily-contorted face for emphasis.

A seasoned street-dweller, Smelly understands the threat. She may be drunk, but believes she's tough enough to handle this hobbled geezer. Her final mistake is to reach across Madame in an attempt to grab the cane. Sensing the move, Madame has positioned herself so that Smelly's arm brushes against her, initiating the contact she senses is an assault. She then defends herself.

The first strike is a sharply-upward thrust of the cane's curved handle, breaking Shelly's nose. Second, the tip makes contact with a knobby knee, which bends Shelly over in order to receive a third "thunk" on top of her head. Smelly melts into a bloddy fetal position.

Shelly's still screaming when the police haul her off the bus in handcuffs five minutes later. Predicting the outcome of Shelly's abuse, Ollie has already alerted Dispatch, who send supervisors and police. Ollie avoids chuckling as he gives his report, but enjoys retelling the story later on the short break he's managed to salvage.

There is no moral to this story. People make up their own morality, and act accordingly. While this is a work of fiction, Madame Guttersnipe is not. She's truly capable of ruining your day if you refuse to yield Priority Seating to her. Don't be surprised if her fellow passengers applaud in response.

Punching Bags to Olive Branches

A nother brother has been attacked. The details are irrelevant. There have been so many assaults on operators the past few years it should become a top priority to stop them.

Our Standard Operating Procedures state: *"Do not respond physically when confronted with threatening, violent behavior or unstable customers unless it is absolutely necessary to defend yourself or a passenger and the degree of physical force is only that which is minimally necessary."*

This is incredibly vague. We're required to "stay in the seat" unless absolutely necessary to protect ourselves. Some believe this means I'm to wait until Joe Jerk punches me before I can leave the seat, or risk suspension. We're instructed to use calm, rational customer service techniques to avoid physical violence. An assistant manager once told me the rationale behind the "stay in the seat" rule is to avoid escalating a situation, and also to stay close to the radio. The trick is to know if and when you need to leave the seat. If we allow our anger to rule, we can make mistakes. Being calm in a tense situation is a tough thing to do, especially when scared. Some violators cannot be "talked down."

Other transit agencies around the country have opted to install cages around the driver's seat. Miami-Dade Transit in Florida has barriers on a small percentage of its buses, but I can't seem to find any statistics as to their overall effectiveness. The cost is reportedly $1600-1900 per bus (From Alameda-Contra Costa Transit District Staff Report). Other means of "protecting" operators, as practiced by Alameda-Contra Costa (SF Bay/Oakland, CA area transit) include random yet frequent boarding of buses by uniformed and plainclothes police officers, training operators in non-threatening customer service techniques, and public outreach. While surveillance cameras on transit vehicles are an improvement, they haven't stopped the assaults.

I don't want to be caged like a zoo animal, cutting me off from the majority of my passengers. Sure, there is a fraction of freaks hell-bent on attacking us, but most people are respectful. To simply throw up a cage might be insulting to those who enjoy friendly banter with operators. It also diminishes our capacity to act as Captain of the Ship by portraying us as cowards. I don't think a barrier can stop a bullet or knife wielded by a determined combatant.

So far, transit officers have ridden my bus only once. In fact, the route they rode a neighborhood commuter run serving a quiet nest of professionals who never gave me any trouble. I asked the officers why they chose that particular route and their response was, "it was just random."

It seems not much thought has been put into ride-alongs. I've driven dangerous routes without benefit of uniformed support. Most runs have been without incident, but a few passengers have tested my customer service skills to the hilt. In fact, I've had to re-evaluate my approach to difficult customers. When someone growls at me, I have a tendency to bark. Normally, I'll give somebody a warning. If they persist, they either leave my bus willingly or in silver bracelets with armed escorts.

After each difficult situation, I'll evaluate how I handled it. Luckily, I haven't been severely tested or attacked. Yet. However, I'm constantly thinking about possible scenarios, hearing other drivers' "horror stories," and combing the web for information. It could save my life someday if I'm prepared for the worst. Some are simply not able to adequately defend themselves against a sudden, unprovoked attack. Take our sister Pam for example. She was brutally beaten last December because a passenger didn't want to pay full fare. Her attacker was basically given a slap on the wrist.

Having met our GM, a decent man in person, I doubt he doesn't care. He just doesn't know how to. He's never driven a bus in service, so he has no firsthand experience or working knowledge of the situations we routinely face. To feel empathy for another, you truly need to have walked in their shoes.

When Pam was severely beaten last winter, nobody from our management showed up at the accused attacker's pre-trial hearing on Christmas Eve. Several union officers and about 25 drivers showed up to support our fellow operator. Our agency's initial response was the usual bluster about offering a reward for information leading to an arrest. However, my feeling was echoed by others: do they actually *care* about our safety?

Our morale suffers every time one of us is assaulted. It feels like we've all been beaten, because it could happen to any of us. The public is largely ignorant of problems regarding our safety. What if our union, in cooperation with transit and local law enforcement, began to educate the public? They could explain the Federal Transit Administration reports assaults on transit operators have increased 144% since 2008, and what penalties people face for this crime. In addition, punishment for assaults needs to be extreme.

Positive media is severely lacking in Portland where transit issues are concerned. For every positive news article about operators, you can count several negatives. It doesn't have a clue what we face out there. We are more prone to work-related injury and health problems than many other professionals. Issues concerning driver comfort and fatigue are being addressed, which is a positive note. However, the disconnect between US and those we serve needs to be bridged.

Educating the public about how to ride transit is vital. Public Service Announcements, with operators explaining basic rules and procedures, are worth consideration. Giving transit operators a face, highlighting our countless good deeds, might bring about a more positive work environment. Other agencies around the country do this (such as Burlington, Vermont and Minneapolis/St. Paul, Minnesota). You'd think Portland, which boasts several transit options, would also consider doing the same. It's also an opportunity for our union to promote the positive things we do daily. We could teach people why buses are sometimes late by explaining what goes on "in the seat." Perhaps then we wouldn't be constantly vilified on Twitter and other media sites. Most complaints are often from the ill-informed.

There will always be passengers who don't care about penalties. There are also good people who come to our defense when threatened or assaulted. Our supervisors are widely spread and it can take several minutes for them to respond. While it is impossible to end all assaults, perhaps we can drastically reduce them.

Portlanders largely depend on transit. We drive this city to work in terrible weather conditions and worsening traffic. Routinely avoiding dangers on the road, our operators are truly some of the best in the world. Ours was once considered the best transit agency in the country. Other transit agencies far and wide once marveled at our efficiency. Now most comments are negative. We've slipped to No. 10 or worse, depending on which reports you read.

While no transit agency can be perfect, we don't deserve being beaten up. Literally or figuratively. We're good people. We work hard and care about our neighbors. Our dedication and good deeds far outweigh the negative publicity we've endured. There's a wealth of opportunity to make transit better for both customers and operators.

It's time we come together, think "outside the box," and regain our place as the best in the country.

⛹ RAW

Joshua wrote:
"My experiences on public transport in Portland have been largely good, and the interplay between drivers and passengers reminds me of my time in Taiwan, where there is as often as not personal interplay between the two, a friendliness that does not exist in many cities in America. The idea of putting drivers in cages "for their own protection" (or, as is often the excuse trotted out in some places I've been, "for everyone's safety") seems a distinctly un-Portland idea."

Clean Buses or Dirty Deke

A spotter once told me a grand total of three (out of 200+) buses at our garage get cleaned each night. I was aghast at this information.

A proper cleaning would entail wiping down every surface and washing the floors. Normally, a bus is emptied of garbage and sent back out into service the next day. At this rate, it takes about 10 weeks to get to each of them. Given that, you could say each bus is in-service nearly three months before it is thoroughly cleaned. Evidently, each bus is cleaned an average of four times a year. Considering the personal hygiene habits of many of our riders, that just adds to the yuck factor.

My fellow drivers say there are a grand total of six bus cleaners district-wide. Each is reportedly given eight minutes to clean a bus. When doing so, they are dressed for it, unlike the operators who spend 8-12 hours driving them. Most buses seem to make it through the wash rack on a regular basis, so they appear clean. But that's only exterior aesthetics; the interiors are often mold-infested, bug-crawling germ factories.

One driver reports, "The sickening reminder comes as I'm walking back to my car, after a long day's work, and I see the brother and sister cleaners wearing full gloves, respirator masks, and practically dressed in hazmat suits just to get safely through their eight minutes!"

My trainer suggested using wipes to clean surfaces an operator touches as part of the pre-trip. This made sense, because the first time I sat in the seat, my first reaction was "eew" when I first gripped the grimy steering wheel. I routinely wipe not only the operator controls, but the rails, stanchions, door handles and stop buttons near the back door. Each time, my wipe comes up black with grime. Some days, it takes two or three wipes before I feel relatively safe, but I'm still exposed to every bug that slithers aboard.

Other operators take their pre-trip wipedown to elevated heights. Several clean the interior windows. In one video, a driver shows a clean rag prior to washing one interior passenger window. After he's done, it's black with grime. There's not time to clean *all* surfaces. The seats are usually the dirtiest. While older buses have cloth passenger seats, the district boasts plastic seats on the new models as being cleaner. This has long been an issue. But if each bus is cleaned only a handful of times each year, bacteria will build up when not properly sanitized.

A 2011 news report chronicled how local university students took swabs off seats in several buses and found alarming amounts of dangerous bacteria growing there. It's abusive to expose us to long hours in unhealthy working conditions, then having to pay for going to the doctor when the filth causes illness.

I wonder what our passengers would think if we donned a hazmat suit to protect ourselves from germ-laden "offices" while we work? If we did wear protective outerwear, we'd likely be written up for uniform code violations. We're already exposed to whatever pathogens our customers bring with them. Another fellow operator states, "I have never been as sick as many times since I started working here."

It isn't the fault of those masked souls who clean up after the hygiene-challenged who ride public transit. But next time you ride a bus, you'll wonder, "when was this bus last cleaned?"

Eew, indeed.

"Roaming Around" responded:

"I retired from another large-city transit agency. I used to take a spray bottle of isopropyl alcohol and spray any part of the driver's compartment that I thought needed some sanitizing. My fellow drivers would laugh and tell me that it would do nothing. However, I rarely got sick. In fact, in over thirty years, I called in sick just once… and that was because I cut my hand and had the whole thing bandaged up. Not that I never had a cold or flu but when I did it seemed to happen on my regular days off. *argh*

"Sure, spraying rubbing alcohol on every surface I touched probably did not do much but psychologically, it probably did a lot to make me 'think' it was doing a lot to keep me healthy.

"Another thing that probably helped more than spraying everything with alcohol was that I kept my driver's window wide open at ALL times. It would not matter if it was day or night, raining, snowing, or 10-degrees out, my window would be wide open. I also kept the foot vent open and both the defroster fan and auxiliary dash fans going constantly. I figured that keeping the air moving around the driver's compartment would in turn keep the germs away.

"Who knows whether those precautions kept me so healthy through my bus driving career or if it was just coincidence."

Lisa added:

"I do the same thing in my train cabs! Everything gets wiped down with Lysol or Clorox wipes!! I can't work in the dirty ick!!!"

A Battle Hymn for Us All

We have a new contract. Amalgamated Transit Union 757's members voted yes this past week by a majority of 82.7% to approve the contract terms, effective two years ago.

It has been a contentious battle. Retirees believe the terms give away what they were promised decades ago: health care provided in lieu of no raises in pay for active union employees. Like a coal miner who breathes toxic air his entire working life and dies early and penniless, a bus operator faces a retirement of health crises on a fixed income. An increasingly vocal public sector erroneously minimizes our skill level and health risks, simultaneously demanding we pay a "fair share" of our health insurance. It's this class warfare which endangers all workers, blue- or white-collared.

Our service is considered so vital to the local economy that our right to strike was legislated out of existence in 2007. Ridership in 2014 is up 10%, with about 322,000 Portlanders using transit daily. Imagine the scenario if we could strike. Another 100,000+ vehicles would jam our roads creating massive gridlock. Those without alternate transportation would be unable to get to work. Without the right to strike, our bargaining position is tenuous. If we disagree with terms presented by the district and vote to reject, our fate lies with a state-appointed arbitrator. If our terms are deemed not in the best interests of the public or the transit agency's financial stability, we are saddled with the district's "last best offer." Oregon arbitration rules state that either the union or the transit agency's offer would be the arbiter's only choice. There is no negotiation at that point. Just either or. Fighting with our collective fists bound behind us, negotiations are heavily weighted in favor of the agency.

It is easier to lose this job than keep it. Standard operating procedures are so ambiguous they are a loose-fitting noose. With each misstep, it tightens. In a reasonable situation, there would be counterbalances. We can be blamed for incidents that may not be our "fault," yet should have prevented because we're *professionals*.

A growing portion of the general public does not view us as such. We're trained to predict the future, based on constantly changing conditions. If a delivery truck smashes our driver-side mirror, we can be assessed a PA if the bus is not completely within lane markers. Rack up five PA's within a two-year period and we face termination.

We're also expected to remain seated while we are spit upon, slapped, punched, stabbed, or threatened at gunpoint. The complaint review process can be insulting, because our accusers often lie. A commendation doesn't remain permanently in our personnel file, but complaints can even if unsubstantiated. Media coverage omits stories of the many good deeds operators perform. It's dirty laundry the corporate sector forces onto the airwaves and newsprint, and a hungry public eagerly ingests it.

It was insulting to read a recent comment posted on a transit-related article. This guy had the gall to state that transit operators are basically "low-skilled workers and their compensation should be commensurate with their skill set." This guy equated us with a "shuttle bus driver at the airport. If you dont (sic) like your level of compensation than (sic) get a college degree or go into a skilled trade that compensates people at a higher rate based on what they command in the market. It really is a simple equation." When you consider a full bus or rail car transports a significant mass of people whose jobs make our economy tick, it is logical to assume our passengers are intrinsically more valuable to the local economy than this uninformed complainer.

For most of the previous century, the blue-collar worker was an American hero. World War II veterans who liberated Europe and stopped imperial Japan from controlling the Pacific theatre were the celebrated American middle class. Unions successfully negotiated with corporate powers, securing improved working conditions, respectable wages and the hope of a decent retirement. These workers produced the goods which American consumers purchased with their hard-earned money. The economy flourished until the greedy upper crust found a way to turn the middle class against itself. Now, many are convinced it is somehow our own fault the middle class is shrinking toward extinction. Instead of punishing those who created economic disaster, we're fighting amongst ourselves. Divide and conquer is an ancient tactic. Transit agencies also use this successful ploy to split union memberships.

The Great Recession caused a massive loss of middle-class jobs. Many who once earned respectable salaries now compete for whatever low-paying jobs they can find. Those who do obtain college degrees are mired in a lifetime of student loan debt. Interest on these loans is ridiculously high. Chances are, today's graduates won't be able to pay off their loans, let alone achieve a salary level commensurate with the effort it took to earn these expensive degrees. The minimum wage job is no longer the exclusive domain of Joe or Sally Teenager. It's now held by Charlie the former computer tech. He's trying to hold three jobs just to make the rent because his decent job went overseas so his former employer's shareholders can afford an extra maid whom they pay... you guessed it, minimum wage.

Small- to medium-sized companies complain they can't afford paying higher wages. They're already squeezed by payroll taxes, over-regulation and shrinking markets. If minimum wage had been raised regularly, the economy would have grown with it. Plus, consider there is no maximum wage. For every action, reason demands a counter reaction. Those criminals who caused the Great Recession were "bailed out" because they're evidently "too big to fail." Actually, they're too rich to jail.

Were *we the people* given equal treatment? No. Instead, we were blamed for a mess we didn't create, left to fight over whatever crumbs remain. The auto industry paid us back for their bailout; the banks have not. Corporate executives have seen their salaries and bonuses increase to the point they make 331% more than the average worker. It's time the *entire* middle class got a raise, not to mention securing the retirement income of those who worked before us.

A bus or light rail operator has passed rigorous training regimens that would flummox the common driver. Over the course of several years driving a transit vehicle, more knowledge is acquired through experience. If you consider the millions of people who enjoy safe journeys every day because of our hard-earned professionalism, our contribution to local economies is invaluable.

Which leads us back to this local contract battle. Unless we reverse current trends, retirement will subject us to extreme poverty. The once-sacred promise of security after a lifetime of dedication seems a thing of the past.

This contract was voted upon by a scant 57% of active union employees. That 43% who didn't vote hurt us all. We owe our retirees the respect they earned working under harsher conditions than we do, using equipment not nearly as advanced as today's. We also owe future hires a commitment to fight for their benefits as well, in the hope they will someday fight for ours. We must insist our transit agency fulfills its obligations, rather than blaming us for its own failures.

Whatever your opinion about the contract, a bigger fight looms. American workers are fighting amongst ourselves, rather than working together to ensure a better future for all. We make the collective economy's wheels roll. Unless we unify, we're all doomed to a fate beneath those wheels.

🚶 RAW

"Anonymous" reacted with this portrayal of today's political climate:

"Here in Mississauga, Ontario it is municipal election season. A local candidate, representing the Troglodyte party, gave a radio interview in which he opined that transit workers were too highly paid. He then went on to say that if he didn't win, he would apply for a job as a bus driver since we make $100,000.00 per year. This was news to me and I was tempted to file a grievance for the missing $35,000.00."

Bouncy Boppin' Board

Driving the Extra Board lately, I feel like a yo-yo. Mornings, then nights, back to mornings again. In the span of four days. It's rough on people to spin circadian rhythms in drunken circles.

Our bodies work best on a regular schedule. Humans want to sleep when the sun doesn't shine. Just when you've achieved a rhythm on the board, your seniority and position sway-drop-roll like Dolly Parton's bosom on a roller coaster. You have to adapt, or find somebody willing to trade your work. Sometimes, people don't want your work, so you're stuck with it.

I sign the board because A) I don't have enough seniority for good runs; B) working overtime is good for a healthy bank account; and C) constantly driving the same runs is about as comforting as the first day of a stomach virus. Lately, I haven't had enough of Part B. I've noticed that PM work comes with more overtime, so I'm tempted to stay on the dark side. Only problem with that choice is I don't see much of my family. Night work allows more time to write and sleep. In night mode, I have to call in for the next day's work before I even begin the current day's schedule. It's a weedy row to hoe. I'm tough, but my blade needs sharpening.

It would be nice if there was one roster for AM reports, and another for PM's. The district seems reactionary rather than visionary. They revised hours-of-service rules in a supposed attempt to give operators more pillow time, but it cut into the overtime extra board operators desire. This came after the scandal-hungry media "exposed" a few drivers who dared make $100,000 a year by working up to 20 hours a day. Some were found to be overly-tired, which is unsafe. But there are hundreds of operators who are in uniform 12-14 hours and only get paid for 10 or less. We're certainly not making $100k; considering a majority of board operators are relatively new, the average salary range is more like $50k.

The glut of board ops is so heavy, there's little opportunity to work on your regular days off. The board is no longer lucrative, and seems this way by design. Rather than trimming the amount of new hires, the district would rather pay thousands of dollars more to train new drivers than pay veterans overtime. It defies the "safety first" credo the district feeds the media, to have inexperienced operators clogging the board. It's also cyclical. Some signups have more overtime available than others, and hours can be plentiful at one garage while scarce at another.

The board should be staffed by operators who have driven long enough to know more than a handful of runs. A new operator might be unprepared to drive a new route with 10 minutes of preparation. It makes them nervous, concentrating on turn-by-turn instructions rather than scanning for possible hazards. An experienced operator, when faced with an unfamiliar run, knows how to balance scanning with reading instructions two or three turns in advance. I read route instructions while stopped, so my attention is on the road. Although I was still a bit green when I signed the board, I had some confidence in my abilities. More importantly, I was no longer on probation, meaning our union would represent me at the accident review board if something happened.

A newly-trained operator is on probation for six months. For me, it made sense to stay part-time while in this precarious no-man's land. As a probie, if you get a third PA, you're fired. All those thousands of dollars the district just spent to train you are wasted if you slip up. I recently heard that of the 20 new hires put in service, about 25% of them don't pass probation. Just a few years ago, new hires had to wait up to five years before going full-time. Nowadays, they're brought up only a few months into their probation. The jump from 30 hours a week to 40-45 is quite an adjustment. The stress of driving as a newbie is hard enough, but when you add another 10-15 hours a week the odds of making a mistake rise substantially.

With the new "block system" of run selections, my low seniority left me with slim pickings. I'm on the board again next signup. Many operators dislike this new way of signing runs. After years of earning their seniority, many believe this new system doesn't honor their dedication. The union will hopefully lobby for improvements.

Perhaps it will go back to the original system. As long as it fairly rewards those with seniority, I hope someday to earn the best work.

HIT COUNTER: 20,000 (October 2014)

Pains in My Butt

My butt hurts, I had back spasms last week, now my knees ache. Human bowels don't respond well to circadian rhythm changes. Head to toe, and I ended up at the butt again. Just part of the job, I reckon.

What does it take to be a good operator? We're not "drivers" in the typical sense. Moving a bus down the road involves much more. A local radio talk-show host said driving a city bus is "easier" than operating a school bus. I don't mean to diminish the professionalism of a school bus operator, but my job is extremely more difficult and stressful. Their passengers are surely precious, but the routes are shorter. Nor do their passengers pay a fare. Regardless, I admire those who transport our children. Even as a parent of three, I wonder if I'd have enough patience to handle some of the little darlings.

To become a "good" operator of a city bus takes many years. There is something to be learned each day. Each day presents new challenges. We constantly adapt to ever-changing conditions. Maneuvers I once thought the toughest to master are now routine. Still I'm often presented with challenges requiring split-second decisions. One slip could result in somebody's injury or death.

Occasionally a passenger will say they know more about my job than I do, simply because they've ridden buses for years. Once upon a time, I thought so too. Having been a bus passenger prior to driving one, my favorite operators made it look easy. On my first day behind the wheel, I realized how truly difficult a bus is to maneuver. Having driven a tractor-trailer rig across country, I believe a bus is harder to drive. A bus has only one pivot point, and that's the dual wheels at the rear. A truck has two: tractor and trailer axles. It is challenging to back a trailer into a dock around several obstacles, but the extra pivot point allows greater rear visibility. Bus operators cannot see behind the vehicle, and it's not advisable to even attempt backing up without a spotter. Also, tractor-trailer operators have cargo that doesn't talk back.

While some operators navigate the same streets daily, others have different routes every day. As an extra board operator, I rarely drive the same route two days in a row. I've done it long enough now to learn 52 lines. Even if you're familiar with a route, road conditions or construction can present constant challenges. Delivery truck drivers habitually park in the worst possible spots, and often make terrible decisions while driving. Marvin Mercedes and Randy Range Rover are impatient. Pedestrians rarely look before darting out into traffic, especially if they want to catch my bus.

Recently I winced as a teenager darted in front of traffic so he could board my bus. A pickup driver had to brake suddenly to avoid hitting the kid and his girlfriend. These juvenile jaywalkers seemed oblivious to the stupidity of their actions, and were miffed when I chastised them. They were indignant, yet I would be haunted forever by the sight of their bodies being mangled into bloody pieces. I was tempted to let them get safely to the sidewalk, then drive off without them.

So just because your operator makes it look "easy," don't be fooled. If their uniform is adorned with Safety Award patches, they deserve your utmost respect. If they growl at you when you board, rest assured you did something that scared the sanity out of them.

Signs on the Bus

🚌 **DEKE'S NOTE:** *I was starting to feel a groove, writing three to five posts a month, sometimes two or more a week. Readership was growing steadily. As I look back on these posts, I can see a progression from rusty writer to one gaining some chops. This particular post has been read 1,426 times, and I was surprised because it was unexpected. It took about 25 minutes to write. Little did I know, FTDS readership was about to explode, with the hit counter doubling in a year.*

Ever wonder why your operator gets irritated, or sighs in frustration? Even though you might think riding the bus is as simple as boarding, it isn't.

Buses operate on schedules. Along each route are "time points," which are specific locations where an operator is scheduled to be. If people board at their leisure, are texting in the shelter and don't look up until you're stopped and then gesture they don't want your bus, it eats a precious half-minute.

You might not understand how this is a problem, but lately it's epidemic. People operate at their own pace; operators are often saddled with unrealistic schedules. If circumstances create time loss on the run, it means our break at the end is cut short. The average rider doesn't ride the entire route. If we're late at the end, our break is cut by the amount of time we're late. Traffic, inexperienced passengers, construction delays... they can all wreak havoc on schedules. Unless there's an Extra Service operator available to fill your run, you'll most likely be running late if you take your entire break time.

Next time you ride, notice the signs on a bus which are supposed to make boarding quick and efficient. Most are focused solely on a tiny screen upon which their entire lives seem to revolve. Reading signs on a bus is not nearly as exciting as whatever meme FaceBook is featuring at that moment. So here are a few signs you may have missed, and what operators think (see comments in italics) whenever they're unseen or ignored.

We've all seen *this* guy. Loitering Larry awaits the bus. Just standing there, Larry is looking at the sky, glancing at his watch. Not a care in the world. As the bus ("finally," he sighs) pulls up, he takes his sweet time navigating the six-inch step up and in. *Gee, he doesn't appear immobile; step up the pace dude.* Then, as he gives the operator the stink eye, Larry just looks around.

Can he go any bit slower?

"How much to ride downtown?" Larry asks.

"See the sign up there?" Ollie Operator replies with a finger pointing above his head. "It says $2.50, unless you're under 18. If you're under seven, it's free."

Perhaps he's capable of understanding that bit of information. Not even mentioning the other fare... he looks as "Honored" as the guy who just paid a buck and smells like yesterday's puke.

Larry begins to dig in his pockets. Out comes the rubbers, Safeway receipts, pot baggie, and finally the money. Of course, it's wadded-up in numerous denominations; a grand total of about $18. As he fumbles for the right combination, Ollie lets out the world's most impatient sigh.

"You know," Ollie says, "it would truly be helpful if you had the fare ready while waiting for the bus, rather than taking two minutes to find it now that I'm actually here. It says 'Please Have Fare Ready Upon Boarding' on that sign telling you how much the fare costs."

Larry takes offense. Who's this stupid driver to tell him how to ride a friggin' bus? For the next several minutes after getting his receipt he rudely badgers Ollie. Questioning his ancestry, nastily trolling anyone who isn't plugged in and tuned out. Ollie begins to whistle, droning out Larry's incessant insults.

Larry can't wait to get off the bus. Unfortunately, he makes a rookie mistake. Ollie hits the first downtown stop at rush hour, and there are about 20 people waiting. Larry, of course, saunters toward the front door where the hordes are coming aboard.

"Please exit to the rear sir," Ollie tells Larry.

Larry gestures a "whatever" and heads to the back door. But

Ollie forgets to push the door handle as he takes fare from the boarding hordes.

"Hey BACK DOOR, driver!" Larry yells impatiently. Ollie twists the handle, but before he can, Larry has started slamming the door. Of course, now it won't open. The green light hasn't appeared overhead, and Larry is angry. Again.

"I said, BACK DOOR DAMNIT!" Larry shouts impatiently.

"Read the sign sir," Ollie replies, "and it will instruct you as to the proper door-opening procedure."

Now Larry stands at the door, having failed to open it prior to the green light, which is now illuminated so brightly people across the street can see it.

"WELLLLLL?" Larry brays as Ollie boards new passengers. Larry's standing there with his palms outstretched, waiting for the door to open. By itself.

Ollie loses his patience. "Push the door, it will open!"

Larry complies. The door is stuck now, due to improper operation.

"You'll have to exit the front then," Ollie says, turning to hide a gleeful smile. The bus is now packed. Ollie secures the bus, runs to the rear and pushes the door shut, zips back in and shuts the front door just as the light is about to change. He watches Larry fight his way to the front of the bus.

Larry is jostled and shoves his way forward as Ollie closes the front door and takes the green light. He steps on our previous heroine Lady Guttersnipe's foot as he passes and gets a cane-cruncher in his groin.

"HEY!" he shouts as he painfully reaches the front.

"Sorry sir," Ollie says. "Procedure dictates I can't loiter in the first position on the transit mall. Gotta go. We'll let you out next stop.

Larry doesn't like this, and stands up at the fare box, yelling into Ollie's face. "You let me out RIGHT FUCKING NOW!" he bellows, his spit spraying the windshield and Ollie's glasses.

Ollie puts his arm out and points to the sign above the windshield. "See that sign? You'll need to move back behind the yellow line, sir, I can't drive with you there, plus I can't open the door while the bus is moving."

"You stupid prick! I wanted out at the last stop!"

"Bummer," Ollie replies. "You should read the signs." *And some manners would help too,* he says to himself. Ollie motions Larry back. Downtown traffic is heavy with all the skateboarders, bicyclists and cars in the bus lane, plus the person crossing against the light directly ahead of the bus, for whom Ollie must brake so they don't become a bloody bike rack ornament. After a few blocks of Larry's lewd linguistics, the next stop looms.

After another round of obscenities, Larry finally manages to exit. A few intelligent passengers exit the rear door, proving it operational again.

A few stops later, Barry Bicyclist exits the rear door. Ollie hasn't noticed Barry's helmeted head bobbing up the sidewalk, and prepares to depart on the impending green light. Just as it turns green, Barry hops in front of the bus. Ollie lays on the horn.

"WHOA THERE BUDDY!" Ollie bellows. He opens the front door as he says this.

Barry shrugs, pointing a finger at himself in a "Who, me?" gesture.

"Yeah, you!" Ollie roars. "Come here for a second."

Barry shakes his head, annoyed a simple bus operator would have the nerve to yell at him. After all, he saves the climate by riding his bicycle six blocks from bus stop to home again, the world should bow to him! He takes his time, carefully removing his $3,000 bicycle from the rack, and pops onto the sidewalk, near the open bus door.

"What?" he shouts.

"You didn't see the sign that clearly states 'Alert Operator before removing bike'?" Ollie asks.

"But I did tell you!" Barry says. "You just didn't hear me."

"Well yeah," Ollie replies. "It's hard to hear somebody going out the back door when people are boarding. Good thing I saw you before I hit the accelerator or you'd be bloodily bouncing around my duals by now. Please make *sure* I hear you. I don't want you to get hurt."

"Yeah, whatever," Barry says with a dismissive hand gesture. After all, he has an MBA in Obnoxiousness and who the hell is a simple bus operator to tell him how to behave?

"Hey buddy, I wanna show you something." Ollie gently gestures for him to get back on board, smiling reassuringly. Barry hesitates yet complies, even though he's embarrassed to note all the riders are watching this exchange.

"See this?" Ollie points to the sign showing the Gross Vehicle Weight of the vehicle. "It should paint a graphic picture in your mind of what happens to someone who steps in front of a moving bus," Ollie quietly tells him. "With all these people aboard, it's more like 50,000 pounds of steel and glass. Multiply that by a speed of five and that's 250,000 pounds of mass rolling at you."

A fly lands on the window next to Ollie. He deftly swats the buzzer flat, bug guts oozing down the glass.

"This could be you, and I don't think all the king's men could put you back together again. Okay? Got it?"

Barry's not satisfied. "Then you should be more careful before you move this bus!" he shouts as he steps off.

"Good thing I am careful, buddy," Ollie says to Barry's departing back, "or you woulda been the bug."

Later, the passenger load having thinned a little, a little old lady with her full shopping cart awaits Ollie's ride. The Priority Seating area is jammed with 30-somethings staring into their tiny device screens, ear buds shredding their cochlear nerves. Ollie tries to prepare them for what awaits.

"We'll need Priority Seating please," he declares as he rolls to the stop. A middle-aged man dressed as if he's down on his luck politely obliges and moves into the aisle. The other two squatters don't hear him, or they're artfully ignorant.

Granny Gilmer boards after Ollie deploys the ramp to make it easier for her to cart $100 of groceries into the bus. Still, nobody seems to have noticed her.

After all he's been through the past hour, including passengers wanting to know detailed schedules of a bus route he doesn't drive, teenagers obscenely arguing amongst themselves, Larry and Barry's antics, and a host of other annoyances, Ollie is now almost nine minutes late to a 12-minute break at the end of the line. His last straw is sucking air.

Turning in his seat, he bellows at Ichabod I-Phone and

WannaBeARapper Wanda, "Please MOVE from the Priority Seating Area so this dear lady can have a seat!" Wanda somehow gets that Ollie is addressing her, and moves her head so she can see Ollie past Granny's rain-soaked head.

"Say what?" she asks loudly, removing one earplug. "You talkin' to me? Whatchu want?"

Ollie is beyond words. He gestures toward Granny.

"I was here first," Wanda whines.

Ollie covers his face and rubs his aching temples, unbuckles his seat belt, stands and excuses himself as he steps past bewildered Granny. He walks up to Wanda, bends over and motions her to remove her other ear bud.

"PLEASE MOVE FROM THE PRIORITY SEATING AREA SO THIS DEAR LADY CAN SIT!" he roars.

"Mister," she bellows, "you don't gotta yell! Geez!"

Evidently, Ichabod hasn't paid any attention, or doesn't care. He hasn't budged.

"Move, please!" Ollie bellows, and motions for Icky to unplug and tune-in.

"Why I gotta move? I was here first!" Icky whines even louder than Wanda. Ollie points to the sign directly across from him.

"I got an Honored card too!" Icky whines.

At this point, our earlier heroine, Lady Guttersnipe, has heard enough. Ollie is her favorite operator. Even though she's sight and hearing-impaired, she knows what's what. Stiffly rising from her seat across the aisle, she raises her cane. Ollie shakes his head (not just yet, dear warrior). Lady lowers it, but addresses Icky in a very threatening manner.

"Either you mind your misplaced manners and make room for this sweet lady," Lady growls, "or you'll learn a painful new dance move, and it ain't gonna be pretty. Now, UP, you ungracious sloth!"

Lady G again raises her cane, and Icky immediately responds. After a few seconds of whining, he manages to rise. Ollie wastes no time raising the seat, and it's settled. Granny thanks him and throws a menacing glare at Icky, trembling in front of Lady G. For good measure, Ollie makes sure to displace another discourteous rider so Granny's overloaded cart remains out of the aisle.

Ollie finally reaches the end of the line. He's three minutes past his departure time. His bladder aches, his sphincter muscle is approaching maximum capacity, and his nerves are shredded.

He pushes "Restroom Delay" on the computer and exits the bus, wincing with each step. Two hours-plus in the seat is strenuous, and his legs complain. Ten minutes later, he emerges from the break room, somewhat relieved. His shift has another six hours to go, and he's already five minutes late. Dispatch will have to deal with scheduling him back into service.

Ollie slowly makes his way back to the bus. Darkness has arrived. The transit center swarms with characters of dubious intentions. As Ollie prepares to enter his bus, he's confronted by a transient demanding to know why he's so late.

He remains calm as he mutters an incoherent "traffic" to the passenger and dispenses a ticket. He hopes the guy doesn't assault him, and ignores the insults. Luckily for Rudy Boy, he's still in a fairly good mood. Still, he wishes there was one more sign: "Beware of Driver."

Tragic

Tonight, we are all stunned by the news of a bicyclist meeting his death on the road, and one of our own was involved. The tragedy of this man losing his life is one thing; how it will be reported is another.

On a very busy 82nd Avenue, where this tragedy occurred, it is extremely difficult to see people. Pedestrians and bicyclists have some very dangerous habits, such as wearing dark clothing without reflective material. When we turned our clocks back last month, few people took precautionary measures to protect themselves on the street. Our transit agency issued reflective vests to drivers for use in our yard to help us see fellow drivers walking to and from their buses. Portland residents seem to take it for granted they will be seen no matter what they wear or where they stand.

In this tragedy, the investigating road supervisor reports the driver saw a man walking his bicycle in the bike lane prior to the incident. Reportedly, this man had no reflectors on his person or bike. The report further states this man was "pounding on the bus" as it pulled away, and came into contact with the right rear duals. The result was a fatality, an operator's worst nightmare.

Even if the operator did as trained, scanning both mirrors and looking over both shoulders before allowing the wheels to roll, how could he be expected to see the bicyclist? People pounding on a bus as it pulls away is an incredibly common occurrence. This is a tragic example of why one should *never touch or otherwise come close* to a bus rolling away from a stop. Intending passengers seem to think if they pound on the bus, the driver will stop just for them and open the door. They're late to the bus stop and demand they be given the same courtesy extended to those who were on time. Those who do this are unaware of the extreme danger involved with touching a moving bus. It's like petting a mountain lion on a hiking trail.

This week I've been practicing my scanning techniques. I've been very hard on myself because there have been a few instances when I wasn't as thorough as I need to be. It takes intense concentration and practiced observation to be constantly vigilant.

As winter approaches, a lot of my driving is done in the dark. During daylight hours, you have the luxury of a street bathed in daylight. When the sun goes down, seeing the lady about to step into the street but is blocked by a parked car is 100 times more difficult. Especially if she's wearing dark clothing. Our eyes are constantly moving from forward to left mirror to sideways to right mirror and ahead again. If you keep your eyes fixed for over a second or two, you lose peripheral vision. When we're trying to see if there's a person at the stop ahead and they're standing beside the shelter or lurking 10 feet away, our attention is diverted from where it should be.

This type of tragedy might be prevented with some intense media coverage about personal safety. Instead of focusing on keeping people safe, there has been too much emphasis on blaming operators for tragedies. Safety is a two-way street. Our union, the district and the media need to work together and create some serious public service films about how to... well, keep our collective pedestrian/bicyclist/motorist heads out of our asses.

Tonight, my thoughts and prayers are with the family of the man who lost his life. Additionally, my heart goes out to the operator who will live with this forever. The media will want to know who he is, what his "safety record" looks like, and what he might have done wrong. It will not, most likely, report on the countless lives he's saved over the span of his career.

Our profession has the most challenged, maligned, and safety-conscious drivers in the world. Portland operators safely transport over 300,000 people daily. Impatient motorists cut us off, oblivious of the danger. We share very narrow streets with pedestrians who dart out in front of our buses and light rail vehicles, and we manage to avoid hitting 99.95% of them. Skateboarders, bicyclists, people using mobility devices... we safely share the streets with all. We're always on the lookout for those who either refuse, or don't know how, to safeguard themselves.

This tragedy is probably not the operator's fault. The bicyclist was reportedly on the sidewalk as the bus left the curb. He made contact with the bus, and lost the gamble. Yet the headlines will undoubtedly read: "Bus Fatally Injures Bicyclist."

We're all deeply saddened by this tragedy. It happened on the eve of our national Thanksgiving. One family will mourn its loss; the operator's family will grieve as well.

Please, be safe when you're out there, people. We work hard to help keep you safe, but the responsibility must be shared.

Paddles and Skirts

🚌 **DEKE'S NOTE:** *Oh boy, was I tired when this was written. It wasn't until a friend of mine pointed it out did I realize the title was amusing. Still, this is just another day in the life, with a fun tale of what can happen when people are "plugged in and tuned out."*

When you've driven a bus for a while, you'll find yourself making silly mistakes. In my case, it just seems funny. Or, it could be the onset of premature dementia.

READ YOUR PADDLE!

After a few runs on one route one day, I was returning to my bus from a remote break facility. Since I had arrived, so had several other buses. Couldn't find mine. It is the 14, right? Quizzing myself is routine, because each day on the extra board is different. Sometimes I can't remember what I drove that morning, let alone the day before. But I was positive today was the 14! All day long, and into the night. What happened here? Did some other driver take off in my bus? I peered into the second bus and saw my belongings inside. But the overhead said it was Line 10. Our onboard computers automatically change the overhead signs. Hmm. When I let myself in, I consulted the paddle and found the rest of my route was, indeed, Route 10. Wow, Blue Boy. Interesting, because I had three minutes left of my break, and I'd never driven this route. Pulling the route description from the pouch, I quickly scanned it, put the turn-by-turn in the cutter, and fired 'er up. Ever since, I scan the paddle before taking off.

WRONG WAY WACKO

Some routes mirror each other for short distances and service stops are shared. One day I drove a 17 for 10 hours. Left on Lincoln, up to Fourth and left onto Harrison. Easy-pleasy, scarred into memory due to countless repetitions. Then I drove an early-morning commuter 35 the next day, packed tighter than Rush Limbaugh in a wetsuit. Took the right onto First and sailed through the green arrow onto Lincoln. Roopsie.

"Hey!" one surprised rider exclaimed. "Weren't you supposed to go straight back there?"

"Indeed," I mumbled in apology. "Okay, how many of you needed Harrison and Second?"

Luckily, nobody responded. One guy got off on Lincoln, politely acknowledging my mistake by saying since it was a nice morning he'd walk the few blocks. Gracious man. I should have hugged him.

Emily Earmuffs, however, finally realized our different surroundings and stormed up to the front, berating me for missing the turn. In my defense, a fellow passenger asked if she hadn't heard my announcement.

"I couldn't hear you!" she bellowed, since she still hadn't removed the fuzzies, which masked the headphones stuck in her ears.

I motioned to her at the red light that perhaps removing the apparatus would be appropriate. She did so and stared daggers into my hopefully-contrite, theatrically-inspired angelic face.

"My apologies ma'am, but I cannot take this time machine backward, only forward, and the next stop is Harrison and Sixth."

"Now I'll have to walk an extra four blocks," she snarled.

"Stupid bus drivers."

It was best not to respond, and luckily the light went green so my attention returned to the street. Another block and Harrison brought me back on track. The expletive she uttered as she left was drowned out by the more gracious passengers who wished me a nice day and let me know my *faux pas* was forgiven.

I had to chuckle at Emily as she departed. Perhaps she would realize, during her six-block power walk, that her plumber's crack was visible because her skirt bottom was stuck into the back of her army boots. Ahh, sweet karma.

Night Vision and Daylight Eyes

Winter is sneaking up on us like underwear that's too tight, along with shorter days and extended darkness. In fact, on December 21, Portland will have daylight for eight hours, 42 minutes and six seconds.

Compared to our 15+ hours of daylight this past June 21, it makes for some tough driving. Granted, our weather has been pretty mild save for the November "Fizzard" which briefly shivered our collective timbers. Downtown this morning, I saw the temperature hovering near 60 degrees; it was colder in Tucson, Arizona!

It's perfectly normal to arrive at the garage in morning darkness, and leave for home in the evening trying to remember if the sun actually appeared at all during the interim. Some folks do not handle our extended star-gazing time very well, and the Northwest has an over-abundance of SAD (Seasonal Affect Disorder). That grumpy passenger might just be SAD or TAD (Transit Angry Dipstick), or just plain MAD (Muttering and Despondent) due to a lack of sunshine. It's amazing how the rain keeps many people indoors, but once we get a sun break bus lines are suddenly slammed with people swarming out of hibernation. Perhaps this is why operators actually cheer when a "Major Winter Weather Event" is even rumored for the vicinity. Fewer passengers equals less headachy, grumpy MADs, TADs and SADs.

You'd think a reduction in daylight would spur our worldly Portlanders to take affirmative action where their visibility is concerned. Nope. As I recently drove a mini route, I counted 11 of 12 passengers who wore *black* jackets. Really, people? Why the need to wear dark colors when you're desperately hoping we can actually *see* you waiting for his bus in yet another downpour? I nearly had a coronary braking for invisible intendeds who were nearly impossible to see.

Maybe some could employ inexpensive yet innovative ways to light up their act. Issuing the entire transit-riding public with our nifty yellow reflective vests might be a bit expensive. There is reflective tape available to affix to a jacket while also accenting Portland's affinity for dark clothing. Perhaps our employer should mount a serious visibility campaign rather than simply putting up a few cute signs on the buses that are ignored. Until recently they used to give us blinking lights to hand out. Nowadays, they don't even provide operators with eyeglass cleaner. Bus operators worry about seeing people (places and things too) in the ever-increasing darkness enveloping us.

Add a few raindrops to the mix, which happens regularly here, and visibility flows down the storm drain. Imagine waiting 20 minutes for your bus in a downpour, when you turn your back to the street a few moments to take shelter. The street noise is intensified as cars splash through puddles, and the sound of a bus can sometimes get lost in the din. We can't see you. Not only do we pass you by, but as you turn around, our massive tires throw a curtain of dirty street water all over you. Now you get to wait another 20 minutes, totally drenched, and thoroughly annoyed the driver missed you.

It's easier to see in daylight. Even when skies are cloudy, our eyes don't have to work as hard at seeing important details. Once the light is removed, our job becomes exponentially more difficult. We strain to see things which we'd quickly dismiss in daylight. Distances are harder to judge properly, especially for pedestrians with a 20-ton monster bearing down on them. Add the fact that many animals are more active at night and tend to dart into the street, and THUMP goes Sally's beloved Meowser. Finally, those who shouldn't be driving in the first place, mainly drunkards, are more active once Happy Hour is past.

Over the course of a two-hour nighttime run, my eyes feel like they've read the dictionary twice over. Although my runs don't usually last much past sunset, sometimes I have to drive until the wee hours. It's the nature of the Extra Board. When your body's circadian rhythm dictates you should be sleeping around 9:00 p.m. and you're actually driving a large vehicle, it is a challenge to remain vigilant. Scanning takes on a whole new perspective when you have to spend more time *looking* at something in the dark as opposed to simply *glancing* at it in daylight.

Next time you're trying to catch a bus after dark, please wear something bright and reflective. It might help you actually catch a bus. It could also save your life.

Holi-dazing

It's December again. People are out bustling and jousting for that perfect gift and delivering Grandma to the store while dodging invisible reindeer. Santa's keeping watch as we alternate between naughty and nice as we negotiate increasingly clogged roadways. I worry about many people who are seemingly unaware their actions could have disastrous results.

Some tend to forget, in the desire to complete their lists, that safety should be their top priority. As my wary eyes constantly survey the surroundings of my mega-machine, I've noticed my fellow motorists need reminders. Here's a few tips from the driver's seat.

SPEED KILLS!
Sure, you're in a rush. Traffic moves about as fast as a turtle race. Darting from one lane to another only increases your chances of getting nowhere fast.

While an adjacent lane may be moving while yours is as still as Congress, lane-hopping gains you no advantage. I've often lumbered by Harvey Hummer several times over as many blocks because he just can't seem to pick the right lane. He darts past me, only to stop at the next light while I time it precisely and cruise past a few moments later when it turns Irish again. He hugs bumpers as if they're endowed with super magnets. Then he slips in behind me as my lane moves, only to slam on the brakes as I service the next stop. Next thing I know, he's flying by me again, sneering. This time, he cuts me off and makes a right turn directly in front of my bus. Bad move, Harvey. I hope he realizes that even though he drives "the big one," mine is fatter and longer. Unless he wants his expensive machine squashed like a bug, he needs to learn patience. And manners.

LIGHTEN UP!

It's dark. A lot. So are people waiting for my bus. They wear dark clothing, stand behind utility poles to escape the wind, and pay more attention to their device than anything else. Several times I nearly missed people at stops because I just didn't see them. Um, duh. Reflective fashions, anyone? Just waving a cell phone doesn't always make you visible if the rest of you is camouflaged by objects you're hiding behind. Please wear something reflective. New rule: if you want MY bus, you'd best pay attention and wave your arms like a crazy person trying to fly, or I won't make a courtesy stop halfway down the block. I will pass you by, because your lack of attention isn't my fault.

"YOU'RE LATE!"

No kidding? Didn't you notice the line of traffic preceding me? Do you think I stopped the bus, jumped out of my seat and sang Christmas carols to my already-annoyed passengers, just so I could purposefully be late? Did I invite the entire city to clog this street just to inconvenience you? Not only are our schedules tighter, they don't take holiday traffic into account because it is typically rare. Makes sense, right? It's logical that when traffic is heavy, we're often late. Buses are in service for 12-plus hours a day, every day; they occasionally break down. Need to be somewhere on time? Please consider catching an earlier bus.

PEACE OUT!

Please remember to show bus drivers some patience. We work hard to ensure you arrive safely. We avoid many collisions because we're vigilantly watching what happens around us. You don't hear about how many disasters never happened because professional drivers are watching for, and deftly predicting, stupid motorist gaffes. The news only reports accidents involving transit vehicles. We keep you safe, even if you're unaware.

Merry Christmas, Happy Hanukkah, Happy Kwanzaa, Happy Winter Solstice. I wish you a safe, happy and memorable holiday season. May peace and joy follow you throughout the year to come.

Red-Suited Freeloader

🚌 **DEKE'S NOTE:** *I just love the holidays. I feel nostalgic, warm and fuzzy, and all the other clichés at that time of year. A bit silly too, when I wrote this one. It was fun, and earned a few chuckles from my readers. Cheers.*

Kris Kringle boarded my bus the other day.

Perhaps he was taking a break from his annual Christmas preparation, took his sleigh out for a test run, and stopped at a brew pub for refreshment. The remnant of a Cuban cigar dangled from his pouty lips, and I wondered what happened to his pipe. This bedraggled elf also had a herd of flea-infested miniature reindeer with him. They milled about skittishly in the Priority Seating area, acting like they had shared a few brewskies with him.

"These are my service animals," he told me as he rummaged in his suit for fare. Seems like there's no dry cleaner at the North Pole, because his outfit was as aromatic as those found discarded under a bridge. And it didn't smell like cloves.

"Okay," I said. "Never seen this many, or this type, of service animal on the bus. Mind telling me what they're trained to do?"

Kris looked annoyed, and there was an edge in his voice as he answered. "Why, they fly me sleigh around on Christmas, you numb skull!" (Perhaps his ancestry is a bit Irish, or he just slips into the brogue after a few pints.)

I winced at his breath. By this noontime, he was pretty much in his own bag.

"If that's so, then where's your sleigh?"

"Damn Portland Police impounded it," Kris growled. "Seems I was parked in a delivery zone, but that is what I do for crying out loud!"

"Okay Santa dude, your fare is a buck for two hours. Please keep your, er, service animals, seated on the floor and out of the aisle."

He paused, sheepishly glancing up at me, and whispered: "I don't have any money left. Mrs. Claus keeps me on a tight budget, you know."

I studied his appearance. I see all kinds of people dressed in red suits during the season. None of them, however, come with reindeer. Something about this fellow had me wondering. After all, I am one of the few who still believe. I decided to take a chance.

"Well, if you're really Santa, do you mind answering a question?"

Several passengers at this point audibly sighed, wanting me to roll the wheels. But hey, none of them had even acknowledged me, let alone said hello as they boarded. I had some time to burn anyway. Despite his condition, this fellow was at least semi-polite and interesting.

"How come, when I was 11 and had been a surprisingly good boy all year long, didn't you give me that Hot Wheels racetrack I asked for?"

Santa studied me intently. He frowned, rubbing his impressively rustic beard. "You're that Deke kid, aren't you?"

Surprised and open-mouthed, all I could do was nod.

"Remember when you tore the head off your buddy's sister's Barbie doll, flushed it down the toilet, and their parents had to have Roto Rooter come out at 11 at night? That's why, you miserable little brat." He spat out the last sentence, completing it with a rotten belch.

Wiping away the offensive by-products of his hops-inspired intestinal explosion, I shot back. "I was framed! Now pay up, or you can try to find an Uber livestock truck. Your service animals just peed on a whole row of seats."

After a little more back-and-forth, Santa exited the bus. His language was not what you would expect of a jolly old elf. He probably read the name on my badge. I was not entirely convinced.

Later, after my downtown break, I began the trek back through the transit mall. As I left a stop, I scanned again. Before I could hit the accelerator, I beheld an amazing sight. Zipping through the air, headed straight for my windshield, was a weaving gaggle of reindeer pulling a portable food-cart, with that red-suited freeloader at the reins. A blinding red light bounced in front of this makeshift contraption, and I thought about running it. At the last moment, it veered off and upward, as it was a reindeer nose. As he rose into the air, I heard the dude exclaim, as his sleigh was a'rockin':

"Merry Christmas to all ye good lil' Portlanders, but that bus driver gets nothing but a filthy Barbie head and coal in his stocking!"

HIT COUNTER: 26,000 (DECEMBER 2014)

Done With 2014, Looking Toward '15

Just over a week into 2015, I will celebrate yet another milestone. Out of sheer boredom waiting for a run, I calculated that in a week I will have seen my 20,000th day. That includes 13 leap years. Considering my 88-year-old father has lived 32,170, that's either mind-boggling or just depressing. Depends on how full you see the whiskey glass, I suppose.

A year ago today, I was still a green driver. This blog was fairly new too. As I read over those early posts, I'm amused. Your Deke is, always has been and forever will be, a goofball. Unfortunately, many of my friends will attest to this.

Whereas most operators have a sharp learning curve, mine resembles my guardian angel's misshapen halo drunkenly stumbling along a rocky mountain path. Lots of ups and downs. Still, I've grown in spite of myself. A bit slower than others, but hey... just because I can write doesn't mean I'm overly bright. At least I try not to repeat mistakes.

Here are some of my goofs these past few years. I'll leave some of it to your imagination, out of sheer embarrassment. If you drive a bus, I'm sure you'll understand.

- Signup periods don't necessarily fall on the first of the month, Deke. The week here runs Sunday through Saturday. Oops, oversleep.
- If you're on extra service and have a layover more than 30 minutes, turn your bus fully OFF. Not just to Day Run. Batteries don't last forever.
- If you want to enter a new Gillig bus through the rear door, hold it open until you're fully clear of the door. If you fail to heed this warning, the door will punish you.
- Try not to give passengers advice if you don't usually drive the route. Especially if you don't realize yours is the last bus to service the stop where they just got off.

- Never trust your eyes at 3:55 a.m. Double-check the bus number of the one you've fully pre-tripped *prior* to taking it out of the yard. Sometimes your *correct* bus number is eerily similar to the one directly in front or adjacent to the one you actually drive all day.
- Keep your fingers away from fan blades.
- When it's been raining heavily for two days straight, make sure there's no old lady in a wheelchair hiding behind the shelter. That way, when you hit that puddle at 35mph, you don't douse Granny at the precise moment she rolls out to flag you down.
- People who live with disabilities don't necessarily want to discuss them with you.
- Avoid negativity when reciting a daily mantra, if you want to keep a positive outlook.

HAPPY, SAFE 2015

Before I leave you and enjoy a particularly splendid New Year's Eve, I must remind you how fleeting life is. A few days ago, I'm not sure exactly where, a lady dropped her cell phone. Under a bus. In a momentary lapse of all reason, she decided to fetch it. In an instant, she was dead. For a phone!

We see carelessness everywhere. Pedestrians glued to their miniature screen as if their life would be meaningless without it. Drivers texting at a red light, who get honked at when it goes green and hit the gas before seeing the car running the red light to their left. Bicyclists texting while riding, blindly headed toward the rear end of a moving bus.

A telephone is only a tool. It can be replaced. Your life is precious, and time on Earth is a gift. You have loved ones who expect you home for dinner. This isn't possible if you're cooling off in a vault at the coroner's office.

YEAR THREE:

DEKE

GETS VOCAL

– 2015 –

It was interesting to read the next few posts, and I wondered where my third year of blogging would take me. The rigors of bus operating were becoming a normal routine. I began paying for regular full-body massages to ease the pain of repetitive motion. For the first time, I took some actual time off from writing posts and began looking inward. How was this job affecting me, positively or negatively? What did I need to do to remain true to myself, while speaking out on behalf my fellow brothers and sisters? How far was 'too far'? Toward the end of 2015, things got a bit testy with bicycle advocates, but we got through the debate with a few bruised egos and no permanent injury. That's how this gig goes.

Which Road? The Write One

🚌 **DEKE'S NOTE:** *I'm reminded that writing isn't just a hobby, it's what I've always loved to do. It's as much a part of me as a guitar is to my buddy Mark. Now I've blogged continuously for a couple of years, and people all over the world have read my words. The reward is being able to speak to fellow bus operators, their passengers and mine. Some live here, others are continents away. After all, the written word is a simple conduit between writer and reader. You're reading my past and I'm in your present, hopefully your future too. Another friend of mine once said that driving a bus is providing "time travel" to people. Perhaps writing is another form of it. Prior to writing this post, I had thought my "well" had dried up, and was contemplating ending the blog. That nagging inner voice the artist cannot ignore harped at me. Ideas started coming again, and I knew stopping at that point would be a cop out. If I could see then what the blog's HIT COUNTER says today, I would not have believed it.*

We all come to a place where, as Robert Frost so gracefully described in *The Road Not Taken*, a choice of direction is warranted.

I cherish this poem. On this first day of a new year, I am confronted with a literary crossroad. I cannot travel both paths simultaneously and hope to find the same reward awaiting me down the lane.

When I began blogging, it had been years since I wrote regularly. My ideas came in jerks and spurts, as did work on a novel born some 18 years ago. I had not practiced my art; many of my tools were rusty. However, the subject of bus operation was fresh and exciting. Throughout my life, when I've been faced with something new, the urge has always been to write about it.

Now, some 80 posts later with 26,000 views, I'm happy with the results. To know that so many of you have not only read my work but actually enjoyed it, is a great achievement and an honor. Writers, musicians, comedians, actors... we're all addicts. We yearn for an audience. As we find people who appreciate our art, we ache for more, and more still, until... well, all drugs wear off after a time.

In the past year, *From the Driver Side* has swelled from a daily readership of 25-30 to a high point of 500-750. Lately, it has dwindled back to a cherished few. It seems Deke has hit a dry spot. I've shared this blog widely, and many of you have done the same. But it hasn't exploded with thousands per day. Considering what I have accomplished, that's okay. I write to a limited audience: those who drive, and others who ride, a bus. While my stories can be interesting to some, there are only so many people who will take time out of their day to read them.

The past few weeks, I've had time to re-visit my posts. Some make me smile, others evoke an artistic wince, a few are prideworthy. The other night as I sat here wondering what I could write, I hesitated. Where am I going with this? I asked myself. What is my ultimate goal? Is there, or does there need to be, an end point? My box of business cards is getting lighter, and I don't know if a re-order is in order. The answers to these questions? Hell, I dunno.

This year's birthday will see me well past the halfway point in my life. It seems I'm flying down the Autobahn of mortality. As a lad, the plan was to publish my first book by the ripe old age of 25. Decades later, my unfinished novel needs dusting and is calling me back into action. My children are nearly all grown. The grey in my beard is nearly as prolific as the growth of management's Rolls Royce benefits. It's time to get back to the business of being *me*.

Over the next year, I will transition from writing mostly as the Deke to creating work as myself. This will leave less time for my alter ego. I have to spread out and file a new flight plan. Sure, I'll post an entry from time to time, but it will only happen when I find something truly fresh to describe. Someday, maybe these posts will find their way into a book of their own. But for now, I think it's a good time to transition away from writing about bus operation.

It's hard to say that, it truly is. I've had so much fun with this blog. It's brought me new friends and boosted my confidence. But my dreams crave fruition, and I'm a stubborn bastard once I've set my mind to something.

Here are a few quotes I try to live by.

"No matter what, have fun every day. It makes life easier to live." – Daddy Blue

"Nothing good is ever easy." – Deke

"Just shut up and write something." – Mom

Cop Tales

DEKE'S NOTE: *Love 'em or not, we need police officers. They protect us when threatened, cite us when we break the law, and chase the bad guys away. People love to hate them, yet no other public servant (except our brave men and women in the military) would take a bullet for us. We need these folks, even if they sometimes piss us off. We could debate their tactics or armchair quarterback their actions for a long time, but if we've never walked a foot in their shoes how can we fairly judge them? They, like us, make split-second decisions the public's safety depends upon. My apologies, gratitude, and respect to local police departments as well as our transit cops for this post. Sometimes however, a driver just has to vent.*

Pulling out from a stop on Broadway a week or so ago, a long line of rush hour traffic sped up when I engaged my trusty (yet oft-ignored) blinking Yield signal. Typical rude driver behavior. I'm used to it. As the fools rushed by me, I spied a city cop cruiser in the mix.

"Ah," I sighed delightfully, "my union brother will let me in."

As I watched with dismay, the patrol car cruised right past me. Not only did he fail to enforce the law, but the doggone copper was fooling around with his onboard computer. I doubt if he even realized my bus was attempting to leave the service stop. I was really upset.

Even if I had noted his car number, plus the time and location of this incident, would it have done any good to report him? Had I nudged out into traffic and been struck by his car, he surely would have cited me. Although we're supposed to have the right of way in this situation, we're also required to take all possible steps to avoid a collision. This means we have to watch out for everyone, even cops. It's enough to piss off the Pope sometimes.

I'd like to know why cops don't patrol the incredibly busy downtown transit mall. Signs instruct motorists which lanes are available, yet they constantly break the law. Only once have I seen a cop pull a car over on the mall. A car was moving against traffic on 5th Avenue, which is one-way in a southerly direction. The cop was stopped as the motorist moved into the bus lane and turned left onto Taylor just across from an officer. Whoop-whoop, Officer Hero lit him up. I cheered and moved on as soon as it was safe.

Every day I drive the mall, it's like following a two-legged dog through a minefield. Cars routinely take the Bus/Train lane and turn right. Directly in front of trains and buses. Even though traffic signs strongly exclaim "NO TURNS." They pull to a stop in our lane as we're just about to exit a service stop, and show us their bird when we draw their attention to the error.

Pedestrians cross against signals or halfway down the block, oblivious to us (or not). Plus, they have a habit of dashing out into the street to catch a MAX train, causing bus operators to brake hard, throwing passengers around like Black Friday shoppers.

Throughout all this madness not a cop is to be seen, except in front of the courthouse. They stand guard in the street, next to their vans of inmate passengers while traffic laws are blatantly ignored. Sure, they're charged with inmate duty and not expected to cite offenders. But where are their brothers and sisters? You would think a city which boasts one of the finest transit systems in the world would put a little more traffic enforcement in its copping.

I once asked a Milwaukie policeman if he had ever enforced Oregon Law 811.167 (failure to yield right of way to transit vehicle).

"No," he replied, rubbing his chin, "I don't believe I have. What is that one again?"

And there you have it. No wonder that Yield light is about as useful as ears on a slug.

Idling Along in Solidarity

🚌 **DEKE'S NOTE:** *In today's fiery political climate, you're either supportive of one philosophy or the opposite. There is no longer middle-of-the-road common sense, honest discussions, or political compromise. In the past few years, racial divides have grown. This is dangerous. It's not conducive to a harmonious society. There is no meaningful or intelligent dialogue. Hopefully, this piece breaks current convention and evokes Lennon's timeless words: "All we are saying, is give peace a chance."*

I'm so white my lineage back to Revolutionary times is blinding. Except for one possible exception, I have mostly European blood mixed with a smidgen of Iroquois. That one exception's name was Mose, a black man from the 19th century.

Early in life, I was taught to look past a person's skin color and into their soul. "If you like what's in there," my mother said, "it doesn't matter what others think or say. Treat others as you would have them treat you." Such a simple concept, I've wondered why it's so difficult for many to grasp.

As a child, I was punished severely when a friend falsely claimed I had called her "nigger." It's a word I've always abhorred coming from a white person's mouth. It's vile. People have died because of this word. The fact my friend falsely accused me of calling her that stung worse than my father's spanking. Even though I vigorously asserted my innocence, Dad chose to deeply ingrain his disgust for that word into my soul so the lesson would never be forgotten.

I forgave him the spanking, because the lesson remains. Rather than be bitter about the false accusation, I resolved from a very early age not to refer to people by skin color. It's uncomfortable for me, to this day, to describe a human being by citing their race. I've made it a habit to include everyone under one umbrella. Those who do not fit underneath it are only excluded for traits I find undesirable.

I do not suffer what is called "white guilt," because I cannot take responsibility for the poor behavior of others. The only moral high ground one earns is through love and respect. Living in the past robs us of future treasures. Ultimately, the reflection in the mirror is our own responsibility. Not having rear-facing sight allows us the opportunity to move forward.

Driving Line 6 a week ago I saw group of about 200 people marching down Martin Luther King, Jr. Boulevard during an organized protest. They were chanting "Black Lives Matter!" and wearing T-shirts sporting the phrase "I Can't Breathe." The vibe was peaceful. They marched down the center of the street, blocking southbound lanes of traffic, for about five miles. They were very organized. Those in the rear included a group wearing safety vests. A van cruised behind the group to block traffic. One man carried a "slow/stop" sign, and was very vigilant keeping everyone safe.

These people were peaceful, and other than annoying a few Sunday motorists, were exercising their right to protest. No cops were around. Perhaps having a police presence could have ignited smoldering passions.

I set the parking brake and settled into an idle. I certainly had nothing better to do. One motorist got out of his car to complain. Meanwhile, I observed reactions of my passengers. A mixed group as usual. Some exited the bus to walk around, or even join, the protest. Several remained and quietly watched. Even though it was my last trip, I was content to slowly follow this march to its end. My bus effectively prevented other vehicles from running up the heels of this possibly vulnerable traffic obstruction. As operators, we safeguard the lives of many every day; this circumstance was equally as important.

"Just as Socrates felt that it was necessary to create a tension in the mind so that individuals could rise from the bondage of myths and half-truths to the unfettered realm of creative analysis and objective appraisal, so must we see the need for nonviolent gadflies to create the kind of tension in society that will help men rise from the dark depths of prejudice and racism to the majestic heights of understanding and brotherhood."

– Rev. Martin Luther King Jr., *Letter from a Birmingham Jail*

Until then, I'd never really seen a Portland demonstration/rally/ protest unfold. Once it arrived at the intersection in front of my bus, the group spread out to block all four corners. They began to chant: "BLACK LIVES MATTER!" and other things I couldn't make out above the noise of my rumbling bus.

I began to study faces in the crowd. Many were white. Holding posters of the late Rev. MLK's words, their actions echoed his eloquent dreams. Half a century has passed since Dr. King implored us to come together, and here was this mixed-race group protesting the fact that although there has been progress, there is much more work to be done.

When I reached the relief point, I explained my tardiness to the waiting operator. He nodded in understanding. Perhaps he liked the fact I phrased it as an opportunity to be part of something positive rather than viewing the march as an obstacle. We're people, after all, like those we serve. To say bus operators are a mixed group is a gross understatement. Those we serve are an even greater melting pot.

People choose to be kind and polite, or they don't. Jerks are not predominantly of one race. Underneath a few layers of skin, we're all the same color. We are the *human* race, and it's not a competition.

Who's That Driver in the Mirror?

DEKE'S NOTE: *Perhaps I'm not the only operator who's ever felt this way, but we all get tired of the job sooner or later. We eagerly await that vacation time. It's healing, cathartic, and spiritually necessary.*

After driving buses a few years, one can become a tad indifferent. It's not an intentional change of perspective, but rather an acquired attitude. This job's array of encounters with patience-challengers tends to warp even the nicest person's disposition, yet we're expected to remain professional under fire.

Over the course of a few years, the average passenger will be driven around town by many different operators. We each have unique styles and perspectives of the transit experience. Naturally, those of us who have seen the worst behaviors might be prone to a more negative attitude. Although we're trained to do the same job, we have our own interpretation of events. Passengers, however, seem to think we're all supposed to behave the same way.

I've recently avoided posting. I needed time to inspect the mirror and evaluate what type of bus driver I've become, versus whom I believe myself to be. I've read my 90 FTDS posts and seen a progression from idealist to road-hardened operator. As a trainer is fond of saying, one has only been here "30 minutes" after a scant few years of service. But my tenure is within the time span my elders warned about in training. One can become bitter if not vigilantly adjusting a bad attitude. While I'm not quite either, I do find it harder to jump out of bed at 3:00 a.m. with the same enthusiasm I once had.

This past week I worked six days straight. Five days of the extra board grind is enough, but six ran me harder than a three-legged rat in a cat shelter. I slept 11 hours last night. Feels like I could use another eight. If I were to allow myself this luxury however, my circadian rhythm would be violated by the time my Monday rolls back around. Usually, my first day off is spent in recovery, with little to no physical activity.

While on report, you sit and wait for work. Our workout facility is across the yard, but even if it were closer to the report desk, working up a sweat and then driving an 8-hour shift wouldn't garner any passenger commendations. My resulting sweat stench would nauseate a garbage collector.

Dad told me when he arrived exhausted from a day's work that sitting in a chair all day is tiring. I laughed. I was then a hormone-charged teenager while he was in his mid-50s. An extra board operator often sits hours waiting for work. Once a run opens up, he sits in the seat up to two hours at a stretch, if lucky has a 15-minute break, then is back in the seat again. This isn't conducive to a healthy lifestyle, which I was accustomed to prior to this job. It worries me when I pull on my pants they are nearly too tight to buckle. I've gained 10 pounds in the past few months. My body is that of a skinny guy. A pregnant one. (I'd hate to see *that* baby.)

Bus operation is one of the least-healthy occupations. Elevated instances of heart disease, diabetes, stroke, and cancer lurk among us. We smoke too much and breathe other toxins in the midst of a hundred bus engines warming up in the yard every morning. We're subjected to disrespect from management, unrealistic safety expectations, and customer complaints that are often false. Yeah, it's not a healthy way to make a living.

Is that what these few years have earned me? Am I now Oscar the Grouch's mentor? Hey, I like to make people *laugh*! How am I supposed to do that if my personality resembles a rectal thermometer?

Recently, I added "Be Calm" to my daily mantra. My vacation begins in a few weeks. My first paid vacation in years. Perhaps some healing will ensue. Until then my dear passengers, be ready to board, promptly pay your fare, sit down and be nice. You'll get there in exactly the amount of time necessary to safely navigate every obstacle placed before my bus.

When I return from this highly-anticipated vacation, hopefully I'll be more relaxed. Maybe I'll smile again. Until then, watch out. My patience is skating on thin ice, and it's warm for February.

A Few Tips

🚌 **DEKE'S NOTE:** *I was going to leave this one out, but when I read it again I was reminded how annoyingly amusing some people can be.*

With the glut of technology these days, vast amounts of information available at our fingertips, I wonder just when we lost our common sense.

Twittering this and Facebooking that, texting our BFF's and adding our SMH's to groaner posts, the basic safety rules Mom and Dad taught us have vanished into cyberspace. Behind the wheel, I'm more apt to SMH when heads-down pedestrians walk out in front of my 20-ton vehicle and FMO (flip me off) when I beep-beep my presence. As if it's AMF (all my fault), they're saying "I KNEW you were there dipstick, shove that horn UYA (definition unnecessary)." But I don't get to respond. That would result in their posting a complaint only a bus operator could LOL at, because I saved them from being ABMUMB (a bloody mess under my bus).

In this day of acronyms for those who prefer modern methods of communication, it's time for a series on How to RTB (Ride the Bus) for DA's. I'll leave you to decipher the latter acronym yourselves.

Paying Your Fare

Nowadays we have phone apps to do everything from reading your email (how quaint) to finding out when a bus is coming. You can also pay your fare with a handy app our transportation district developed. Problem is, PPL are TFB (too freakin' busy) TXTing to PTF (pay their fare) ahead of time. They stand either just outside the door pecking away on their screen with facial expressions like that of a pooping dog, waiting for the fare app to load. I work on the "Be Patient" part of my mantra every time this happens.

I say: "Please get on, walk behind the yellow line, and show me your fare when it comes up."

I'm thinking: *I'm running 10 minutes late and have two buses directly behind me which you failed to notice because you had your nose buried in the bosom of some YouTube pole dancer. And you have the gall to raise your hand to me in a "Just a Moment" gesture? From just outside the door? GAG (get a grip)!*

Really folks, it's not that hard to have the app keyed up and ready to press "Buy" as I'm pulling up. You're not gaining fare by waiting until you're officially on the bus, but you are wasting my precious break time. How? By not having your fare ready when you board. People who pay with that old-fashioned cash stuff usually have it in their hand. They're professionals. You may be a pro with your phone, but when you waste everyone's time by waiting for the not-so-perfect app to complete its task before boarding, you're a transit novice. Some operators won't wait if you're phone-stoned. They're apt to close the door in your face and move down the line. That way, at least you're early for the next bus.

Preparing to Board

As a bus approaches your stop, one of the worst things you can do is move closer to the curb. You're not doing us a favor by getting that much closer to us. Stay well back from the curb, near the bus stop sign, and stay put. Many people see us coming in for a landing and they move toward the bus. Stay at the pole, please. By moving, you're taking our attention from our "landing" to avoiding smacking you in the head with the mirror. It's our job to align the bus to facilitate safe boarding; it's not wise to meet the bus. Let us come to you.

Boarding

Once you've paid your fare, don't stand next to the fare box. Step behind the Yellow Line, folks. It's there for a reason. I can't see through you, and I need to avoid closing the door on that lady who just ran up to the stop. When the bus is moving you should be seated or safely holding a stanchion or grab handle. If you're in front of the Yellow Line and I have to stomp the brakes, you might have a bloody encounter with the windshield.

I am not the tourist information center. Don't hold my door open to ask which bus goes where or when it arrives. If you have a question, ask a fellow rider. Habitual riders know the system better than the average operator. On any given route, there could be three Fred Meyer locations, a few Dollar Stores, two methadone clinics, and 10 marijuana dispensaries. Your operator might know what stop you need, but it's not our responsibility to plan your trip. Our job is to maneuver a bus safely from A to B.

Stowing Your Bike

There are only two spots for a bike. If there are already two bikes on the rack and you're the only person at a stop, the bus will probably pass you by. Waving your wings like a beheaded chicken won't make us stop to explain the obvious to you. And no, you can't bring it on board "just this one time," unless my bus is the last one of the service day and it's safe. It's too bulky and it could injure somebody if we stop suddenly. *Fuhgeddaboudit.*

As the bus arrives, don't step off the curb before we've stopped. There is a special procedure we follow for bicycle loading, using steps designed for your safety. You're at risk if you step in front of an oncoming 20-ton vehicle. Do you truly want to be squashed flatter than a sand dollar on diet pills?

One of the most important things cyclists forget is to remind the operator, *as you are exiting the front door,* that you will be removing your bike. If you sit in the back, then exit the rear door and walk outside the bus and jump in front of it just as we're about to roll, it tends to scare us stinky. We give rides to hundreds of people a day, and don't always remember the guy with the bike was wearing a *"Make Portland Normal"* T-shirt and multi-colored spandex shorts not complimentary to his physique.

Plan Your Stop

You may know your stop, but your operator likely does not. We cannot read your mind. Several times a day, somebody will pull the stop cord too early. Bringing a bus safely to a stop is a precise maneuver. We don't like to waste time. Unnecessary stops are time killers. It's polite to say "sorry, next stop," preferably *before* we pull over. An ornery operator might push the "Cancel Stop" button when the cord is pulled again and just roll on. The guilty one then usually yells "HEY YOU MISSED MY STOP!" Busted.

Be Nice

You've been waiting for a bus for an hour, and should have been at work 27 minutes ago. You're angry, and worried what the boss will say when you finally show up. Things happen with public transit. Buses break down. Trips are cancelled, and traffic can be heavy. Your driver could be a rookie. Is it a good idea to berate the operator who finally does pick you up? It's usually not our fault when we're late. We've likely heard complaints from the 42 people who previously boarded. If you ride transit daily, chances are your boss is aware of the Gumpism we all know well: "it happens."

Bike Chronicles

My driving saved two bicyclists' lives last week. One was a little boy who didn't know any better. The other? A neuron short of firing.

The bike lane on Williams was recently moved to the left of the travel lane to allow vehicles and bicycles a bit of harmony on a chaotic street. As a bus operator, I believe it's a great idea because we don't have to wait for gaggles of riders to pass before we service a stop. So far, it seems to be a positive change. Even though some motorists squeeze past my bus by encroaching on the bike lane, there is more visibility of bicyclists.

One lad of about seven years was riding his bike just behind his mother's as we crossed Weidler. At this point, the bike lane passes over the traffic lane. Keeping the two bikes ahead of me, I eased into the right lane as we approached Broadway. Mom hogged the center of the bike lane, so Lil' Fella was outside in the traffic lane. I gave the horn a beep-beep, a driver's friendly way of saying "Hey, there's a bus behind you."

Mom saw what she thought was my bus bearing down on her son even though I was a good 10-feet behind him. She scowled at me. Because she did this, she almost missed the yellow-to-red light and stopped just short of becoming the hood ornament of a speeding delivery truck. Then the banter began. Our conversation went something like this:

Mom: You don't need to be such a jerk.

Me: Sorry ma'am, I was just trying to alert you of my presence. Your son...

Mom: I don't need you telling me about my son!

Me: I'm not trying to argue, or be a jerk. I just wanted to tell you he was in the traffic lane and I honked to let you know I was there. That's all, not trying to argue or anything. She hung her head a second, then instructed her son to stay in the bike lane. He appeared to tell her to make room for him.

Mom: Oh, okay, sorry.

Me: It's okay, I just don't want to see the little guy get hurt. Have a nice day!

It's a huge responsibility to shepherd 40-60 people in a 20-ton monster, while also avoiding anything that could come into contact with it. People do not realize how many lives we save every day. All they hear about is the tiny fraction of people or objects "struck by a bus." It's an irresponsibly lazy media technique to omit the "other guy's" responsibility in a headline, or it might read "Bicyclist Runs Stop Sign and Hits Bus." Or, "Texting Driver Swerves and Hits Bus." It's more sensational to lead with events being our fault. Even more insulting, they tend to insinuate the driver needs "more training" to ensure these accidents don't reoccur.

We're watching, gauging distances, scanning, predicting and being proactive out there. We're diligent while most motorists are not. Besides, one slip on our part and a life could be lost. Public safety commands every second of our work day.

This leads to the other bicyclist whose life was spared because I predicted his actions. As I crossed an intersection, he was weaving along in the traffic lane and then moved to the sidewalk. Just past the intersection was a bus stop with intending passengers. Planning my approach, I accounted for the possibility that Chance Armstrong (Lance's slower brother) would do the worst possible thing, which of course he did. Just as I was gliding into a smooth landing, Chance blew off the sidewalk into the street, not 10 feet in front of my bus. Since I was braking anyway, a bit more pressure on the brake saved him. I beeped at him to say "Hey watch out!"

The gentlemen waiting for the bus, having watched it all in living color, gaped in amazement as Chance didn't even look back. He left a parting gift though. His one-finger salute made my passengers shake their heads as they boarded.

"That dude's a dumbass," one of them said as he paid his fare.

"Yes," I replied, "but he at least he's a *live* dumbass."

Tough Tiddlywinks

🚌 **DEKE'S NOTE:** *As I read this post, it was a toss-up as to whether I'd include it here. Then I realized it chronicled how I was feeling after two years of writing. Since that's why I write the blog in the first place, here it is.*

This blog is like a friend of mine who listens, but says nothing as I ramble on about the job. It doesn't mind when I bend fundamental grammar rules. It doesn't whine when I forget something to write about while driving Line 4. It doesn't judge pieces I write... it merely displays them.

FTDS is here because I created it two years ago. Now it is a living, breathing entity whether I feed it or not. Even when I neglect it for other creative outlets, I hear its heartbeat. Like an echoing whisper, or the breeze at on favorite hillside, or the voice of my mother... it now resides within my soul. When it cries out to me, I come back and massage it with more stories. It feeds, then rests. Y'all come and go, but FTDS remains part of me. That is just weird.

In these past two years, I've changed because of this blog. Life as Deke transcends normalcy as I keep two of me healthy. I created this pseudonym to protect myself from possible recriminations resulting from speaking my mind. It's a paranoid reality borne of working for "The Man" for several decades. He can say one thing, while meaning quite the opposite. What *he* doesn't know can't hurt *me*. Or so I'd like to think. So even if you know the Deke's identity, I appreciate that you all keep me to yourself. Whoever "rats" will be the one who kills FTDS, because I don't believe "I" have the same freedom of speech to which Deke is entitled. I don't believe I've written anything insulting enough to warrant discipline. When I stray from the norm, my lady is there to slap my hand and remind me to behave.

Lately, I've had requests from readers to explore topics not suited for this avenue. Political in nature? Usually no, thank you. Worth risking my protection under "Freedom of Speech" rules now weighted toward Big Brother Transit Agency? Absolutely not. Dealing with life as a bus operator? Now you're talking! If for some reason what we "feel" out there as operators annoys management, that's transit normal.

So the following is a cringe-worthy paragraph, addressed to management.

We make the wheels roll, folks. Y'all are just bean counters and overpaid paperweights. We're out in the trenches, straddling the line between fare informers and code enforcers. When something happens, we're expected to make snap decisions which are heavily investigated by management, the media and public. If we over-zealously defend ourselves when we're attacked, our actions are hyper-scrutinized by lawsuit-paranoid management and dirty-laundry hungry media. In the spur of the moment, when we're not sure of our attacker's true intentions, our biological fight-or-flight mechanism results in grievous injury to our attacker, we're disciplined. We're supposed to be perfect drivers, but when we make mistakes, we're lambasted, chastised or even fired. When our GM retires, he has nothing to worry about. His job doesn't deal in life-or-death situations. Interestingly, he has the Rolls Royce benefit package while ours is beginning to resemble a rusted Gremlin.

I could go further, but I'll leave that to others. It takes a while, but every operator comes to a point where we realize we're not as important as we're told. Hold that thought the next time a manager makes a show over you. Those who have driven a few miles in the seat might be genuine in their concern; the others can be an unfavorable jury.

HIT COUNTER: 30,000 (April 2015)

Venting Old Fogeys

A newbie mentioned this week she had skimmed through this blog and found it to be "like someone who is venting... I get enough venting from all the old fogeys in the bullpen." Well then, it sounds like I've prematurely entered fogeyville.

I entered this profession late in my working life. I've had several careers before this one. Many operators have done amazing things in their lives, and this is where we landed. For some, transit has been their sole occupation, and I have great respect for them. How they've taken decades of abuse without becoming snarling, drooling beasts is beyond me. Our district, and fellow drivers, should bow in respect to their dedication; instead, management actively plans to make their retirement reminiscent of Oliver Twist in the orphanage. When little Oliver poofs up his cajones enough to ask for "more, please," the warden (management) morphs into the worm in Pink Floyd's *The Wall*. When senior operators vent, they've earned the right.

Conversely, it's amusing how newbies gather around the same table in the bullpen. They share "war stories" with one another, highly amusing any veterans within earshot. Noobs believe their experiences are unique. I should know. It wasn't that long ago my classmates and I shared that table. As you progress in this job, one quickly learns that only extreme stories are worth sharing. Otherwise, it's old news. We deal with a wild assortment of the public, rivaling the variety that cops and those in the medical profession attend to. After a while, little surprises us.

Veteran venting is a product of their decades of service. Maybe this new driver hasn't yet been spit at or verbally abused. It takes a while, but we all get that treatment eventually. Sure, I "vent" quite a bit in here. Hold it all in, and it's bad for the cardiovascular system. If you read some of my early posts, you'll see a gradual transformation. I began with a flowery attitude. Then shit got heavy. Contract negotiations made us all tense. Operators were attacked, several times. Heavy hours on the extra board took their toll. Your Deke has evolved, yet it hasn't all been for the positive. This job is tough, folks. It wears on you. So does management. Photos of me as a newly-minted rookie compared to those today show I've aged considerably more than the three years spent on the job. Kind of like a president.

So yes, perhaps my venting here annoys some readers. This is my therapy, folks. It's where I tell you what it's like to be me. That's all it is. Some would rather not read these posts after a hard day behind the wheel. Can't say as I blame them.

Many operators say this blog expresses how they feel. Perhaps I'm just a dryer vent for other drivers. If the vent gets clogged, the steam can't escape, and the whole works explodes in a fiery mess. Thanks to this outlet, I've remained somewhat sane in this profession.

This is my last career, unless my decades-long book project proves lucrative in the end. After all the years fighting to make rent and feed the family, I'm looking toward retirement. Like most people who reach their mid-50s, it's a shock to realize I've entered this stage of life. Goals once put off suddenly jump back onto the abbreviated Bucket List. It feels as if I've been young longer than I actually was. That juicy 401k from the last job? Spent as a result of mass corporate outsourcing, which left me unemployed an agonizing three years. I had never been without work more than two weeks before then.

This job is vital to my family. People my age, even with decades of life experience, are not favorable in the job market. If you're young, perhaps keeping the job isn't as vital as it is when you've lived a few more decades. With Congress wanting to gut the Social Security system, retirement is becoming a scary prospect. When management cuts benefits every contract negotiation, the future becomes terrifying.

My father-in-law just retired yesterday, at 71. He's tired of working, and I don't blame him. He's toiled over 50 years, and he should be rewarded and allowed to enjoy himself. Instead, he worries if they'll have enough to get by without his steady paycheck. They have to depend on Social Security and what little savings they've been able to put away.

Our General Manager, who already makes three or four times what I do, is assured a fat bonus upon retirement, free health care for the rest of his life, and $16,000 per month. He's never worked in the driver's seat, which I believe should be a requirement for that position. Throughout contract talks, management talked about union benefits practically bankrupting the transit agency. Actually, their mismanagement of, and failure to fund as promised (and as legally required) the pension plan, is not our fault. Yet we'll pay for their misdeeds. Each contract negotiation seems to yield more for management, less for current and prospective retirees. Instead of savoring our golden years, we'll be sweating aluminum.

Yeah, "old fogeys" vent a lot. We've earned the right, through the decades of hard work and dedication to our careers. Life in the sixth decade presents problems younger folks don't understand. When their bodies begin to fold after years of physically-punishing work, they too will vent. Hopefully in the meantime, they regularly clean their collective lint trap so they don't explode themselves out of a job.

Time to Update the GM Position

🚌 **DEKE'S NOTE:** *I believe that if you haven't driven a bus, it's impossible to understand this job, let alone make decisions which affect us. This post found me a bit playful in addressing a serious topic. I was pretty annoyed at the antics management employed prior to and during our contract negotiations. Perhaps if our GM had ever operated a bus, he'd better understand our predicament. One can always dream.*

Bouncing around in an ancient Gillig operator seat gives one many opportunities to wax mischievous. Aches give way to pains, and more grey hair appears. Balancing my monthly bills while trying to plan for a not-too-distant retirement, the antics of management creep into the mix and well, I get a bit ornery.

My first union contract negotiation was educational. Having reneged on its promise to fund decades of retirement obligations, management refused to take responsibility. Instead, it embarked on a public relations campaign designed to convince the public we are overpaid gluttons greedy for more than our share. It wouldn't have been so bad, but the public bought this tripe. It infuriated me to have passengers tell me we make too much money for "just driving around all day." The corporate-owned media loved using the term "Cadillac" to describe our 1975 Pinto benefits. We gave up more than they did, and our GM was given a raise and a pat on the back. I found this insulting, especially considering our "raise" is offset by higher insurance costs we all have to absorb now.

It's sad to see so many people die shortly after retirement. This job wrings the best out of our bodies, leaving a broken shell when the job is done. Union members were once promised we'd never have to pay insurance to care for the bodily damage we endure. Many people probably read this and think we're "greedy" for expecting "free" insurance. It *ain't* free folks. We pay for it through years of mental and physical trauma. Transit operators have some of the highest amounts of stress, cancer, cardiovascular events, repetitive motion injuries, and back problems of any profession. It's akin to taxing the food I eat then again when it becomes waste. None of us start the job with the expectation of "easy money." Our sacrifices should be worth a respectable retirement. When you consider what an operator's (or mechanic's, for that matter) body endures during a typical career, it's insulting for us to pay as our job makes us sick.

Our GM enjoys a six-figure salary and a golden nest egg awaits him when he leaves his ivory tower: a six-figure yearly pension and free health care for life. Really? For what? While we sweated negotiations, news reports focused on a few drivers who had the gall to earn $100,000 in one year, in an effort to make us appear over-paid. If an operator takes in 100k over 12 months, he or she certainly *earned* it through excruciatingly long hours in a poorly-designed seat. I'm sure a GM's job is fraught with annoyances. However, ours is far more dangerous and physically demanding.

We have union elections this month, and I have an idea for our leadership when contract negotiations begin again later this year. Long hours in the seat have me fantasizing about remodeling our GM's job, office design and benefits package. I polled some co-workers, and their responses were surprising. Here are the recommendations of this unofficial, ad-hoc committee of tired-of-being-insulted transit workers.

Training

Prior to running the show, GM candidate must successfully complete the bus training program. His salary and benefits package will be identical to a trainee's. If the trainer doesn't think he can cut it, he's "let go" just the same as anyone else.

He must pass each exam and obtain his Commercial Driver's License, subject to the laws we all must obey. He must be line-trained and become a mini-run operator for the duration of his six-month probation. If graduates with a clean driving record and his sanity intact, only then would he be able to resume the duties of GM.

Each year, he must perform six weeks of in-service bus operation on the most challenging bus lines. His starting times will fluctuate from 4:00 a.m., getting later every day until he is working nights, then back to a report time of 3:00 a.m. at the beginning of the next week. He will be allowed no more than two Preventable Accidents; any more will result in termination and forfeiture of district benefits.

If he is late for any shift by one second, he loses his work for a day; two oversleeps result in disciplinary action, up to and including termination. After his in-service work is complete, he must spend one weekend day each month scrubbing the interior of buses for 10 hours, at the going rate paid to those who currently do this job.

Each month, he must meet with operators to discuss working conditions. He is subject to random drug and alcohol screenings, and must carry a valid medical certificate.

Office Remodel

His cushy executive office chair will be replaced with an operator's seat from a retired 1600-series bus for a period of one year. While at his desk, Mr. GM must be seat-belted at all times. Mechanics will install a device to replicate the driver experience. It will bounce, jar him sideways and vibrate. If he complains of back pain, a workmen's comp doctor will refuse his claim by maintaining it is an injury from a previous job, and will be denied benefits. He cannot leave the seat for over two hours at a stretch. He will only have three breaks of 15 minutes each, then it's back to the seat. If a phone call or meeting runs late, it will cut short his break.

All day long, diesel fumes will be pumped into his air conditioning vents. Transit riders will have 20 minutes a day to stream into his office, without screening for weapons, and lodge phony complaints about him. Several times a year he could possibly face physical attacks without benefit of immediate protection. If he leaves his seat to defend himself, he's subject to discipline or termination.

When riding transit, he will be required to wear a special orange vest with "BOSS" written across it. As a passenger, he will also be expected to inspect fares, de-escalate heated arguments, and field complaints about service cuts. If winter weather turns icy, he will be expected to help maintenance crews chain the buses and assist operators who become stuck on the road.

Benefits

His salary will be reduced by one-third, including the paltry wages he was paid as a trainee or operator. No bonuses will be granted, unless the same amount is passed along to every union employee. He cannot become vested in his pension until his 10th year of employment. Upon retirement, he will have the same benefits as provided union members in the most recent contract. I might have been more lenient with his pension, but hey, we forgot to fund it for 30 years. Oh well.

Vacations will be accrued identically to ours, and he cannot have any more "lost time" than union employees. He will have whatever benefits the least-senior drivers are given. He is allowed only as much vacation as his seniority allows. If he uses more than 32 hours of sick leave, he will be counseled on his lost time, and it will negatively affect his performance review.

Uniform

His corporate suits will be replaced with orange plaid uniforms made of heavy wool. Any time he is caught out of uniform, he will be sent home without pay.

Board of Directors

The board shall consist of five people elected at large by the public it serves, plus one retired and one current union employee. Each time one of them utters the term "Cadillac benefits," a mild electric shock will course through all elected bodies until an apology is offered.

Hey, it could be worse. Making the rounds in the bullpen the other morning, I put this topic out for discussion. Mr. GM, your employees are much more generous than I have been here. A few sympathized with our "upstairs" relations, going so far as suggesting we trade places with non-union employees so we feel empathy for what they go through. However, I've been employed by corporate America, and I can tell you this job is much harder.

We hear often from management as to how much they "appreciate" us. They pick a few to get recognized for their accomplishments, and lavish praise upon them. That's nice, but more of our operators deserve this. It's good for morale. Yet this seems all for naught when contract terms are released and we see how much disdain management has for front line laborers. It's insulting to give our GM free insurance for life when he retires, yet nothing for new hires when their bodies are used up and disabled.

Mr. GM, while you're in training and in-service, one or more of us will take over for you. Perhaps if we trade roles on occasion, we'd have more respect for each other. Until then, please don't patronize us by saying you "appreciate" what we do. Because respectfully, I don't believe you truly understand our position.

We're the Good Guys

Recently, one of my fellow drivers came upon a fight in a North Portland street. Somebody opened a 55-gallon drum of whupass on a kid, and our heroine 'Scout' (she somehow reminds me of a childhood friend with this nickname) didn't like what she saw. With bus horn blaring, she scared the offenders off. Scout deserves kudos for this, but knowing her generous and kind soul, she's not the type to toot her own horn.

Bus operators are often falsely accused of dishonorable acts. While we're not perfect, we work very hard at keeping people safe. We consider it our duty to protect folks from the possible carnage caused by their own inattention. Downtown on the transit mall, pedestrians dart out into the street against the signal. Light rail, bus and streetcar operators keep a constant eye out for the errant jaywalker. When you hear about a tragedy occurring involving transit, it seems we're automatically blamed. Yet there are no headlines about the hundreds of lives we save daily. It's a sad commentary on our society that we'd rather see gore rather than the miracles of life.

Each vehicle has a horn, which we're trained to use only to warn of danger rather than out of anger. Plenty of people test our patience many times each day. It's difficult to resist the temptation to honk and throw a one-finger salute. If we gave in to this urge, the "offended" party would likely whine in complaints of road rage. This results in reprimands from our managers, who might scold us even when they know the complaint is likely bogus.

Of every 100 calls to our customer service line, about 99.5 are complaints. Compliments are rare, but prized. On my bus one day, two ladies were talking about the "horrible" bus operators they've experienced. They continued until I couldn't take it any longer.

"When was the last time a driver did something nice for you?" I blurted out. "I mean, are you saying we're all jerks?"

Silence. I feared the worst. Had I overstepped, earning myself a complaint for complaining about their complaints? At that moment,

I felt angrier than a badger with hemorrhoids. Simultaneously, I was more nervous than a hungover groom at a shotgun wedding.

"Well," one of the ladies said, "no they're not. I mean, you aren't."

"Thank you for that," I said with a smile. "I was beginning to worry."

"But the other day," the other lady began quietly, "I was waving for a bus to stop because I was late, and he just kept on going." By the last syllable, her bravery returned along with the volume in her voice.

I discovered that she left her house late, and was across the street on a busy street at rush hour.

"You know why he probably passed you by?" I offered.

"Yes," she replied testily, "because he's an asshole, and he made me late to work."

"He's an asshole for possibly saving your life?" My voice rose an incredulous octave.

"What?!? He didn't *stop*!" She was indignant.

"Sure, I get that," I said in a softer tone. "But you admitted you were late, that's one mark against you. Another, you weren't even near your stop. I wouldn't have stopped either. Unless it's a time point, we don't service empty stops. Since you were across the street and not in the crosswalk, you were only a blip on the radar. To stop would have encouraged you to cross that busy street against the light, possibly not even in a crosswalk. You could have been injured or even killed. Encouraging dangerous behaviors tells everyone else on the bus that it's okay."

"Hmm," she replied thoughtfully. "I didn't think of that."

"We're not taxis, Miss," I added. "We have rules to follow regarding stops, and they're centered around your safety."

"Yes, but it's your *job* to pick us up! I'm usually there and he's late!" Her anger had returned.

"Evidently," I replied, "not as late as you were. Our job is to drive safely. We pick people up who are waiting at the stop. Everyone on that bus had evidently arrived at their stop on time. You, on the other hand, were simply early for the next bus. Was this your regular driver?"

"I don't know," she said. "What does that matter?"

"If not, he didn't know you're a regular."

"Don't you people talk to each other? I mean, about who rides the bus?"

"Only when they're rude or dangerous," I answered. "If the driver is on the Extra Board, the regular driver didn't make it to work that day. The driver has no way of knowing *who* rides the bus. There are nearly a thousand of us, hundreds of thousands of riders, and it's statistically impossible to know every regular on every line. Plus, we usually only have 10 minutes to prepare for a run on the board."

The air seemed to have left her argument. She paused a minute to digest this information.

"Nobody's ever explained these things to me." Her tone had softened. "I appreciate your kind manner."

This shocked me. I thought my pissed-offishness was shining brightly, and decided to tone it down a bit.

"We're mostly concerned for your safety. We're sorry if you miss the bus, but we can't risk your safety, or that of others."

By that point, we were at the end of the line. The two ladies thanked me, a bit more profusely than I likely deserved. I wished them a nice day and moved on down the line.

A month or so later, I received a commendation from one of these ladies. She said she didn't realize how people complain so much about drivers, and also complimented my safe driving and patience. I was humbled, because I had interrupted their conversation and was a bit testy. Perhaps I touched her guilt button, and she forgave my sins.

Often, I wonder if Scout's interference was ever appreciated via a commendation. She, and our many other drivers who do good deeds daily, deserve more praise than we receive.

I was lucky that day. The next week somebody complained that I flipped them the bird. I did not, but at that point I wished I had. They probably deserved it, but I never give into road rage. That's not how I roll.

Stingy Neighbors

Having just finished driving Line 6, what strikes me most is not the hordes of passengers who ride daily. It's not the shenanigans some of the riders pull, or the horrid traffic. It's Washington motorists who either don't know our traffic laws or simply don't care. After today's work, I'll wager it's the latter.

On C-Tran (Vancouver/Clark County, WA) buses, there is a sign on the back. It's a triangle, with the mere suggestion that drivers yield to a bus as it re-enters traffic from a stop. Over 90% of Washington drivers seem to have a "Yeah, right" attitude regarding Oregon traffic code. Why shouldn't they, when C-Tran's lame attitude of just putting a sign without a warning light like our agency does, just encourages drivers to ignore it?

Dealing with the traffic on I-5 northbound is dreadful. The backup begins around 2 p.m. every weekday, and doesn't subside until after 7:00. It is ridiculous that a metropolitan area with over 3,000,000 people has so antiquated a freeway system, often down to two lanes in some of the most congested areas. Many of the commuters call Washington their home state, yet Oregonians foot the biggest bill for road upkeep and repairs. When Oregon asked Washington to pony up some cash to replace the antiquated I-5 bridge (the Columbia River Crossing project), their legislature at the last minute decided it was too expensive. As a result the traffic continues to get worse with no plans for relief in the immediate future.

Washington motorists are some of the most reckless drivers on our roads. They totally ignore our flashing 'Yield' signals easily 5-to-1 times more than Oregon drivers. They cut us off with regularity. Whenever I drive Line 6, I have to be especially careful crossing the street at Jantzen Beach, because the 90% of cars with WA plates haven't been taught that every Oregon intersection is a legal crosswalk. I've almost been struck by drivers who routinely shout obscenities as they careen past me in their quest to get to the next red light. This isn't very neighborly behavior, considering many of them shop on our side of the state line to take advantage of our lack of a sales tax.

Since they can't abide by Oregon laws yet take advantage of our fair state's ample generosity, I have a few suggestions. First, we should levy a toll on all bridges linking our states. Evidently, there was one some time ago. If we charge them to use our roads, perhaps we could resurrect the CRC project and make some critical improvements to our freeways. They use our roads, why shouldn't we charge them for the privilege?

I would add a 2% sales tax on purchases made by Washingtonians (or all out-of-staters) in Oregon. It might be difficult to determine residence, but maybe not in this digital age. We're taxed to the hilt as Oregon residents, but our neighbors to the north simply thumb their noses and laugh at our polite examples such as "the zipper" (traffic merging from one road to another: one merges, next car goes).

Of course, many of my fellow operators live in Washington, and I suppose some will find my rant offensive. They pay our hefty Oregon income tax, and I appreciate them. My brothers and sisters aren't the culprits here, however. It's their fellow Washingtonians who need driving lessons. To be fair, we have our own share of asshats; today I witnessed a local taxi driver blow through a light that was red a full second before he arrived.

With Portland's metro area forecasting steady growth for the next few decades, something must be done. Unless Washington takes some neighborly steps, I'm in favor of forcing them to pay their share. Until then, I'll continue giving WA cars a wide berth.

Fun with Fussy Britches

🚌 **DEKE'S NOTE:** *I try to keep it light out there, or it becomes oh so... tedious to be a bus operator. I choose to have my fun with a dish of orneriness on the side. I heard about this prank from a fellow operator shortly after printers replaced old-fashioned tickets from the cutter, so I decided to try it on my route one day.*

Rude teenagers annoy me. You know the ones. They have their earplugs in, don't look at you when boarding, etc. There are plenty of kids who have great manners, and kudos to their parents.

When Miss Fussy Britches boarded my bus the other day wearing clothing too revealing for a 15-year-old, complete with orange hair, nose studs, snotty face and attitude, I was a bit miffed. Not at her appearance mind you. I've come to accept if people want to look like a bad carnival act, it's their business. Nothing fazes me any more.

Miss FB put in her money, but I did nothing. I hate being ignored.

The time clock was early, and I needed to kill some time. I decided to have some fun. My thumb poised over the CAD, I waited. She sighed, hands on hips. Gave me the stink-eye. I raised my eyebrows as if to say, "Yes, smartass?" Instead, I motioned for her to remove the earbuds.

"What?" she snarled.

"First," I replied in my Nice Operator Voice, tinged with a tad of over-sweet sarcasm, "good morning, Miss. Second, the machine doesn't read minds. What type of fare would you like?"

"All Day Youth, of course!" she replied, pouting while rolling her hideously made-up eyes. The other passengers appeared to be silently enjoying the developing scene.

"Well don't tell me," I said. "It's the machine that gives you the fare, tell it what you want."

Miss FB sighed again and leaned into the ticket printer. "I said Youth All Day!"

Still, no ticket printed.

"Did we leave our manners at home today?" I asked. "This machine *abhors* rudeness."

"Watch what you call me dude, or I'll report you!"

A few chuckles erupted from some passengers in the front seats. Stifling laughter, I upped my English.

"Please and thank you are the preferred responses to a Voice-Activated Ticket Dispensary, Miss."

One of my elderly passengers, with whom I'd earlier enjoyed pleasant conversation, snorted laughter and covered her mouth. Miss FB turned around to see Granny grinning down at a book in her lap. Granny looked up at her and said, "This is a wonderful story, you might enjoy it."

Nice cover-up, I think.

"I don't read, old lady."

Granny nodded her head and raised her eyebrows as if to say "obviously."

A full minute had ticked off my clock, and it was time to roll.

"Well Miss, which is it? After a certain amount of time, the farebox eats your money and won't give you a ticket."

"Fine!" she shouted. Leaning inches from the ticket printer she said slowly, enunciating clearly but not too loudly, "One Youth All Day ticket, please!"

Instantly, I pressed the corresponding button on my screen and the ticket printed. Miss FB actually jumped back in surprise. She recovered, took the ticket, gave me a petulant look and walked back to a seat.

Turning to my side window, I chuckled.

A few minutes later, two more teens boarded and the young lady sweetly asked, "May I please have two Youth All Day fares, sir?"

I had already seen the $5 bill in her hand before they boarded and pressed the corresponding button, so the tickets printed instantly. I sat there with both hands on the wheel, watching Miss FB. She now had her mouth open a little, stunned at how quickly their tickets printed.

The fun over, I glanced back at my passengers. Granny had sported a full grin ever since Miss FB's fare printed, and she let out a hearty laugh as our eyes met. Miss FB herself scowled at me, and once I thought I even saw an extended middle finger.

Miss FB exited before Granny. As we rolled away, Granny wagged her index finger at me.

"You naughty, naughty man!" she said with a chuckle.

"Come on now ma'am," I said, "do you really blame me?" I winked at her.

"Nicely done," she replies with a sharp nod. "Haven't seen many drivers with such a wicked sense of humor! Loved it, actually. It was all I could do to keep from spitting my chewers onto my lap."

Dangers of Operating

It seems lately that many folks are easily annoyed. Passengers are upset their normal line and train didn't show up and they had to wait longer. Operators are verbally abused virtually every shift. Dispatchers are often overwhelmed, cops are elsewhere when needed, road supervisors are on the other side of their district. What does Ollie Operator have at his disposal to determine how to handle each situation as it occurs? Himself, and his wits.

This morning, I read about a lady operator whose breast was grabbed and twisted roughly by a passenger with autism. Here are the facts as stated by our operator:

1. The operator had come to the end of her line, and noticed a group of developmentally disabled people with chaperones waiting for a different bus.

2. As she stood up from the operator's seat, one of these individuals jumped onboard and roughly grabbed her breast and twisting her nipple. She fought him off, with the aid of three chaperones. When he finally let go of the operator, he moved to the back of the bus and sat down.

3. The chaperones had to coax this individual off the bus.

4. Sister Operator immediately contacted dispatch by telephone.

She gave a description of what happened, at which time her attacker exited the bus.

5. Operator requested Dispatch alert drivers of other lines as to what had happened, especially the operator of the bus her attacker intended to board.

6. Dispatcher asked driver if she was okay, to which she gave a reply she described as "flip" or perhaps laced with sarcasm. "Yeah, as long as I keep telling myself he's autistic and not just some ass."

7. No road supervisor responded by the time her break was over; police did not respond either.

8. She continued her route, and found out her Station Agents had not been notified, nor was there an incident number assigned.

I'll start with the assault. This operator's breast was grabbed "roughly." From the sound of her account, the guy just wasn't going to let go without a fight. As this is a highly-sensitive area in normal conditions and extremely painful when assaulted, I would imagine her reaction was intensified due to pain and shock. The assault left her bruised, both physically and mentally. Yet it wasn't treated as an assault on an operator?

What if she had seriously injured her attacker in response? Had she broken his arm, would that constitute "reasonable" force? I mean come on, who hasn't been on the receiving end of a nipple twister? As a male, sans breasticles, it's painful enough, but for a woman... YEOW! Would she be arrested for assault for simply defending herself?

When you're attacked, you don't have the luxury of determining how much force is "reasonable." What if she had reacted to the painful assault by breaking his nose? Would she be on trial for assault? Would the media play up the fact the assailant had "special needs" and turn the operator into a villain? There is too much ambiguity where it comes to the term "reasonable," because a person is temporarily unable to gauge an appropriate response while under painful and sudden assault.

This attack left the operator, as a fellow union brother stated, in a "diminished capacity" to safely drive her vehicle. Without benefit of road supervisor to assess the situation, the operator could not determine her own ability to safely continue.

The human body's response to an attack is a biological "fight or flight" condition. The body's normal sense of equilibrium, or *homeo*stasis, is temporarily disrupted. The mind is not tuned to produce rational thought at this moment; in fact, people are not "normal" for hours, days or even weeks afterward. The body is so primed to ward off an attacker, the energy this state consumes is enormous. Depending on the intensity of the body's reaction to attacks, hormone levels can remain imbalanced for several months. In the case of an operator with a compromised cardiovascular system, it could possibly trigger a heart attack.

The safe response here would be for the operator to refuse going back into service for at least one day, citing safety reasons. It is difficult enough to ignore the many slights and insults we're subject to each shift. But when we're physically assaulted, it's time to take care of ourselves, not worry about our transit agency's schedules.

It's no wonder our profession is deemed one of the most stressful. When you consider how many times every day some operator has experienced a stressful passenger encounter, it is amazing we continue to safely operate our buses.

Another troubling aspect is that her Station Agents weren't aware it had happened. The fact there was no incident number is disconcerting, considering we're instructed to report practically anything abnormal that occurs on our shift. Our dispatchers know what we go through, as they have driven buses themselves. Their job is difficult too as they manage operators, supervisors, mechanic calls and extra service operators. They are sometimes under-staffed during peak hours. They have enormous responsibilities, and they usually do an outstanding job under extreme circumstances. I haven't heard about this incident from their point of view, and I refuse to lay blame at their feet.

There are any number of explanations, and it is a common response for us to blame someone when we feel wronged. We're isolated out there, and want to protect our brothers and sisters.

However, operators are but one of the lug nuts on the bus; we're part of a team. Our best response is to educate one another, increase solidarity and preach consistency.

My fellow operator and union brother, Henry Beasley, has put a lot of thought into operator health following an assault, and has offered the following points for consideration as additions to our SOP's. If one of my brothers or sisters who reads this is assaulted on the job, please do the following.

1. Notify Dispatch immediately, and request a road supervisor and police response.

2. Call your union rep as soon as possible and ask for advice and assistance. Ask the rep to contact all who should be aware of your situation, including the Station Agents at your garage.

3. Write down what happened as soon as it is safe to do so. We tend to forget important details if we wait too long.

4. File charges against your assailant; we cannot expect the public to behave if we let it slide. Remember, if we do anything wrong, we're almost certainly called on the carpet. Why should we always be the nice guy? For your sake as well as for your fellow operators, insist your assailant be held responsible for his/her actions.

5. Refuse to continue in service. Your body, mind and soul have suffered grievous harm, and you need time to recover. If you decide to drive again, you're setting yourself up to fail because your mind won't be concentrating on safety, mostly the events you just experienced.

6. *Stand Your Ground.* Don't be bullied into doing something you shouldn't have to.

7. Take the time you believe necessary to heal before going back on duty. Your passengers and fellow operators need you to concentrate on driving safely, and you cannot do that if you're upset, injured, or in shock.

Another operator was so terrified one night she reports "hiding behind a tree, running for my life, scared out of my mind" during her route, only to be disciplined later for parking her bus on the wrong track in the yard. Why did she even have to drive again after this incident? Even more infuriating, she was confronted by a manager who reportedly didn't even ask her if she was okay, and reprimanded for parking the bus in the wrong place. Hell, she should be applauded for getting the rig back without a scratch, considering she was likely on auto-pilot after such an event!

Sadly, operator assaults are a common occurrence. When our management refuses to acknowledge that we operate without protection, and then insults us by reducing our contractual benefits, we feel isolated. There should be a concerted effort to support the frontline workers by management, the public, law enforcement and the legislature. Laws should be enforced, and violators should be severely punished.

I hope that if I'm confronted with an attacker, that my response is "reasonable" enough to save my life, keep my job, and recover my sanity. My hopes and prayers remain, as always, for the safety and protection of my fellow operators.

Busted!

🚌 **DEKE'S NOTE:** *Sometimes it's difficult to remain anonymous, but I've been lucky except for a few close calls. Luckily, my brothers and sisters are protective of my nom de plume.*

A dear sister operator, whom I haven't seen in quite a while, approached me the other night at the garage as we finished our runs.

"Can I ask you something personal?" she asked.

"Well," I replied, "I suppose so JuneBug. What do you want to know?"

"I was reading *From the Driver Side* the other day, and I think I made a connection. Are you the Deke?"

Wow! Slammo! Zing! Busted. So much for that pseudo anonymity that has accompanied my self-perpetuated dual personality. There was no question as to which one of me would respond.

"Um," I stammered, "what makes you ask that?"

"Because, if it's you, and I think it really is, you talk just like you write. It *is* you, isn't it?"

There it was, laid out on the table. My dual persona, revealed. Yet all was not yet lost. Several people know my true identity, and JuneBug is about as safe a friend with my secret as anybody. It was just a bit unnerving that she made the connection. I mean, we're friends, but we haven't spent much time getting to know each other. She's one of those people who you feel as if you've known each other for years. Easy to talk to, really sweet and kind.

"Well," I told her, "You guessed right then. But I had no idea..."

JuneBug laughed. "I knew it!"

"Really though?" I asked, incredulous. "I actually write how I speak?"

Evidently, I do. My wife doesn't see it, but perhaps that's because she's so close to me. It's fascinating though. I've written since I was about 10. It's always come naturally, and I reckon my style is akin to you and I just sitting here having a conversation. It seems comfortable to write as if you're right across this desk watching me type.

Only problem is, I hate people watching me write. You might just guess who I am.

What Happens if the 'Big One' Hits?

I wonder what it would be like if The Big One hit Portland. According to seismologists, we're due for a major earthquake in the Northwest. A big 'un, so they say, 8.0 or more on the Richter Scale. And when it happens, our fair city will be a horrific mess.

A fellow driver asked if I knew our transit agency's plan in case of a disaster. I don't, and I doubt if the talking heads do either. It would be pretty chaotic, to say the least, if disaster struck our fair city. When you consider there are hundreds of buses out at any point every day, we would be the eyes and ears for emergency crews needing to know what routes remain undamaged and/or passable. Depending on the time of year, we could have our buses utilized as shelters or first aid stations.

Chances are, if an earthquake of major proportions strikes here, it will cripple the entire Northwest. Devastation for hundreds of miles, tsunamis, volcanic activity. Utter chaos. Scientists lately have been really talking this up, and it's a major concern for many. However, I haven't heard much about disaster planning from our transit agency.

Earthquakes shake the hell out of everything. Bridges collapse, freeways become impassable, tsunamis tear up the coast. People are stranded, their homes demolished, cell towers are inoperable and we're unable to contact loved ones. And of course, many are injured or killed.

I could be cruising along on a rainy winter's night when all of a sudden, the road starts moving side-to-side. I slow down and stop, but things are still moving. Everyone on the bus is scared. Bridges are swaying, some collapse. A huge fissure opens a few feet in front of my bus and we start sliding down toward the Willamette River. Whoa, what the hell should I do now?

First, I'd want to make sure my passengers and I are as safe as possible. Unless we're upside down or under water, I'd urge people to remain inside. A bus weighs 20 tons and is about as structurally safe as anything else you could find in that situation. With power lines likely down all over, I'd hate for anybody to run screaming from my safe haven into a human cookout. If our antiquated radio system remains online, I'd have communications with Dispatch. We'd most likely sit tight and offer refuge to any wandering or injured souls who venture near.

Many of our bridges were built before building codes required earthquake stability. They will likely collapse. Except for our new Tillikum Crossing. The new Sellwood Bridge was engineered with a large subduction event possibility in mind. For the most part though, our roads and bridges will be impassable.

Depending on the scope of the damage, we could be stranded for days. How would we survive? There are no emergency provisions on board, except for the snacks and water I keep in my backpack. We're not allowed to keep weapons on our person, so we'd be at the mercy of any wandering marauders. I'm sorry, but the thought of fighting off an armed lunatic with nothing but a fire extinguisher or a fare punch gives me the willies.

Road conditions here are often atrocious. The idea of anyone "evacuating" in an emergency is a sick joke. While buses can run a whole day on the fuel on board, this comfort zone disappears when the tank is emptied. Once conditions become safe enough, we could all be facing a long walk home.

The City of Portland has thought of the 'what ifs,' and they have a very informative and helpful preparedness guide online ('The Big One' Survival Guide). I have not been able to find anything put out by the transit agency as of the publication of this post regarding bus operations.

Surely my readers have pondered this scenario. If our transit agency has, it's a secret to me. I'm curious to know what our southern neighbors in California have to say about transit worker preparedness.

Meanwhile, I'll just keep on tooling along, ready for whatever happens.

Singers and Complainers

There are all sorts of characters who ride my bus. I've heard wild stories about particular exploits, arguments between passengers, and seen extraordinary acts of kindness just when I was losing faith in humanity.

As operators, abuse comes with the territory. We get yelled at for being late, even if it's just two minutes. People who miss the bus because their phone is more important than watching for us call in complaints if we roll past their inattentive buns. But this complaint takes the cake.

I recently had the pleasure of driving Line 30 to Estacada, a small town about 20 miles southeast of Portland. It's a pretty drive, through forests, along a curvy stretch next to the Clackamas River. There are farms, wildlife and wonderful vistas to behold. The passengers are usually nicer than the inner-city folks I usually pick up on different routes. They don't mind when we turn off the interior lights when it's dark outside. In fact, they remind us to do so. It removes glare so we can see the road better.

As we entered Portland, a gentleman startled me by coming up behind me as I did a traffic check over my right shoulder.

"Whoa!" I exclaimed. "Howdy there, sir."

"There's a guy back there singing," he said softly.

"Yeah?" I glanced at my passenger mirror to see a young man with headphones, softly mouthing the words to a song on his iPod. I could hardly hear him over the bus noise.

"And this bothers you?" I asked.

"It's terribly inconsiderate," he replied.

Well, now. Considering it was pretty quiet that morning, I didn't consider it problematic. Phone conversations create more noise pollution than this guy softly singing to himself.

"I'm sorry you feel that way," I said, and left it at that. The passenger sat down. I glanced at him in the mirror; he saw this and pointed at the musical criminal. I just nodded.

As I drove, my ears became more finely-tuned to this 'problem' singer. He wasn't going to win any talent contests, but he could hold a tune. I didn't recognize the song, but it wasn't profane and nobody else complained. I just let it ride and concentrated on safely operating my 18-year-old bus.

A few stops later, the young man exited. Afterward, the older guy repeated himself.

"I think it was just inconsiderate of him to be singing," he said.

I just nodded. No comment.

"Sir," I said a few moments later, "I've had a lot worse happen. People scream at each other, or at me. Couples have arguments over what to have for dinner. Several people try to tell me how I should do my job. But seriously, a young fellow softly singing to himself is not what I'd consider a problem."

"Well," he said, "I just thought it wasn't very polite of him."

"Duly noted," I growled. "Just be glad it wasn't me doing the singing, or you'd really be upset."

I could have belted out some of my favorite sordid tunes by Chuck Wagon and the Wheels. Sometimes on my deadheads, sans passengers, I'll let loose my warbling voice on the unsuspecting ghost riders.

Truly, if I had sung my favorite ribald tune, there would have been numerous angry calls to Customer Service that day. Regardless, I thought his complaint was silly. If that's the only problem I have to deal with on a run, I'll take it.

Just a Bus Driver

🚌 **DEKE'S NOTE:** *I don't recall exactly who said it or where, but someone truly annoyed me with a statement about how "simple" our jobs are. One thing folks know is that you don't want to piss off an Irish/Scots fellow. This is the result.*

I am sorely annoyed. Somebody said something truly foolish on social media and insulted bus operators everywhere. Stomped on our profession, smashed us into the dirt and kicked us when we were down. Of course, he could not have been entirely serious, only belittling our profession using the broad brush of a fool.

"Any trained orangutan could drive a bus," he said.

Really? You could train an animal to do this job? I've heard they might have buses which drive themselves in the future. But an orangutan as a professional operator? Puh-leeze. If you think human drivers are a surly lot when passengers test our patience, imagine a primate's response if it gets spit on or assaulted! Transit agencies worldwide would be destitute from lawsuits stemming from the instincts of a wild animal fighting back. They bite, too. All we're allowed is "reasonable self-defense," whatever the hell that means. Orangutans don't have the mental capacity to gauge the response necessary to safely stop the bus while keeping attackers safely at bay. Any self-respecting primate would jump on the violator like a hungry fat dude on a free donut.

Surely it was just a lazy attempt at humor, a figure of speech. But those few words are sadly the opinion of many people. It takes a lot of skill and fine motor control to navigate a bus through these city streets. Even though we have power-assisted air brakes, it constantly requires a few hundred pounds of controlled pressure to stop these beasts. At the same time, we're scanning over 200 degrees of a visual plane for possible dangers. Passengers create distractions by thrusting their trip planners into our faces at the most inopportune of times, asking "Where do I get off the bus for this address?"

So yeah, I was sorely annoyed to hear that. I'm open to good-natured ribbing, but when you disrespect transit operators, I show no mercy in my response. We work extremely hard every day. We're expected to smile and remain calm, even when abused.

I read recently where a driver in another city was attacked as his bus was in motion. A passenger with a doctored pass was angry when the operator wouldn't honor the fare, so he grabbed the wheel of the bus and repeatedly struck our brother. With the aid of other passengers who briefly subdued the attacker, he finally brought his bus to a safe landing. He was battered and injured, but he kept everyone safe. Instead of being concerned about the driver's well-being, his transit agency actually suspended him for five days without pay. Why? Because he didn't take his beating courteously. Talk about adding insult to injury! Not only was the operator traumatized and injured by the assault, his transit agency refused to back him up, instead choosing to demoralize and insult their own "valued employee" because he had the audacity to defend himself.

So yeah, I went haywire at this "friend's" remark. Needless to say, he's no longer welcome to discuss anything with me, let alone my profession. If I ever saw him waiting for a bus, I'd tell him to wait for the next orangutan to pick him up. Good luck, buddy.

My Butt Hurts

Dad was right. When I said that all he did was "sit all day," he told me I would find out someday how tiring it can be. He was right. My butt after an 8-hour shift is so sore I can't sleep on my back. This is a good thing because Mrs. Blue says I snore like an unmuffled backhoe at full throttle.

There are things out there however, which make me smile, cheer and generally forget about my pain from time to time. Today on the downtown transit mall, an out-of-state motorist was in the bus service lane for several blocks. I beeped at him and opened the door when he rolled down his window. We're not supposed to participate in road rage incidents, but I was friendly in tone and manner. Perhaps this fellow hadn't seen the miniature signs prohibiting his driving decisions.

"Pardon me sir, do you see the signs up above that say 'No Turns' and the ones on the street that say BUS ONLY?"

"No, I didn't. And I don't care." Window goes back up. Smug little prick.

He blithely continued down the service lane with me behind him. I was trying to service that stop. Evidently this prompted him to ignore the multiple signs instructing drivers how to behave on this street, and he swerved in front of two cars to get into the auto lane before anyone else could get to the red light. Then he turned right, from the far-left lane, directly in front of my bus, onto the one-way street. The wrong way on the one-way street, I must add.

Later, heading the opposite direction on the mall, I saw another motorist in the Transit Lane I was trying to merge back into after servicing a stop. This time, I saw a cop in the auto lane. I motioned to the officer as if to say, "See? Can't you help me out here?"

Our brother in blue nodded, then flicked on his blues and reds, pulling into the Transit Lane behind the offender. The motorist turned right, directly in front of me and beneath the "NO TURNS" sign, with cop right on his bumper. Cop pulled Mr. Ignoramus over and hopefully cited him.

VICTORY!

There is some yin and yang out there. Poetic karma. But hey, it's the first time I've seen a cop stop a violator on our transit mall.

I just wish I could have heard the conversation between the cop and motorist. It might have gone something like this:

Motorist: "Sorry officer, I'm from Seattle."

Cop: "Don't they spell 'Bus Only' the same up there? Here's your citation."

Signup Shenanigans

Signups are a stressful event, especially these days. For the first time in years I was able to jump off the Extra Board into some work I truly enjoy.

As you put in years as a bus driver, you expect a few things to happen. First, as the miles pile up, you gain more experience. This increases your skill and safety. Years of driving are also supposed to give you seniority. I've been gradually climbing the ladder, but I defer to those who have toiled at this for centuries. (One year as a driver can age us 3-5 years, so if one has been doing it 20-30, yeah I'd say it must feel close to 100.) With seniority should come the "plum" runs, the juicy ones that are off early and pay nicely. Senior drivers have earned the right to pick these.

When your transit agency alters runs so that senior drivers are forced to drastically alter their schedules, they feel cheated. A sister friend of mine said she had to sign something that's out six hours later than she did this time. That's not right. Now she has to scramble to rearrange her life, even after decades of service.

Apparently, there were supposed to be two options hung at the garages, so operators could compare, then vote on their preference. This did not happen.

I've only driven a few years, so I don't expect the cream of the crop. We all have to earn our seniority. However, this time I ended up with three runs totaling over 10 hours overtime a week. This is something I shouldn't expect for a few years. Even though this is good for my bank account, I feel as if I'm cheating my senior brothers and sisters out of something they should have.

One of the powers that be at our agency is on vacation this week, so no resolution is immediately foreseeable. An option for this mess is to scrap the whole signup and start over again, or to keep what we have and try to change it for next time. The latter solution is certainly not a popular choice.

If this is a ploy by the agency to set union members to squabbling amongst ourselves, it's working. The union meeting a few nights ago was full of grumbling senior operators. The executive officers could only tell us to fill out the survey forms and voice our frustrations there. Since union leaders agreed to this mess without our approval, the membership is highly upset.

Newer drivers have some of the best picks this time. While I truly like what I picked, it feels cheap... stolen. After putting in 10-15 years or more, I would feel cheated as a senior operator. I hope that once I get there, I'm not thrown under the bus like they have been this time. It's a terrible way to treat our most valuable operators.

I'm sorry this happened, my senior brothers and sisters. Fair is fair, and I respect your seniority. You've earned it.

HIT COUNTER: 40,000 (OCTOBER 2015)

Just Drive Asshole

It's been a particularly rough week. Without going into details, I was the victim of a brutal verbal assault. It happens from time to time, but rarely on my route.

I'm used to rudeness by now. People seem to think I'm there to serve them, as if I'm their personal chauffeur. What they don't understand is that riding a bus is a privilege, not a right. Just because they plunk down a few bucks and change doesn't give them the right to boss me around.

When I'm behind the wheel, it's *my* bus. Not the transit agency's, not the public's, not those riding in it. I am the captain of the ship. It is my duty to safely transport passengers on a specific route to their destination. Abiding by our Standard Operating Procedures, I am paid to operate a vehicle that demands my full attention. In addition to following the law, it takes concentration to maneuver through narrow streets originally designed for horse-drawn carriages.

A person of average intelligence knows it's a bad idea to annoy, insult or assault a bus operator. But there's about one percent of the riding public which seems to delight in doing so. Professional jerks, you might say. They might be mentally ill, but whatever their excuse, they still don't have the right to put everyone on (or around) the bus in danger. Our attention must be strictly focused on safe operation, not unnecessary distractions.

Sometimes, I will chastise a passenger if they're chatting too loudly on their phone, or if I can hear the music in their earphones.

It's distracting, and takes me out of my safety zone. General conversation on the bus is white noise, like the diesel engine. When a passenger erupts into a vile, profane and ignorant tirade after a bus operator asks them to abide by agency rules, they have put the entire bus at risk, and everyone within it.

When some guy who is highly impressed with himself decides he doesn't have to obey the rules, things can instantly turn sour. By cursing, shouting and screaming at me, he hasn't just dented my safety zone, he has demolished it. Rather than elaborate on a recent heated exchange, here's what I dearly would love to say to one of these imbeciles, but cannot if I want to remain employed.

Jerk: "Shut up. Don't tell me what to do. I pay your salary, so shut up. Just drive Asshole." (Comma omitted on purpose.)

Me (over bus intercom): "Ladies and gentlemen, at our next stop I must ask you all to disembark from this bus. I've been instructed to 'just drive Asshole.' Since there's only one person on this bus fitting that description, I'm sorry but all you polite and decent people must leave so I can carry out his command. Thank you for riding, be sure to thank Asshole for your inconvenience."

Instant Karma Strikes Again

After another tough week, I managed to remain courteous and upbeat. It was my Friday, and I was determined to make it a nice day. Of course, there's always someone ready to sour my mood.

When an aggressive driver zipped past both my bus and the car behind me as I pulled from a service stop, he broke three traffic laws. First, he was speeding and driving aggressively; he passed in a turning lane; and he failed to yield to a transit vehicle. A minute later as I scanned ahead leaving the next stop, I saw his truck sideways in the middle turn lane, with another vehicle angled in front of his. Although neither vehicle was damaged, he was screaming at the other driver through his passenger window while banging on his car for emphasis. The other driver appeared to be calling the police. After I cruised by this road rage, a cop car sped past, evidently in route to the scene. My only regret is I didn't stop and offer my services as a witness. The cameras on the bus surely captured his antics, but I didn't see what happened. Hopefully, he was cited.

Later as I boarded passengers at a stop shared by different lines, Bonehead #2 stood with his back to the bus door, talking to someone. He made no effort to board my bus. Nor did he signal that he wanted to. So I closed the door. At this point he gave the common arms up "HEY!" response, so I reopened the door. Big mistake.

"You're two minutes late and I need to get to work!" His manner and speech were terribly rude. I remained unruffled.

"No sir, I'm exactly on-time," I said with a grin.

"Don't argue with me asshole, you're late. Now just shut up and drive." Then he walked to the back of the bus, a typically arrogant move to show he need not treat me with respect. I shrugged it off. One more run and my weekend was on. His rudeness rolled off my shoulder into the trash can.

After I made the right turn onto a major street, he jumped up and shouted, "Hey this is supposed to be the 79!"

"No sir," I replied calmly, "it's the 33." I realized I was going to enjoy this next exchange.

"Your sign said it was the 79."

He apparently hadn't looked at the overhead signs or never learned to read, so I got out and checked. Sure enough, the signs were both correct.

So not only did I let him off several blocks from the nearest 79 stop, I made sure *not* to give him a courtesy stop. You don't treat me like crap and then get a bonus. His rude behavior resulted in his walking four blocks to catch a bus that would surely be gone by the time he finally got there.

He disregarded all safety concerns and darted across five lanes of a busy street, cursing me the whole way. As if it was my fault he's a jerk, fool and imbecile all rolled into one.

Not sure who lit their fuses on their tampons, but I would imagine both were pretty short to begin with. It was rewarding to see the karmic results.

I Hit the Jackpot (Not!)

The recent readership explosion of this blog has also shown a marked increase of advertising revenue. Numbers of "clicks" have exploded, leaving me with a giddy sense of excitement thanks to added income to my struggling coffers.

This has me dreaming of exotic vacations. Shall I return to Hawaii? A trip to Ireland, Italy, Spain or the coast of France? Will Deke realize his dream to emulate Steinbeck's cross-country odyssey in a brandy-new camper-adorned pickup truck? Can I finally roam carefree in our national capitol, spending a week or two exploring the Smithsonian and all of DC's wonderful sights?

I reckon not. Since I sneakily allowed ads on my blog earlier this year, I've made a whopping buck-fifty. Not exactly a bundle. More like a haphazard mound of pennies. Just about enough to plunk a few quarters down and take a few spins on the Redneck Retirement Plan (lottery) slot machines.

Seems I'd have better luck dressing in ratty clothes, sporting a makeshift sign out of cardboard reading "Anything Helps... My Retirement Fund is Woefully Short" and standing out on the street with a tin cup.

It's off to the shower with me. Time to don the uniform blues and make my way downtown to catch... I mean drive... a bus.

Using Common Sense to Avoid Tragedy

While this job pays me well, there are often times the income doesn't keep up with the bills. This income disparity leads me to be a taxi driver in my personal car on my nights off. Of course, I'm still bound by Hours of Service rules, but in this signup I have plenty of wiggle room.

The other night was Halloween, which is very lucrative for taxi drivers. I must have ferried a few dozen intoxicated and costumed revelers. It was fun. Unlike the drunks who often ride my bus, these people were kind and considerate. I'm happy to provide a valuable service to our community. Even though a taxi ride can get a bit pricey late at night, the other option is the very dangerous choice of driving while intoxicated. Sadly, I witnessed the result of what can happen when people drive when drunk.

Just before 1:00 a.m. that evening, as I drove two fellas to their home, we came upon a ghastly sight. A man lay motionless in the middle of the street on Lombard at Peninsular, and a nearby vehicle was engulfed in flames. We safely detoured around this horrible scene, having arrived moments after it occurred. A witness was checking the man's pulse... but he evidently died at the scene. My heart was heavy, and I was sad to know the family of the deceased would soon be informed of this senseless tragedy.

If the public had the same training as we do, our streets would be safer. Perhaps those who think they're "better drunk drivers than sober" should wise up. It could save their life, or that of the poor pedestrian I saw lying in the street the other night. Call a cab, and let a sober professional get you home. It could prevent your loved ones from answering that dreaded late-night knock on the door.

Newer Rides, Older Joints

🚌 **DEKE'S NOTE:** *New vehicle models usually have some bugs. When I wrote this post, we had just received a new generation of Gillig buses. I wrote about the problems I had noticed. Our bus design committee must have heard our complaints, because the newest buses now have the kneeler switch on the door handle. While it can be a bit tricky to use sometimes, it's much better than reaching forward a few hundred times each day. I heard the buses with the dashboard kneelers are someday going to be retrofitted with the new design, and I applaud this decision.*

The verdict on the new buses is in. Some have 100,000 miles or more, and this operator would much rather drive the older models.

Somewhere along the line, a design team decided to add a few feet to the front of the bus. This added more vision barriers. We already have to "rock and roll" in the seat to make sure we don't miss something, but with several more barriers to scan around, it's more like bobbing and weaving while dancing to a Michael Jackson tune.

In addition to the added vision barriers, the driver's seat is still uncomfortable. If you're over six feet tall, the edge of the seat cuts off circulation just above the knees. The adjustable pedals are a nice touch, but on some models the turn signals are too close, making it so you have to actually move your foot onto the turn signal rather than simply pivoting your heel between them.

The kneeler control is on the dash, requiring the operator to lean forward in the seat to lower the bus. On a typical route, we can kneel and raise the bus hundreds of times a day. Drivers are suffering from repetitive motion injuries, because it's quite a reach even when you have long arms. If you're shorter of stature, it's more than just a reach.

We're impressed with drop-down chains for the maybe once-a-winter snowfall in Portland. However, one driver had to crawl his bus over a curb one day, breaking the chain anchor. Show me a driver who has never driven over a curb, and I'll show you a true service animal: they're equally as rare.

Another thing I've noticed is the back door opens differently. Instead of pushing when we activate the door, passengers are supposed to just *touch* it between the handles. Sometimes passengers slam through the doors. Problem is, these newer buses don't like a heavy hand, and they tend to slam shut on their assailants. This earns us angry stares, as if it's our fault they can't bother to read the instructions.

There are some good things about the buses on order. One helpful feature is kneeler and mobility device ramp controls are combined with the door opening lever. This is much more ergonomically-correct for operators. The engines burn cleaner and are more fuel-efficient, with a smaller carbon footprint. A fascinating feature is an exhaust burner, which incinerates particulates and results in virtually zero emissions. The route signs on the new buses are larger and brighter. Curb illuminators come on when we activate turn signals, making it easier to see around corners at night.

Many operators prefer a return to the flat-faced models which incorporate the operator-friendly features, rather than the ugly new ones with too many blind spots. But hey, I'm just a bus driver... what do I know?

Blame Sharing for Tragic Incidents

🚌 **DEKE'S NOTE:** *Oh my, how Portland cyclists hated this one! A local bike blogger happened upon this post and decided to write a review of my blog. He took note of my "thought bubble," which while it insinuated I'm passive aggressive, was simply frustration venting through my fingertips. The result was a backlash from many of his readers who were angry with my calling out their often-dangerous habits. Some even called for my termination. Such is the result of free speech: if it pisses people off, then they want to ban the messenger. Too damn bad, I say. I don't write with the goal of coddling; I tend to shoot from the hip, and it needed to be said. People are loathe to admit when mistakes are made by the injured, and quick to blame transit operators.*

This one touched off a firestorm of debate between passengers, bicyclists and operators. My goal here, as always, was to raise awareness while fairly spreading the blame for tragic incidents which occur involving public transit.

A recent post was the result of a "Re-Certification Class" our agency has once a year for all bus operators. This one will discuss what constitutes safety, and whose responsibility it ultimately must be attributed to.

Our local transit-blog muscle man, Al Margulies, recently posted a video on this subject. A retired bus operator, Al is well-known for blasting our district for its blunders and shenanigans. It's good to keep grinding the agency for dragging its feet, especially where the word "safety" is concerned. While he's correct in lambasting the agency for its lack of action in lieu of a passel of fancy words and finger-pointing, my belief is "Safety is a Two-Way Street."

I've stated many times that transit operators save lives each trip, on all lines, every single day. You won't hear about that in the media, because safety doesn't sell. When something bad happens, you hear about how the agency needs to "train its operators more" or "study safety solutions" and blah blah blah.

Oh sure, once in a while you get the "Operator Good Guy" feel good story, but most of us don't tell the Public Information Office (PIO) about all the good things we do. Why? Because it's all part of our job. The "news" would most likely not be interested if it were inundated with "nice" stories, and most of us are just simply... well, too modest to talk about it. After a shift is over, we just want to go home and put that day's work behind us. The next day, we often forget what happened the day before. This is also how we deal with psychological detritus thrown at us every day. In order to drive safely, we have to let it all just roll off our shoulders, good or bad.

When you hear about transit tragedies, such as "Lady Doesn't Look as Train Approaches, Loses Her Leg," people are quick to point at the operator, especially the media. Do you think my headline is what the media would say? Of course not! That would be putting the blame on the poor lady who lost her leg! We operators address the pedestrian's responsibility. If you read the quote in the article by a police officer, it speaks volumes about blame.

"Witnesses stated (she) had a hoodie on, and looked to be wearing earbuds as she crossed the tracks," the policeman stated. The train blasted its horn in warning, a signal everyone else but the victim seemed to hear.

We see this type of behavior every day, everywhere we operate buses or trains. People act as if the world is responsible for their safety, and if they wear earbuds it's up to another to watch out for them. Unsafe bicyclists especially are guilty of taking foolish chances around transit vehicles. Newer buses are much quieter than the old ones, especially when riders tool along with earbuds blasting their favorite music. However, when we alert them of our presence with a firm "beep beep" of our horn, their idea of thanks is often an extended middle finger. Oh, how I'd love to see someone bend that finger back until it snaps! But no. Can't do that. We're not allowed to respond. At all.

Yes, I get a bit testy when the public, or the media, questions our "safety training." It's quite adequate, thank you. The public's, however, is severely lacking. There are no media spots on How to

Ride a Bus. I rarely see any Public Service Announcements on how to BE SAFE. People won't even read the signs on our buses. I get it. It's a personal responsibility thing. But wait... whatever happened to that? It blew away with the advent of the smart phone, I'll betcha. Plugged in and tuned out. That's what society considers normal these days.

When something bad happens involving a transit vehicle, BAM... blame it on the operator. They're overpaid monkeys anyway, right? I mean anybody can drive a bus! Well evidently not everybody can walk down the street without doing something ridiculously reckless, but that's beside the point, I reckon.

I had a Recertification Class recently. The trainer was a veteran with many years behind the wheel, somebody I respect and admire. I learned some things that can help me become even safer. Bus operators are human. We develop bad habits that need correction. We need to be kept informed about different safety procedures. This class is really a good idea, even though the district probably wouldn't have done it if not for a fatal incident a few years ago. Yes, we get regular training. Does the public? No, because it is assumed people are responsible enough to conduct themselves appropriately.

One thing about the class that bothered me was a demonstration by a man who works in the Safety division. We were subjected to a terribly patronizing video outlining such things as what constitutes a "slip, trip or fall," and other such things we all learned as children. We listened politely as this chap told us how "safety is our culture," yet the talk of the town was how this pedestrian lost her leg when she was hit by a train because she didn't look before crossing in front of it.

The people at our agency who are most concerned with "safety" are the operators and other front-line workers. Management seems to love the sound of it. It's a pretty word to them, but when they're slapped in the face with obvious safety-related fixes, they "study" it. They study something really hard. Unfortunately, they often fail the test.

Take our new Orange Line, for example. Cost to build: just under $1.5 billion dollars. Yet with all this money, and a supposed "safety culture," the end-of-the-line boarding approaches are straight lines with feeble warnings (on the ground) to "Stop and Look." No herding passengers left, then right, before crossing the tracks; like they have on some of the remodeled approaches on other lines. Brand new line, horrible design. No gates to save people from their own stupidity. Sure, the trains there are poking along at 5-10 mph. But if you make contact with a slow-moving object that weighs 100,000 pounds, it could quite possibly result in your death.

We all feel terrible this tragedy happened. Whenever we hear about an injury, or a fatality, you can be assured that at least a thousand operator voices are raised in prayer for the victim and family. We're human, we truly care about our riding public.

Pay attention folks. We sure do.

🚶 RAW

Trolleypup:

"Passengers earn their accidents...just as we do... We say here 'If you didn't save someone's life by 10am, you probably called in sick!'"

Frankie B:

"Just want to say as a member of the public who rides MAX and bus on a daily basis that I think you operators do a damn good job every day. Incidents like the one described where a person is struck by a train or bus is not the operator's fault. I see idiots everyday who don't pay attention and walk right in front of your vehicles without even an inkling of thought. There are more than enough safety precautions in place, as well as VERY safety conscious vehicle operation going on. I see this on a daily basis with operators. Especially considering everything an operator faces, unfriendly motorists/pedestrians, deplorable traffic conditions, abuse from passengers, it's a testament to your professionalism and concern for safety that these type of incidents don't happen more frequently. Keep up the good work, and know that there are many of us out there who respect and appreciate you getting us safely to our destinations every day.

Al M:

"Hey I think this blog readership is about to really take off. Just saw you get listed on BikePortland."

Anonymous:

"Look, the trams all over Europe have little protections between the people and the train. We shouldn't be dependent on barriers. We should be paying attention."

Nathan H:

"Thanks for reminding people about all of the training you folks receive. I certainly do not envy any operator for taking on (and evidently internalizing) all of the conflicts that the transportation system creates.

"However - a lot of your venting is non-productive. Maybe you are a singularly angry person, but this post paints a picture of a culture of anger amongst (agency) operators.

"Breaking people's middle fingers? Lame. Threatening people on the web is lame. It is never productive.

"Does (agency) provide or facilitate therapy for anger problems in the operator community?"

Deke:

"Nathan, this blog IS my therapy, thank you. Y'all take things WAY too seriously. You expect us to be perfect, but this is not a perfect world. How many times have you said "Why, I'd like to..."? But you don't mean it. Neither do I. However, to remove this from my post would be literary cowardice. If you take it literally, then you're not reading how we keep the finger-flippers safe, and gladly so. They are someone's love/son/daughter/husband/wife/brother/sister, etc."

Anonymous:

"Hey Deke found your blog on Bike Portland. I ride a lot, but really have no beef with bus drivers. It doesn't take a genius to figure who has right of weight. I don't envy you guys, Traffic is unpredictable and road users are stupid. Thanks for taking safety seriously."

Rants and Reviews

🚌 **DEKE'S NOTE:** *Yeah, I 'rant' a lot in my blog. Like I responded to a reader, it's my therapy. Yes, we're offered free counseling. Horrible things happen to us, and it can be very helpful in the most trying times. However, I don't believe that sharing my opinions qualify me as passive-aggressive. Quite the contrary, according to a friendly psychologist. In this post, I heartily defend myself in the aftermath of the "Blame Sharing" post.*

Wow, what a week. First, this blog was reviewed by Jonathan at bikeportland.org. On one hand I appreciated the publicity and many great comments which gave me insights from the cyclists' point of view. On the other I was amazed at how many of those readers are simply boneheads. Some can't distinguish venting from reality, for one. Others seem liberally-infused with an unhealthy dose of hypocrisy.

While many appreciated what we do while keeping people safe, others questioned my professionalism. Somehow, we're expected to be emotional robots when we avoid colliding with them, saving their lives whether or not they realize it. As our adrenaline level rises after a near-miss with an errant bicyclist, we're often treated to the one-fingered salute. How many of you can honestly say that if you saved another's life and they flipped you off, you would nod and just say, "Bless you, child"? Not many, I'll bet. All because you used your horn to alert them of impending disaster. Some bicyclists' rants are silly, childish, and contraindicative of the majority of intelligent and attentive bicycle-riding public. Because I have the audacity to call stupid behavior just that, I'm labeled "angry" and "horn happy."

My good friend and brother, The Rampant Lion, was astounded another would refer to us in such a manner. In fact, he took it a step further.

"If you're a f-ing scofflaw, and you're doing something stupid and unlawful, like riding your bike across a crosswalk, then, without either signaling or looking first, you swerve back into the traffic lane in front of my 40,000-lb. machine, you bet your sweet bippy I'm gonna honk at your ass!" The Lion roars much louder than I do.

For those who cannot maturely interact with the world into which they blindly venture, I'll jump back to their formative years and treat them accordingly. I'll wash their 'binky' in a politically-correct organic antiseptic, so this nasty old bus driver's epithets won't infect their fragile temperaments. (We're cursed and belittled all day, every day by ignorant ne'er do wells, but we tough it out.) Then I'll buy them a soft little bunny to cuddle. (Personally, I prefer my bunnies fried or in a finely-seasoned Welsh Rarebit.) Then, I'll give them a ba-ba infused with a ganja smoothie to mellow them out. Finally, I'll tuck them in with a rancid blanket made of street detritus, singing James Taylor's *Damn This Traffic Jam* until they settle into a fretful nightmare.

Folks, I won't sugar-coat what we face out there. If I wake you up or even piss you off, I'm doing my job as the author of this transit blog. Maybe you'll read something that could possibly save your life. I truly desire to help you be safe. You're 100-200lbs. on a 20lb. nearly-invisible two-wheeled self-propellant sharing the street with a 40ft., 11' tall, 9' wide 20-ton monster operated by a vigilant professional. You're most likely safer near a bus, if you follow basic commonsense rules, than you are amidst passenger or delivery vehicles.

We're actually very nice people. If my 'ranting' offends you, I heartily suggest *you* seek counseling. I'm not always negative, but as traffic gets worse each year, our jobs become proportionately harder. Yes, I pounce on stupid behavior. But you may notice I also have a softer side. There are some funny bits here and there, so I've been told. I'm not a growling, spitting, finger-bending ogre who eats little kids for dinner followed by cute kittens for dessert. If you don't like it when my truths offend your fairy tale image of life, too damn bad. Go tell Stephen King to chill when his characters chop off limbs or think firestorms upon various pissers-off. You don't see him acting these stories out in real life, and to lambast me for a finger-bending thought bubble is ludicrous.

Yeah, I rant in here. It keeps me safe, sane and able to treat passengers to a courteous and safe ride. When FTDS was reviewed, I had 42,000 hits. An overwhelming majority of responses have been positive. Many of my readers also drive a bus, and they say my writing usually mirrors their own thoughts. People all over the world read this blog to the tune of 4,000 a month. From humble beginnings to this point, all has gone well. I'm very grateful for this opportunity, and I thank you for your honest opinions.

One thing this experience has taught me is that I've reached that point in a bus driver's career where I need to step back, take a deep breath, and not allow things affect me so deeply. If I seem angry to you, it's only because my fellow Portlanders practice ignorance at the worst times, and when they do so around my bus, it's highly stressful. Any sane person would be affected by a near-miss. It happens to us regularly. If you believe these are all the fault of bus operators, you're horribly mistaken.

For the first time in my career not long ago, I had to stop driving in the middle of a shift because I was verbally assaulted. Nobody has ever spoken to me in that manner, tone or with such cruelty. I was so upset that had I driven further, the memory would have been such a distraction I couldn't have concentrated on safe driving. When I stepped off the bus, my hands were shaking, my soul was in turmoil. I was glad I made the decision to call it a day. Even though they were inconvenienced, my passengers understood. Some even thanked me, and said they were sorry I was treated so poorly. Such kindness brought tears to my eyes.

Peace be with you this holiday season. I hope all your ups and downs are in bed.

🚶 RAW

Just a few comments of note. I wanted to heal the evident rift between operators and cyclists by separating the dangerous from the safe. Some incidents truly elevate our blood pressure, and these two posts were surely the result of a few knuckle-biters.

Rampant Lion:

"First, let me say that I gladly share the road with bicyclists who willingly follow the same rules and laws that I do. I'm trained to allow you a safe distance when you're in proximity to my bus, I willingly yield to you the right of way when you occupy the lane in front of me, and very much appreciate it when you signal your intentions that I may anticipate your movements.

"If you expect anyone else to share the road with you, then you must share an equal responsibility to abide by the same rules and laws that are written to keep us all safe when doing so. If you do, you won't hear a peep out of me.

"But, when you screw up around my bus, when you deliberately scoff at the law and cause an unwarranted risk to others, I will roar like the rampant lion. The least you will hear is the sound of my horn warning you of the danger you're posing, and that you'd better pay closer attention to the risks you're presenting. If that shakes you up, then GOOD!!! Maybe you'll look twice before doing that again."

Anonymous:

"Hi there. I am a new reader. I followed the link from Bike Portland. And I want you to know that I appreciate your skill and obvious care. And I do ride a bike much more often than transit. When I read your words from a couple days ago, 'We're always watching for dangers, predicting behaviors, altering our speed or making slight alterations in our course to avoid accidents. People do stupid things around our buses so often we're used to it.' Thats exactly how I ride my bike. And pretty much the same words that I have often used when talking about *staying safe on a bike. So, we have a lot in common."*

(Then, Bike Portland chimed in with a gentle chastising on my choice of words.)

jmaus:

It has been great having you comment on BikePortland and I've enjoyed meeting you via email this past week. I hope we can use our respective platforms to foster understanding and awareness among different types of road users.

"On that note, I was very disappointed to see that you chose to refer to some people as "boneheads" and hypocrites in your opening paragraph. Name-calling is not a good way to set the example for everyone else. Hopefully you'll be more careful with how you refer to other road users in the future."

Deke:

"Thanks Jonathan. But while some of your readers didn't pull any punches either, I'd say the name-calling stats are about even. Let's move forward, but remember... I calls 'em as I sees 'em. If someone pulls a maneuver which puts my passengers in danger, I'm not going to sing them a lullaby. Let's just keep it safe out there Portland! Peace."

Time for Some Innovative Re-Design

Portland's downtown transit mall is a mess. It's the major hub of our transit system. North-going buses, light rail and streetcars use Sixth Avenue, and southbound use Fifth. But the signage instructing motorists is horrible at best. It's an unruly and dangerous place for anyone to be. Nobody will speak up about it. Except me. I've had enough, and it's time this debacle is dealt with.

There are three lanes on the mall. Painted onto the street are "BUS ONLY" or "LRT BUS" with double solid white lines as recommended barriers between transit and other vehicles. Signs at streetlight level inform motorists the right two lanes are for transit vehicles only, and that right turns are not allowed. These instructions are not bold enough to keep confused (or inattentive) motorists from obeying the lane restrictions.

The result, especially at rush hour, is pure madness. Vehicles regularly clog our service stops or transit lanes in hopes of beating obedient motorists to the next light. Bicyclists weave in between buses and cars, run red lights, and often turn right directly in front of bus operators leaving service stops. Some cyclists mistakenly believe the right lane, as it is in other places, is also a bike lane. Pedestrians routinely ignore the walk signals, or simply refuse to look up from their phones long enough to deduce it might be unsafe to cross. And then there are the skateboarders, taxis and kamikaze delivery trucks.

Trainers devote a good deal of classroom time teaching operators the rules of our transit mall, followed by practical training behind the wheel. A bus driver's senses, which are always on high alert, perk up even more once we turn onto the mall. One missed scan at any given moment can spell disaster for any of the thousands with whom we share these streets. The average person doesn't realize how many safety protocols are involved in a single block of operating a transit vehicle through the mall.

All this begs the questions I'm about to ask.

Why haven't there been widely publicized safety assessments of the transit mall, with suggestions as to how to fix the many problems? Most likely, it's easily summed up by our city leaders using the age-old excuse: we don't have the money. Where the public safety is concerned, I'm sure an enterprising grant writer could find the funds necessary to make vital changes. The transit agency was warned in 2006 when it was designed, according to news accounts at the time, but it chose to ignore pleas for changes. A decade later, the need for a re-design is paramount for public safety.

Why does local law enforcement turn a blind eye to blatant traffic violations on the transit mall? From what I hear, city government is afraid of offending tourists by issuing citations. What a flimsy excuse, when you consider how treacherous it is to navigate our bustling downtown. City leaders should devise better methods to keep people safer in the downtown area. Seemingly nobody except transit workers seem to understand the safety issues on the mall. People have been injured and killed due to Portland's shocking willingness to leave conditions as they are. When accidents happen, the blame seems to be thrown upon US.

Over 40 bus, four light rail, and two streetcar lines, along with Lift vans and other vehicles use the mall every day. It was designed to avoid total chaos with all the transit traffic combined with private and commercial vehicles. Each bus line has specific stops to service, and transit workers do an admirable job working together to transport thousands of commuters daily. But it's not easy, nor is it a safe environment for anybody. And it's getting worse.

Why isn't our transit agency leading the way in innovative solutions, which is what once made it one of the best in the country? If our management employed creative energy, it would have long ago improved the "culture of safety" it spouts at every media opportunity. It would prove a commitment to safety rather than giving it mere lip service.

It's a mad world out there. If the City of Portland truly cares about all who live or visit here, they'll find a way to fix things. If they would simply enforce the law and fine offenders, it would create a culture of safety to protect those who visit the area. If transit truly believed "Safety is Our Core Value," it would push city leaders to action. Instead of trying not to offend people, it should take a stand and insist that obeying laws is vital to assure public safety. In a city this beautiful, boasting one of the finest transit systems in the world and a spectacular new transit-only bridge, it's disconcerting we have such a dangerous transit mall.

Here's a few of my ideas, take 'em or leave 'em.

Cite motorists, bicyclists or pedestrians who blatantly ignore traffic laws. Try regularly patrolling the mall. Design and print brochures explaining basic traffic laws and procedures, and distribute them to information centers, hotels, and shopping malls. Produce public service announcements discussing how we can all safely co-exist.

Re-design the transit mall and be creative about it. White markings are mere suggestions; make yellow (or red) double lines separating regular from transit traffic, install flashing signs (light rail designers had the foresight to do *that* right) as warnings. If people knew Portland was serious about "safety," perhaps they would finally pay attention. If violators paid a few fines, it might just save some lives further down the line. Better yet, ban all traffic except transit vehicles. Quit being passive about it.

Build that new bridge across the Columbia River, and charge tolls on all the bridges between Oregon and Washington. If our neighbors won't pay their fair share willingly, then it's time to force them. Some of our bridges are built on timbers, some over 100 years old, and that they could collapse in a seismic event. It's time to take action, not whine about our neighbors' refusal to pay its share of replacing these disasters-in-waiting. Tolls could also help pay for street repairs. Bus operators collectively feel each pothole thousands of times a day.

Portland seems inattentive to safety. Tourists and our own citizens are at risk because rules have become mere suggestions.

Sure, maybe I'm just a crackpot bus operator. What do I know? Well here's one thing I *do* know: we waste money dreaming of bridges to nowhere, while we could be spending on those which could make everyone safer.

My Christmas Wish List

This time of year can be particularly stressful for some. Many of us see it as a time of reflection, a season to show our loved ones how much they truly affect our lives. Already, I've had the greatest Christmas present a blogger could ask for. Since this time a year ago, FTDS's hit counter has almost doubled itself, surpassing 21,000 hits in 2015 alone.

People from Russia, Australia, Canada, Japan, Belarus, United Kingdom, France, Germany, Ukraine, Ireland, and Poland have read my words. I am truly humbled. Even though bus operators are scattered across this gorgeous blue marble, we're united by what we do for a living. I realize not all my readers are operators, but I hope by reading this blog, you understand us just a little bit more.

What do I truly "want" for Christmas this year? I've already had to change the heating system in my house. Santa wrote that he had to order a rail car to deliver all the coal to my house. So that leaves me at your mercy, dear readers. Hope you can help me out. Here's a list of 10 things I would love for Christmas, and the entire year.

Pay it forward. When someone (like a friendly bus operator) does you a solid, do somebody else a favor too. I believe in the domino effect. It's amazing how easily you can help somebody, and the result is often smile-inducing. Even if your efforts aren't immediately noticed, kindness can be contagious.

If a bus operator growls, barks at you, stop and **think** *a moment.* There's usually a hidden lesson here. That operator's demeanor is likely the result of something you did that is downright dangerous. You probably scared him/her. Don't argue. If you'd like an explanation, first apologize, then ask what you did to deserve such a tongue-lashing. Remember, your infraction has already passed through the operator's busy task list. Chances are it's forgiven. We can't hold on to things very long because our emotional trash can must be quickly emptied so we can continue giving you a safe ride. Be humble and honest with yourself; your safety is truly our number one concern.

Call the agency's Customer Service Department when you see an operator do something nice. Out of each 100 calls, 99.5 of them are complaints. Surely, we deserve more than half a compliment out of 100. People are quick to criticize, yet slow to praise.

Put your phone away for a bus trip, and watch what we do. Pull the earbuds out. Watch how other motorists treat us. Chances are you'll see something that evokes wonder, shock or even awe. Imagine how you'd feel sitting at the controls of a bus. See how many things your driver did just to make a simple turn? Did you see that pedestrian dart out from between parked cars? The bus coming to a sudden stop will look and feel entirely different if you see it from our perspective.

Read the signs on the bus. They are there for a very good reason. Most are meant to ensure an efficient, smooth and safe ride.

Be kind to your fellow passengers. Treat them as you would a revered grandparent, even if they're rude. Fights on the bus involve police. Police involvement requires lawyers. Lawyers are expensive. Physical aggression can be painful, no matter how badass you think you are. Hospitals aren't cheap either.

Remember that just because somebody appears "different" doesn't mean they are any less a human being than you are. We're too divisive and judgmental a society these days. Practice kindness, and it might be returned to you a hundredfold.

Smile. It's good for you. It takes more muscles to frown than it does to smile, and it's healthier. I try to smile at everyone who boards my bus. The basic human response to a smile is to return it. I love it when I see a bright one.

Even though you're having a rough day, week, year or life, remember there's always somebody else who has it worse. Had a bad day at the office? That guy in the seat across from you who smells bad hasn't had a bath in a long time. Why? Because he's homeless, and that's not necessarily his fault. That lady who just hobbled onto the bus and took extra time to sit down may have recently had surgery, making every step painful beyond your understanding.

Please... be... careful. This is my biggest wish. There are people at home who love you. They count on your coming home safely, every day. How would they feel if you were hit by that train or bus? They would be devastated, and so would the vehicle's operator, the investigating supervisor, the transit dispatcher, transit and city cops, paramedics and any witnesses. We're all a team, and we want you transported safely. Safety involves being aware of your surroundings and following rules even if they seem ridiculous.

There you have it. It's actually an easy list, and won't cost you a thing. I'm a cheap date, or so Mrs. Blue says. It will be a fun Christmas this year, especially when I turn the Grinch movie off just as he's finished stealing all the goodies. This is where I tell my kids the story ends. I'm kinda like that ol' Grinch. Even though I sometimes growl and scowl in here, my heart is full of love and kindness.

Merry Christmas, Hanukkah, Kwanzaa, Winter Solstice or whatever holiday you celebrate. May all the peace and joy of life fill your days and nights as long as we are blessed to have you here with us on Earth. Peace be with you and yours.

HIT COUNTER: 48,000 (DECEMBER 2015)

YEAR FOUR

GRIZZLED AND PATCHED

— 2016 —

By this point, I had enjoyed a major jump in readership. By summer, my monthly stats soared to 5,500 hits. I had been snubbed by London bus enthusiasts but gained new ground elsewhere. I used fewer words to get my point across. My posts became sporadic, but I was still having fun. My creativity either ran a bit dry or went wild. In the final part of this book, there are a few surprises. By August, FTDS recorded its 70,000th hit. Not bad for an ornery old bus driver.

Spinning Wheels Got to Go 'Round

🚌 **DEKE'S NOTE:** *I love* Blood Sweat and Tears. *People my age recognize that old band, and even some younger folks may know the tune. This year started with a bang, just what experienced operators love and newbies dread: inclement weather. It's our chance to shine, a challenge to keep rolling when others cannot. We get people where they need to be more often than we're given credit for. Here's a post about the Silver Thaw of '16.*

"If you don't like the weather in Oregon, then wait a few minutes." Portland sees about 35 inches of precipitation each year, most of it as rain. This past weekend, it came in the form of an inch or two of the frozen white stuff. Snow? Yeah, that's it. We get some every few years. Two years ago, we got a boatload of it. This time, just a dusting. The next several hours featured freezing rain. That's when things got treacherous.

Operators in other parts of the world may laugh, but when Portland gets a snowstorm, the aftermath is anything but picturesque. It is almost always followed by freezing rain. We call this a "Silver Thaw." If we only got the snow, then sunshiny warm temperatures to melt it away, life would be grand in this lovely city of rolling hills. But no. Snow is easy to drive on. Ice on top of it makes for white-knuckle driving. It sticks to the bus mirrors and windshield wipers. Sidewalks instantly turn from safe havens to broken bone zones. Power lines become ice-encrusted, making light rail travel unreliable. Tree limbs, already saturated with the 15 inches of rain that fell in December, become so heavy and brittle they break away in the accompanying 50mph winds. Our fearless power company workers get kudos from me for all the emergency situations they respond to. Tree limbs seem to love falling onto power lines.

Driving to work on Sunday morning was lovely. The snow was billowing, drifting along the road. Picturesque expanses of white floated down upon us. Made me want to cuddle with Mrs. Blue in front of a fireplace while emptying a bottle of Merlot. I rolled into work, ready to get people where they needed to be. My line was on an abbreviated snow route, so the first half of the day came with extended breaks. Then the snow stopped. After a few minutes of lovely silence that cold winter morning, I heard the telltale "snap crackle pop" of freezing rain. I inhaled deeply on my vape. I knew the rest of the day would be a challenge.

Portland is a disaster zone when it comes to inclement weather. The lack of planning is astounding. Freeways are the first to receive attention, but the rest of us have to wait. We're expected to be at work, ready to drive, no matter what the weather is. Where's our public support? I've read a lot of Tweets ranting about how we "suck," but when there's icy weather, who is out there taking Portland to work and home? WE are. Transit operators, supervisors and maintenance crews risk injury to serve an often ungrateful public.

A frustrated rider Tweeted they had seen buses sliding off the road and wondered "how much winter driving training do they get?" We are told *what* to do, but *how* to do it can only be learned by *doing* it. To maneuver a bus without sliding on wet ice requires incredible driving skills. Keeping it away from those who shouldn't be out in the first place involves intense skill.

People armchair quarterback what we do, yet they can't operate anything more complex than a video game controller. In the real world, you don't get a "do over" or an "extra life" after crashing. We're playing for keeps out there. It takes mental toughness to operate a bus in normal conditions. When you add ice to the equation, along with many motorists who have no idea how to drive in it, our job's difficulty is compounded 100 times. It's a relief to set the parking brake at the garage when it's all over, knowing you have returned without a scratch. I saw numerous cars slip and slide, crash and smash; 4x4 big truck drivers who hadn't a clue how to let their vehicle do the work for them; people slipping and falling in the worst possible places; and numerous stunts by reckless daredevils. I was so exhausted after that shift, I slept 10 hours straight.

While driving on snow, your entire body tenses. The mind works overtime. You're constantly measuring stopping distances and multiplying by the ice factor, using your feet in an operatic melody between brake and accelerator. The steering wheel and the seat of your pants become highly in tune. The slightest slip of the front or rear of the bus is met with a coordinated response, with the mind's computer constantly problem-solving to keep all six wheels in a straight line. Add the confusion of traffic around you doing everything it can to make your situation even more difficult, and these tasks are magnified.

When you come upon a dangerous situation, you have to use problem-solving magic. Normally, when I'm not sure how to handle a situation, my support line to Dispatch is a lifesaver. During a storm, they're too busy to respond quickly. You must carefully think situations over and act accordingly. If you can't figure it out, you stop and wait for Dispatch to call. Operators are excellent at problem solving, but sometimes it helps hearing another voice of experience giving you another set of options you may not have thought of.

We only had a dusting of snow, but also about three inches of ice. I had a question I didn't think important enough to bother our brother and sister dispatchers. They were dealing with true emergencies and I didn't want to interrupt someone else getting help. So as many others of us did that day, I sat and thought it out. Logic, experience, and a ton of grit comprised many decisions. Luckily, I didn't end up in a ditch. Nor did my bus make contact with anything or anybody.

My day was almost over. I was maneuvering through a busy mall parking lot to our break area, artfully avoiding pedestrians and sliding cars, when a perplexing incident unfolded. An oncoming bus and mine were stopped at an intersection when from off to my left, a little car started spinning donuts in between us. This driver narrowly missed the other bus as he attempted to show the world what a "pro" he was. He zipped past a few terrified onlookers and headed for a deserted patch where he continued spinning around like a dizzy bumblebee. Some kid, most likely. Oblivious to danger and invincible.

Unluckily for some operators, they slipped and fell on icy sidewalks. One reportedly suffered a serious head injury requiring surgery. Other ops were surely bruised and battered from trying to keep upright in their quest to use a restroom at the end of their line. I nearly slipped and fell, and I had ice trekkers on.

Instead of daring Mrs. Blue to brave the horrific conditions to ferry me home that night, I rode light rail home. I stood 40 minutes in the freezing rain waiting for it. We were within 200 yards of the end of the line when the train stopped. For another 30-45 minutes, we endured a fascinating game of back-and-forth as the operator and a supervisor worked to inch the train forward. Ice on the lines was interfering with the electric current. They delivered us to our destination and a bus whose operator graciously waited for us.

My stories of this "event" pale in comparison to some I've heard. But the hard work of everybody shows just how dedicated our transit community truly is. From the mechanics and chain crews, to the heroics of operators, tremendous support of supervisors, tireless coordination of station agents, incredible organization of dispatchers and rail controllers, and invaluable assistance from trainers... it all worked out in the end. We kept Portland rolling in the worst conditions possible.

Many of my passengers graciously thanked me for working that day. Conditions were terrible, and they were thankful for the safe ride. But some are never satisfied. They say horrible things about us as we're doing our best to keep people moving safely. I won't give these people the satisfaction of repeating their foolishness.

I do know one thing: we may not be perfect, but when the weather's so bad nobody should be out there, WE are. Bank on it.

Wise Cracker

🚌 **DEKE'S NOTE:** *Bus operators often have a warped sense of humor in the bullpen. Especially this one.*

My dear ladybuds were gathered at the Extra Board table one day when I came in to do a quick work-related errand. A few minutes later, I was outbound.

"In and out so fast?" Karen asked.

"Well," I replied, "if that's the *only* time a lady asks me that, I'm doing pretty good."

Bus Stops and Body Parts

It's a good job, but a tough one. Sometimes it gets to me, and I grump at people for the crazy chances they take to catch a bus. Other times, I just smile and shake my head, glad I was able to avoid potential disaster. Still others, I curse myself for making mistakes and compel myself not to repeat them.

We're often lambasted for being "greedy," since all we do "is drive a bus around all day." Wow. Really folks, is that *all* we do? Every action we take is part of operating a bus, and there's a lot more to it than most realize. We're not sitting behind the wheel of your fancy new Lexus, with a seat programmed to remember your pampered body. It's a monster of metal and glass, with a seat designed back when Abe Lincoln was driving a bus in Springfield. (Okay, so I sometimes exaggerate.)

This is an enormous responsibility. Each weekday, bus and train operators transport nearly 400,000 Portlanders. People on their way to work, mothers toting their precious cargo, elderly headed to medical appointments, countless others to whatever destination awaits them. Each passenger is our responsibility, their safety entrusted to our skill and instincts. No matter what Mother Nature throws at our windshields, we brave conditions to provide millions of safe rides every year.

Very often as I glide along in my mega ride, I'm treated to a lovely sight. It could be a dazzling snowy Mt. Hood illuminated by a full moon, downtown Portland bathed in the shades of pink and purple during a grand Northwest sunrise, or deer grazing along an emerald green roadside splashed with the splendid golden rays of a setting sun. I marvel at the kindness of my fellow Portlanders who see somebody using a mobility device struggling to cross the street and push them to safety. Rush hour traffic affords the opportunity to observe the Portland "zipper," where merging vehicles are allowed in one at a time in a show of solidarity. Yes, there are many good things we see out there. Somehow the good balances the tougher moments of our everyday toils.

Like anything good, it's challenging. Often, it's extremely difficult. It's also physically demanding. By the last day of my work week, it seems each joint of my aging body has been subjected to a triathlete's training regimen. One night I recently counted how many times my foot depressed the brake pedal to stop the bus. In one 80-minute ride, the busiest of my shift, I stopped 90 times at service stops, traffic lights, pedestrian crossings or stop signs. Since that's on the high end of things, let's say I average 65 stops an hour for a total of eight hours of driving. That means I stop the bus 520 times each shift. When you consider how many muscles in your lower back, hips, thighs, knees, calves and feet are used to perform this maneuver, you get a better idea of why we might be a bit grumpy at the end of the line.

Our brake pedal isn't as soft a touch as a car's. It takes a few hundred pounds of pressure, plus intense fine motor control of our legs and feet, to smoothly stop a bus. Multiply 520 by five nights and you'll see I stop 2,600 times a week. Ouch. Yeah, our parts can wear out quickly, especially those of us who've haven't seen our 30s in a few decades.

We earn every penny. It's harder to keep our job than it is to get fired from it. Too many complaints get us "counseling sessions" from managers. If we're involved in a collision, even if it's not our fault, our actions prior to the collision are studied by panels to see if we did everything reasonable to avoid it. If not, we're assessed a PA (Preventable Accident). Get five of these in any two-year period, you're done. We're constantly on the alert out there as a result, and that's usually a good thing. However, the mental combined with physical make for stressful working conditions. The rigors of the road age us two or three years for each one in the seat. Our health insurance was once covered 100%, as transit agencies realized the toll this job takes on the body. We've been paying a small percentage of our premiums but we're still getting beat up out there. Something's got to give soon, but chances are it'll be my knee joints before the agency grants us any healthcare concessions. Some say we're too expensive, but we're worth every cent. Imagine a city's economy and traffic without us.

Tips for New Drivers

We all were newbies once upon a time. A lot we've had to learn on our own, but once in a while I pick up a tidbit from another operator. If you don't learn something new every day, you're just not paying attention.

When I'm pre-tripping a bus in the yard, I'm always reminded of the basics. They apply to life on the road too. Here are a few things I'd like my newer fellow operators to remember.

SAFETY first!

Once you've stopped your bus, set the parking brake and put the transmission in neutral. Make it a habit to do this before anything else, whether you're in the yard or at the end of the line. Say it as you do it: "Brake and Neutral." So many operators have been injured (one recently in our own yard), or sadly even killed, because of carelessly forgetting these basic procedures. Yeah, you're at the end of the line and need to pee. But it only takes one mistake to end somebody's life.

Be Considerate

Turn everything electrical OFF before shutting the bus down. That way, you or the next driver isn't met with a blast of air from the heating/cooling system, fans set on high blasting hot or cold air at you, or windshield wipers squeaking away on dry glass.

Close the Driver's Window

We've all had the bus where the previous operator left the window wide open, then Mother Nature dumped a few gallons of rain onto the driver's seat. Often times it could be sunny and gorgeous when you jump off the bus at the end of a run. In the Northwest, the weather changes quickly. No amount of paper towels can sop up a sopping wet cloth seat. It's a bit embarrassing walking off the bus with a dark stain on your navy (or worse, tan shorts) pants and having someone say, "Did you pee yourself?" Unfortunately, some of your fellow operators have soiled their pants because they didn't reach a restroom in time. The memory of this can be embarrassing. Something as simple as closing a window can be important to another operator.

Early at the downtown transit mall?

Burn time before you arrive or at the last position of a shared stop, not in the first position. Recently, one operator would arrive two minutes early at the first transit mall stop, throw on his flashers, and let his clock burn down. I came in behind him right on time, and picked up my passengers. I closed the door, waiting to take the first position. My bus was already full, and this operator sat for two light cycles. Now I was two minutes down. At the next stop, if the operator was still early and burned time in the first position, I'd be four minutes late. The bus behind me might also be late, and we were upset with our brother up front.

We all know schedules are imperfect at best. Regular operators quickly learn where the "bubbles" are on a paddle and the best spots to burn time. Extra Board operators don't have this luxury, because they get different work of varying lines and trains. If you're unsure where to kill extra time, ask other operators how they drive the route and you'll likely also learn other valuable tips.

Don't know what to do?

STOP AND LOCK. If presented with a situation that you cannot immediately decide how to handle, this is a simple solution that will help you safely determine how to proceed. Often, we're afraid we'll be berated by our passengers or fellow operators, so we just plunge through a safety concern depending upon our lucky stars. This is when stuff happens. *Bad* stuff. Whenever I've counted on my lucky stars, they've usually fallen.

If you stop and lock, perhaps the delivery truck driver bearing down on you on a narrow street while he consults his cell phone will hit your mirror. There's a BIG difference here to the incident review panel, which is especially important if you're on probation. It doesn't matter what other people think if you stop and lock; what matters is you safely maneuver your hulk of metal and glass from Point A to Point B. Remember your trainer's first lesson: Don't damage the equipment. Using your best judgement requires a lot more caution than the average driver uses.

Yield to those closest to the end of the line.

If you've just started your run and you cross paths with an operator who is nearly done, yield to them in tight spots. Maybe they're running behind. It's important etiquette, and it shows consideration for your brothers and sisters.

If something is wrong with your bus, report it.

Some things we fix ourselves because they're minor, or are not "mission critical" to waste time asking for a bus trade. But if you have a wobbly mirror that is hard to see out of, an "idiot light" on the dash even though the bus is running fine, or a burned-out headlight, send Dispatch a "Mechanical Rolling" message.

I once had a bus that nearly stalled as I slowed to a stop, but since it didn't quit running I didn't report it right away. At the end of the line, I took my break and just let it slide. On my next trip, it stalled at every stop. Instead of blowing it off, I should have let Dispatch make the decision. My delay in reporting it inconvenienced passengers when the bus wouldn't start again and we had to wait for a replacement I likely could have had before they even boarded.

If your ticket printer is low on paper, change it.
The CAD (Computer Assisted Dispatch) shows a warning in red letters once the roll is down to 25 tickets remaining. Don't leave a short roll for the next operator to drive the bus. Always leave your bus as you would like to find it. It's truly annoying to find little or no paper in the printer at the beginning of a shift.

These are just a few tips, and I hope they help you. A lot of this job is just common sense. You'll figure it out as miles add up. Some of you are seasoned veterans who don't need me nagging at you about stuff you've known for years. Besides, according to Bishop, I've only been operating for about 45 minutes, a wet-behind-the-ears smartass in comparison to my respected elders. But hey, I'm also getting old, and according to the late, great Richard Pryor, "you don't get to be old bein' a fool."

Transit Tax Would Hurt Employees

🚌 **DEKE'S NOTE:** *Transit agencies are always searching for more ways to bring in money. Fares alone don't generate enough to pay for the many costs involved in transit operations. But this idea is like charging shoppers to ring up their own purchases.*

Fellow bus operator Kent rode my bus the other day. It was nice to see him again because he helped teach me a run when I was really green, giving me tips I remember to this day. He told me about a bill currently being considered by the state legislature, which would allow transit to tax local employees, in addition to their employers who pay transit taxes within the transportation district. This is wrong on many levels. Here are a few reasons why.

The employees of companies within this district already pay enough taxes. Local, payroll and property taxes are very high in Oregon, with the only saving grace being we don't have any sales tax. However, those who rely on public transportation to travel to and from work, if not provided with passes by their employer, already pay fares that have basically doubled in the past 20 years. When you factor in wages that have not risen proportionately over that same time frame, worker bees are getting the shaft.

Without plunging into today's rich vs. poor debate, it is still safe to say that a flat income tax on employees is *regressive*, meaning it disproportionately affects lower income residents. If a low-wage earner buys a $5 day pass every day, that's roughly $100 a month. When you factor in car payments, fuel, insurance and maintenance on a vehicle, it's still cheaper to ride a bus. However, when you start taxing people (0.185 is the bill's proposed rate) in addition to this, they're paying a lot more to spend hours on a crowded, stinky bus. You're also charging them for services they may not need to use. Those who are just making ends meet but don't ride the bus would be paying this tax too. Such a tax would definitely be tougher on the folks with two minimum-wage jobs than it is on our agency's

$100,000+ per year executives, who would most likely be exempt from this tax. (Logic dictates that transit employees wouldn't be subject to a tax to fund their own agency, but I won't bet on it.)

Our transit agency argues this proposed tax would be used to expand service to keep up with increasing demand. It also says it would partner with local municipalities to build safer transitions from transit to pedestrian/bicycle pathways, help provide lower income/disabled people and students with reduced fares, and purchase more buses.

However, according to Chris Lyons of the Clackamas County Board of Commissioners, this tax would make it harder for local government to raise monies necessary to fix our failing infrastructure.

"Clackamas County and many other local jurisdictions struggle to find dollars to maintain their roads," Lyons wrote in a statement against SB1521. "Our greatest tool to achieving these funding shortfalls is through vehicle registration fees and increased gas taxes. SB 1521 will make it challenging, if not impossible, to garner public support for these critical transportation dollars. Dollars imposed from SB 1521 will not improve roads or add critical infrastructure, but rather will increase the number of large buses driving over these failing transportation facilities that desperately need additional maintenance dollars."

Lyons says this would not sit well with the voting public. "We believe the employees of these businesses, many of whom do not use public transportation, would reject the fee if posed to them by ballot," Lyons said. "Our fear is that the Legislature will not give employees that option."

With transit accused of bullying over the past several years, its support of this money grab puts its operators at greater risk of abuse. Would people retaliate against the operators? Our union already faces an uphill battle when new contract negotiations begin in December. Transit has a history of painting us as greedy. I hear plenty of riders lambasting operators for negotiating better wages, with one having the nerve to refer to me as "rich." At the time, I was at the bottom of the pay scale, which I can assure you our GM hasn't had to endure while employed at the agency. Even now, at the top of our wage scale,

I could scarcely qualify as wealthy by any means of the imagination. Somebody who makes what I do is a working stiff, and would suffer taxation without representation if this tax were implemented.

Management keeps hiring overpaid executives while complaining about union workers' pay and benefits, an extremely hypocritical position. Instead of increasing existing service, transit keeps pushing more expensive light rail projects many don't want. It buys more buses operators have determined are dangerous because of vision barriers, telling us to "rock and roll" in the seat more, which increases driver fatigue and repetitive-movement injuries. It also minimizes our safety concerns as attacks on drivers nationally increase every year, while its safety course teaches us the difference between "slips, trips and falls" rather than giving us tools to protect ourselves.

Hey, I love my job. I'm paid well, but I'm worth more. My body takes a beating every day and I strive to be even better than expected. I'm courteous, smooth-driving and law abiding. Each day on the job I'm self-evaluating, learning hints from fellow operators, and making my best effort to provide excellent service. But if you tax our fellow citizens without giving them a voice in the matter, we will feel the push-back. That's one hell of a regressive tax burden.

The Smoker

It was bound to happen sooner or later. I smell all kinds of stink as people board, but thanks to fans and windows, the odor usually dissipates quickly. People often exhale that critical final puff as they board, much to my chagrin. But this guy...

One evening I detected an odor usually found at poker games. Glancing into the passenger mirror I tried to discern the source. I couldn't tell. Then I heard one of my fellow operators, who was headed home after his shift, call out a passenger.

"Please put that thing out," he growled loudly. "I don't want to smell that the rest of the trip."

I'm a bit slow, I know. But it finally hit me. CIGAR SMOKE!

Over the bus loudspeaker, I bellowed: "Is somebody SMOKING on my bus?"

Another glance into the mirror revealed three fingers pointing out the offending desperado. Returning my gaze to the road, I pulled inot the next bus stop.

"Sir," I said, "here's your stop."

"But I don't want to get out here!" he whined. "I put it out, won't do it again, promise."

"That may be true," I replied in my pseudo Southern drawl, "but it's agin the law to smoke on a bus, and I'm refusing you service. You can get off voluntarily, or in handcuffs. Your choice."

He hesitated a few seconds, head bowed in either shame, anger or both. I waited patiently; my time clock showed me running early. Then he slowly rose, shaking his head, and bolted out the back door.

The smoke and stench lingered, and my remaining passengers obliged me by opening some windows to clear the air. I think they were blasted awake by the sound of my normally-kind and friendly voice taking a sharp detour. I'm polite to all who board my ride. It puts people at ease; even the hardest-looking cases usually return my smile and thank me for a smooth ride.

Now I struggle with a forthcoming dilemma. When Stogie Man, who's a regular himself, boards my bus next time am I going to warn him not to repeat his crime? Or should I let my previous action speak for itself? If I see him standing alone at a stop, I'm tempted to pass him by. But this seems like an unnecessary power trip. Sure, he smoked on my bus. His fellow passengers later told me it seemed he'd forgotten he was still aboard! Wasted, perhaps? While it's a bit more serious than farting in an elevator, it's hardly a capital crime.

I've been the victim of a bus passing me by, even in uniform. However, given Mother Nature's propensity this winter for dispensing large volumes of water from above, I take pity on my fellow soggy Portlanders. Yeah, I'll give him another chance. But just *one*.

HIT COUNTER: 50,000 (MARCH 2016)

Nice Folks Ride My Bus!

🚌 **DEKE'S NOTE:** *Since I wrote this piece, Darius and I have been getting acquainted. He's an artist, reader and movie buff. We have some history in common, both having experience in typography and graphic arts. I miss the folks I met on this run, and that's partially why I signed it again. It will be nice to pick up where we left off. Meeting new people is one reason I wanted this job. Driving a bus gives me the opportunity to mix with a great cross-section of people with whom I wouldn't otherwise have contact.*

Sometimes people board my bus who intrigue me. It's usually their eyes which shine with the intelligence I'm drawn to. Operators know the type we usually deal with, the ones who don't even look at us and curse freely every sentence. When I board a person who is friendly, greets me warmly and thanks me when they leave, it feels like I've won the Bus Operator Lotto.

Lately I've had two gentlemen regulars I've had the great pleasure of meeting. One of them rides home after a long day of work in a warehouse. He stands patiently and insists others board before he does, showing the manners not always visible in the bus riding public. He's a big guy, perhaps in his early 40s. The first time I saw him, Darius smiled and greeted me as he boarded. His eyes shone with kindness. His eyes also betrayed some sadness, but we all travel life's bumpy roads. I look forward to him being on my bus. Whenever somebody can brighten my day, I let them know about it, without being too forward. Spread a little kindness to me, and I want to repay it. Darius, if you're reading this, thank you for being genuine. I'm sure you're a great friend to many and harbor a gentle, wise and kind soul.

Then there's Johnny Stingray, as I like to think of him. A cool, funny, and decent young man in his 20s. He too has the eyes of a much older soul, and a smile that lights up an otherwise dark bus. He spent his youth caring for family members with health challenges, and now he works at a care facility. I've always admired people who do that job. It takes the patience of a gentle soul, one who understands the hardships of others and makes great effort to ease their discomfort. Every night we have great discussions, and even though a generation gap exists between us, he's very intuitive, thoughtful and an intelligent conversationalist. Plus, he's blessed with a sharp sense of humor and gentlemanly manners.

Decent people realize the job we do is full of stress. Our eyes see so much more than the average driver, and sometimes we see more than we care to. My heart and soul ache for the bus driver on the west side of town earlier this week who witnessed a man crossing several lanes of a busy road get struck by a car, all because he wanted to catch that bus. When kind people ride, say a few friendly words and thank us for doing our job, these simple gestures can make even the hardest days considerably better.

Thanks Darius and Johnny, for making my last run of the night an elixir for what usually is a rough day. I look forward to seeing you, and I miss having you on board when our schedules don't mesh. I wish more of my passengers were like you.

I Forgot the Ball and Chain!

Humming along to Susan Tedeschi on my way to work, I was enjoying having the car for a change. Usually, my beloved keeps our only wheels, but sometimes she relents and I get to avoid riding transit to drive transit.

As the song ended, I thought it would be a great time to call Dad, since I only had 10 minutes before arriving at the garage and he's usually good for talking just about that long. Nice new car, it allows one to place a call via voice command while keeping both hands on the wheel.

Uh oh, my attempt failed. Lady Hyundai's immediate refusal to obey my command went something like this:

Me: *Call Dad.*

Car: To place a call via Bluetooth, a device must first be paired.

Me: DAMNIT! I SAID CALL DAD!!

Car: Look dumbass, connect your damn phone and then we'll talk.

Hmm. Checked all my pockets, no cell phone. Double checked, no luck. I was more than halfway to a 10-hour shift with no cellphone. Oh well, I decided it was time to break the fixation.

I'll just text the wife... no big deal.

Duh. Text my wife to tell her the phone I can't use is sitting on the desk next to her? Really? C'mon, Einstein. Geez.

It is painfully apparent how attached I am to that damn thing. Sit on the toilet, check the emails. Wait for MAX, scope out arrival times on PDX Bus. Waiting for my bus to arrive, play on FaceBook, check the weather, look at FTDS blog stats. See something cool in and around StumpTown, take a photo for this blog. Missed the Trail Blazers game last night, check the highlights. Wow. I was jolted by the sharp slap of reality. No phone, no mindless play.

What did that leave me to do? Think, for one thing. Walk and think, actually. What a concept! Walking is my favorite exercise anyway.

I have blathered on before about people and their cell phones, scoffing at how addicted they are to them. Yet here I was, wondering how to live without it. Not quite a year ago, I clung to my flip-phone with middle-aged stubbornness, not wanting to become one of "them citified smart phone fellers." Besides, I thought then, what good is a phone except to text or call people? Who needs all that fancy stuff anyway?

Evidently, *I* do. Well some of it anyway. I don't play games or read books on it (except my novel-in-progress), and the apps I have are either practical or stuffed away in a folder labelled "BS." I've become addicted like everyone else.

As I drove my bus today, I found myself getting cranky. Was I having withdrawal symptoms? Nah. We're strictly forbidden to use phones while driving. At the end of the line, I decided it was time for a quick attitude adjustment, so I took a walk. My legs and butt thanked me. Instead of the head-down slow amble, I actually stretched out and zipped around the block. In the pouring rain. For the first time in 10 months, I felt truly refreshed. I didn't care about all those doodads on that dad-burned contraption! I also read my nearly-finished copy of a Mark Twain book. Yeah, that thing made of paper pages.

The only thing I truly missed was the banter with my beloved better half. We're sickening. If you ever saw our text strings, the amount of cute little emoticons we use might make you gag. It is nice however, to make sure she's okay, find out how horribly the dog farted or what came in the mail, what's for dinner. Domestic stuff. Once an evening, I give her a call just to chat about our day. That part I was able to remedy, because I still remember how to use an old-fashioned contraption that's wired to the wall in our break rooms. It had push button numbers, but even if they were on a rotary, I could still use it.

After our usual three-minute conversation, we ended it like this:

Beloved Blue: "Purple, pink, blue and red hearts, smoochy face."

Me: "Nerdy glasses, hearts and roses, Cupid arrow in heart, smoochy face too."

Good grief. I hope nobody else heard me.

Cleansing Our Political Energy (COPE)

Not wanting to fully engage in our union's political arena, I will say it's time we reverse the trend of dirty campaigning. We see it every day on the national political scene, and it is disgusting.

I encourage every ATU 757 member to vote their conscience. The question is simple: which candidate has the best potential to do US the most good? We don't come to this conclusion by battering those with whom we disagree. It is nobler, and more conducive to unity, to emphasize the good. To tear down another is gruesome, hurtful and painful to watch. It does nothing to foster a unity we need to become stronger; it does everything to weaken our union.

Each of the three running for union president have strong

qualities. However, I rarely hear about them. What blasts forth is mostly negative. *So and so did this to such and such long ago,* etcetera, *ad nauseum.* Many seem to have some sort of dirt on the other two, while elevating their preferred candidate to sainthood. It's like saying "Candidate A smells worse than B, so I'm voting for C." But you know, each individual has a unique sense of smell. Candidate C might smell better than the other two put together to me, but all three might positively *reek* to you. You can't judge a classic novel by its musty cover, any more than you can convince me that eggplant tastes anything but bitter. I will not begrudge you your fondness for eggplant, and you cannot convince me your coveted recipe for it will send my taste buds into culinary bliss.

One President of the United States whom a great majority of Americans will agree was the finest we've ever had, Abraham Lincoln, faced what many believed an insurmountable task in keeping the Union together. At the time he was elected, the United States was balanced upon the precipice of failure. When he campaigned against Stephen Douglas for Illinois Senator in 1858, he included a profound biblical reference to one of his most famous speeches. "*A house divided against itself cannot stand,*" he stated. When asked why he would invoke one of Christ's most quoted statements (found in the gospels of Luke, Matthew and Mark), he said: "*I wanted to use some universally known figure, expressed in simple language as universally known, that it may strike home to the minds of men in order to arouse them to the peril of the times.*"

Our employer seems intent on rendering the union powerless. We do this without any help, by constantly tearing ourselves apart while fighting battles of no benefit to the whole. The peril we all face is our employer's desire to chip away at our livelihood and benefits with each new contract. Retirees feel betrayed, as well as our newest members, from the last contract, so we've already seen our unity ripped apart. Recently, some retirees wondered if they should form their own union. If we can't protect either group today, can we logically expect the newbies to protect US in years to come?

Abe's words ring true today, whether related to ATU 757 or the United States of America. We're fighting amongst one another when our energy and commitment should be to unify, become ONE strong force, and push forward... together.

"A house divided cannot stand." I repeat this to stress a vital point. Once this election is over, are we going to continue arguing over who we think should have won, or put aside our political prejudice in order to facilitate a powerful and unified force for the good of ALL union members?

I've made my choice who to vote for. Once the election is over, I will add my own strength to the victor to help build the power necessary to affect change. It is my fervent hope my resolution becomes our collective battle cry from this point forward.

The Verdict Is In

I've been busier than a one-toothed beaver in a lumberyard. Just last night I began deciding which FTDS posts might work best in the book I hope to publish, wondering what to name the collection, and asking your opinions on whether I should "come out" from under my pseudonym.

My FaceBook friends have voted 3-1 in favor of me remaining under cover. My wife thinks my dual personality is tiresome and silly. But she understands, as many of you do, that I don't want to lose my job. I work for a municipal corporation governed by itself, where freedom of speech isn't exactly a "core value."

I've been injured by corporate bullies before. In another job I held, a certain executive put his name on an article I wrote for our department's newsletter. I was told to swallow my pride or lose my job. It was a tough chew, but I choked it down. It left a terribly rotten taste in my mouth. I wanted to confront the plagiarist, but I learned to take "freedom of speech" with a large chunk of sodium from that point on. When I signed on to this gig and their information officer tiptoed around the "free speech, except..." concept, I just smiled and nodded. More corporate doublespeak for "don't rock the bus or you'll end up underneath it."

When May arrives, this blog will have its third birthday. I've had a lot of fun. Some of you might not agree with what I have to say, but that's human nature. I can't be everything to everybody; to be honest about what I feel is all this is about. It's also been great practice. Blogging is my stress steam kettle. As time on the job rolls by, a lot of tension builds up. Wordplay as the Deke helps keep my blood pressure down.

As I read some of the earliest posts last night, I had to chuckle. A friend of mine who started driving about the same time I did, said she has followed my progression from wide-eyed greenhorn to semi-veteran. She told me I write what she feels, and it's better than any drug. There are some posts that are gems while a few leave me wondering "Why did I write THAT?"

Yeah, the jury is in. It's not a unanimous vote, but I have to agree anonymity is the best row to hoe. For now. Less weeds, more yield. No toxins or bugs to worry about either. For now, if you know me, please keep it close to the vest. I'll be rolling anonymously a while longer.

🚶 RAW

The Rampant Lion wrote:
Just a couple things. We work for a "Municipal Corporation," with taxation authority, its own police force, and its own district attorney. This corporation is governed by state law, and a board of directors which is appointed by the state governor. Corporate managers and administrators have no accountability to any elected official whomsoever. The corporation is not an agency of any elected government, but rather a rogue bureaucracy ruled by agenda-driven elitists."

Safety vs. "Customer Service"

🚌 **DEKE'S NOTE:** *Corporations tend to study issues for long periods without learning much. Action is taken by informed, decisive people. Inaction is the product of foolish enterprise. I get angry when I see my fellow operators assaulted while our management utters corporate sound bites rather than working toward creating strong deterrents for operator abuse. The next two posts deal with "Safety" from the viewpoint of operators who remain at risk from the society's lowest common denominator.*

"Safety is our core value," says our management. "Bullshit," says I.

I'm reminded of a scene in *The Shawshank Redemption* where Red comes in front of the parole board for the final time. They ask if he's been "rehabilitated." His response is that of a tired old man, irritated with their nonsense. His plea has been rejected twice before, and after 30 years behind bars, Red doubts if he can make it on the outside.

"You know," he says with a sigh, "I don't have any idea what *that* means."

Parole board guy starts to say something, but Red interrupts.

"I know what you *think* it means sonny," Red says. "To me it's just a made-up word. A politician's word, so that young fellas like yourself can wear a suit and a tie, and have a job."

This is exactly how I feel about my employer's "safety" statement. It's so easy to say: "We value safety." Easy, that is, if you're sitting behind a desk pulling a six-figure salary instead of doing what we do for much less. Operators not only *think* safety, we taste and breathe it. We devour and digest, rinse and repeat it. Safety is our first sense, from the time the alarm interrupts our rest until pillow time returns. Each moment we're responsible for a transit vehicle and those within, it's the main subject of every thought we have or move we make. Our personal safety seems less important to management than for those who ride.

I had a discussion with my manager one day about whether I

should board someone who runs across a busy street directly in front of my bus. Most operators will say "they're too stupid to ride the bus, pass 'em by." Not according to management. We're supposed to throw safety aside along with caution and common sense to give them a ride. All in the name of "customer service." If I do as they say and board this passenger, it says to everyone on the bus, "It's okay to do stupid stuff because they'll let you on anyway." It's a terrible example to set. Safety be damned, we're customer service representatives now.

Once upon a time, professional drivers were respected. Now, that idiot who nearly became pavement paint is catered to, rather than taught an important safety lesson. To management, boarding that passenger is a "safety procedure."

Usually, when somebody boards who has narrowly avoided death, they insult the operator. They don't thank us for putting everyone's safety at risk to cater to their risky behavior. Passengers think we're machines, but we have an obligation to advise against jaywalking to catch a frequent-service bus. It doesn't matter if we're 10 minutes late; they don't know, nor do they care. The next bus could be a few car lengths behind, but they have to catch *mine*. It's a "me first" mentality many employ. If we drive off without them, you can be sure their next call will be a complaint.

The extended front end on the new Gilligs has vision barriers. The "A frame" windows obscure our vision of side streets and crosswalks. Instead of heeding our warnings, the district bought another 70+ buses with the same design flaw. Management's remedy? Rock and roll, baby. We do this anyway. But to do it several more times a minute than in a traditional flat-front vehicle adds extreme amounts of stress and fatigue to our bodies.

Bus operators suffer repetitive motion injuries with alarming regularity. Our right foot pivots from accelerator to brake thousands of times a shift. New boot heels are worn down after only a few months. Our legs, and our whole body behind them, depress the brake pedal hundreds of times a day. It takes hundreds of pounds of muscle to slow and stop a 40,000-pound vehicle with air brakes.

There are many arguments to be made about Operator Safety.

If "Safety is our Core Value," why did the district quit providing eyeglass cleaner? Isn't our clear vision a safety concern? If safety is vital, why not ensure something as simple as eyeglass cleaner is readily available? Sometimes the simplest things can save somebody's life. Is a few thousand dollars a year for eyeglass wipes more expensive than a lawsuit? Methinks not.

Many operators have been assaulted, then forced to continue driving. This is not conducive to safe operation. When an attack occurs, it triggers the body's "fight or flight" response. Faced with danger, our brain sends commands to all parts of the body. Adrenaline increases, blood flow concentrates in the central core, hormones race, the heart pumps faster, breathing becomes rapid, muscles tense, senses like eyesight and hearing intensify. This is the body's natural response to a threat. We are slapped and punched, spit and puked upon, screamed at, threatened, stabbed and shot at. I've been lucky when faced with dangerous situations and have been allowed to "call it a day" without repercussion or time loss. Other operators have not been so fortunate. A few months ago, one operator reported an assault yet no police responded and she continued her route. Another operator's bus was riddled with bullets, yet she had to finish her shift. When her manager granted a day to deal with post-traumatic stress, she says she wasn't paid for it.

As my brother Henry so aptly describes it, a driver with diminished capacity "is a safety hazard to themselves, passengers and the general public." An operator who has just been assaulted isn't thinking "safety" once the wheels are rolling again. They're thinking about what just happened to them, and are experiencing strong emotions best dealt with at home. A soul needs time to recover, and if an operator is forced to continue operating a bus carrying even one passenger, everybody's safety is compromised. This seems to be of no concern to the district.

Our supervisors and dispatchers know what we go through out there, and they have always been extremely supportive of me when something out of the ordinary happens. I'm usually given the option to continue on route or take recovery time. I'm very grateful for them, for they know how it feels to do this job. The problems seem to lie with those managers who have never driven a bus in service. They haven't been screamed at by a manic passenger who might just have a weapon under that jacket. They don't have to make split-second decisions that could save a life yet throws a passenger to the floor, resulting in a PA. The managers who have driven a bus actually understand what we go through, and I'm lucky to have one of them. But if management truly cares about safety, they won't insist we give rides to risk-takers. It's not safe to reward foolishness.

The higher up the management, the more detached from reality they are. I have always known that the higher you climb, the less oxygen there is. When I saw my sister Pamela's bruises inflicted upon her by an assailant who beat her over a few bucks in fare, I wept. Not only for her, but also because it could happen to any of us, any time. As she trembled facing her accuser, I was proud of her for speaking up. At the same time, my anger intensified due to management's conspicuous absence in the courtroom. When her attacker wasn't dealt the harshest of sentences, my confidence in the law's protection was wounded.

I'd like to know why a mobster is a more vigilant protector than our employer or the judiciary; at least he kicks ass when someone messes with his employees.

Another Hit

Just a few hours after I published my recent post about safety, one of our bus operators was punched in the face.

This assault happened when the operator informed a passenger who paid $3.00 for the $2.50 fare that we don't give change. Nor have we since Jackie Gleason portrayed a bus operator on a 1950s television show, *The Honeymooners*. So instead of just eating the $0.50, this punk punched the operator, who was simply doing his job. We don't yet take credit cards, and the fare amounts are plainly posted on the bus next to the front door.

Predictably, the district put out a statement on the assault which sounds good to the public, but makes union operators sigh and shake our heads in utter disbelief.

"Our operators provide a vital service every day, getting riders where they need to go safely day in and day out. We ask riders and the public to treat our operators with kindness and respect," was the district's statement. You *ask* them? And when they say no, then what? Tap them on the fingers and give them a time out? These people need to be p-u-n-i-s-h-e-d, and severely. Jail time, and an exclusion from ever riding transit again is my idea of treating us with respect. There is no excuse for this increasingly violent behavior.

What's it going to take before Portland gets tough on crimes against transit workers? Must one of us die before they actually stand up behind their rhetoric? Must we carry one of our own corpses in a black bus hearse before some authority raises its outraged voice demanding violence against us be met with fierce retribution? Lip service doesn't protect us from assault. Only action does, and I'm not talking about some cage around the operators; that's like a tiny bandage on a gaping wound.

If the district is serious about operator safety, it should insist the prosecuting attorney push for felony prosecution. Maybe then the public will realize that punching one of our operators will result in serious consequences.

Transit Pancakes, Silly Questions

Sometimes people say the silliest things. Today, I had a few such gems.

First, the ugly. Some old fella left his cane on my bus, but by the time I realized it I had already left the stop. Downtown. Can't go backwards or stop in the intersection. The transit mall was packed with buses, trains, streetcars and confused motorists. I took an abbreviated break at the transit center and hit the road again.

As I proceeded through a traffic light adjacent to a MAX train, the lady who had accompanied the caneless gent stepped into the transit way, between my bus and the train, screaming at me to stop. In the middle of the intersection that is, so she could berate me for "stealing" the cane. Sorry lady. I waved her to the curb, and not recognizing her from earlier, rolled on when she was out of harm's way. I'm not going to stop, open the door in a dangerous place and allow you to yell at me. Plus, she came close to becoming a tragic transit pancake. Strike two on you, bubbaloo. Cane will be waiting at Lost and Found in the morning. Top o' the day, now get the hell out of the transitway. Your safety should trump inconvenience.

Later, during rush hour on my outbound trip, traffic was typically backed up for about 15 blocks. At the end of the line of traffic lies a particularly busy stop. A sulky-looking teenaged girl mumbled something directly behind me. It sounded like a question, but I couldn't be sure. It was a warm day, the air conditioning thinks it's still winter in Portland so I have two fans blasting, so I looked in my passenger mirror and asked "Hmm?" This time she walked up and stood directly behind me.

"When are we supposed to get to the stop?" she asked. It was obvious this 10-second traffic signal wasn't going to oblige my already-blown schedule, as I'd watched it cycle about five times before I got within striking distance.

I frowned at her and replied, "We were supposed to be there about 10 minutes ago, but I reckon we'll make it sometime before sundown." She wrinkled her brow into a sulk and sat back down. When she finally exited, there was no "thank you."

At the next major stop an older gentleman (I use the term grudgingly) asked me to give him a courtesy stop a few blocks up and around the corner. Explaining to him it wasn't a safe place, I gently refused. "I'm sorry sir, I can't let you out there." His response was vulgar. He cursed me, then suggested I perform an impossible act upon myself. "Have a nice evening sir," I replied through gritted teeth as he exited. I dearly wanted to help him exit with the heel of my boot, but I resisted the urge. Not good customer service, I reckoned.

Just a bit later, I came upon a young man with a fascinating question. "Hey, the bus that was supposed to come didn't come," he said. "When is it coming?" Hmm. No details here. Let's see. Either I could verbally spank him for asking such a thing, or take a gentler route. "I'm not sure sir, I'm not driving that one."

Finally, on my last trip out of downtown, one lady came up to my door just before my light turned green. I sighed emphatically. "Yes ma'am?" I said in my most controlled voice.

"The board up there says my bus won't be here for another 29 minutes, so when can I expect it?" This question, in addition to the day's previous gems, just floored me. I hung my head a moment, thinking of the best reply.

"Well ma'am," I replied with a smile, "It'll be here in about 28 minutes and 14 seconds." Then I shut the door and floored it.

It can often be a long, frustrating day behind the wheel of a bus. But sometimes, it's just entertaining enough to keep me smiling.

Shocking Operator Stalker

Recently, after my post "Safety vs. Customer Service" was published, another operator came dangerously close to being physically assaulted. We're all vulnerable, and since our protection doesn't seem a priority to anyone but US, I'm speaking out. Again.

In an exclusive one-on-one with the victim/driver, I could feel his remaining anger, fear and feelings of isolation and frustration after what was a sadly common occurrence for bus operators. He asked not to be identified, as he is the victim. His eyes told their own story as the words poured out of him. Alternating between anger and shock, he was able to paint a very real and disturbing picture of the incident. Here's how he described it, with my questions in bold type.

"I was driving Line 9 on a Friday night, and was coming to my stop at Hall and 5th when I heard a commotion near the back on the bus. One voice stood out, and I asked this man to please quiet down. He refused. In fact, he came to the front of the bus to yell at me. Feeling threatened, I told him to leave the bus. He refused again, and would not stop yelling at me. He went as far as to say I was an Uncle Tom and the only reason I 'picked on' him was that he was black. If he had actually read the story, he'd know the character 'Tom' was black! I'm not. It was a moot point, so I deduced there was something else going on. Dude seemed a few quarts shy of a gallon.

"I asked Dispatch for police to come and remove him. He was very loud and threatening, standing in between the fare box and the door, refusing to leave. I remained in my seat and spoke with Dispatch, who reassured me help was on the way. When police arrived, he had left the bus and my doors were closed. An officer came in, asked a few questions.

By then, I had been told by two passengers that this man had been verbally harassed by other passengers and was angry about that. I wasn't aware of this, because I was keeping an eye on a different passenger who appeared to be in distress. When this unruly dude raised his voice to others on the bus, his was the only one I heard. I felt bad for him even though he had verbally assaulted me. All I wanted was for him to get off my bus so I could finish my run and take a break. He hadn't touched me, so I asked Transit

Police to warn him not to interfere with my job. I thought the guy just had a bad day, and as it is often the case, took it out on me. As long as he was off my bus and out of my face, that's all I cared about."

(It took a few moments for him to continue. He took a deep breath, collecting himself.)

"The police cleared me from the scene, so I informed Dispatch I was heading to the end of the line. I was a little rattled and very late by then, but just needed a little time to clear my head before making my last run. When I emerged from the break room, I finished talking to my wife on the phone and returned to my bus. Guess who was waiting for me?"

This guy left the stop at Hall and 5th and took light rail to North Terminal before you were ready to leave? What happened next?

"Well, yeah he was stalking me. And by then, he was even more agitated. He was waving his arms around and yelling at me, stepped between me and my bus, throwing one helluva fit. I told him he was trespassing and he had to leave. I told him to leave me the fuck alone. I was done with him at Hall and 5th, didn't press charges, but this guy came all the way to our break area just to mess with me? I called Dispatch and asked for the cops again. I was nervous, thought I would be physically attacked. I was preparing to defend myself. He even harassed a lady driver who had come in for her break. I told him to leave her alone. She was trying to calm him down but I told her just to GO! Luckily the cops arrived just then."

Did they arrest him this time?

"I thought they had. They put him in handcuffs, and I was out of earshot so I couldn't hear what was said. I didn't want to be anywhere near him, obviously. By then I was extremely upset. I mean, really? This guy came 40 blocks up there to mess with me again? What the hell? When the cop came over to talk to me he said he'd 'dealt with this guy before' and 'he's off his meds and can be violent,' I thought 'oh great.' I was sure the dude was under arrest! For trespassing at least. Another driver came over to me and said he'd dealt with the guy on his bus too. 'Yeah, he's a royal pain in the ass,' he told me."

He's messed with other drivers too?

"I guess so, from the way the cop acted."

Right. Like we have any idea who is excluded from riding. That dude should have been banned before, but we all know that's

about as effective as a bald porcupine fighting a wolverine. Let's finish this up. What happened next?

"You won't believe this. I'd seen the cops handcuff the dude and thought he was in the police car when I finally left the lot. I was done for the night, too stressed to safely continue my route. Remember, I had been in fight or flight for about an hour by then, so I wasn't going to put my passengers at risk by driving in a diminished capacity."

He paused, head bowed in deep thought, then added, *"I would have thought about this shit all night instead of being able to be vigilant and drive safely. So I told Dispatch I was done for the night and they cleared me to head back to the garage.*

"But then before I could get even get three blocks down the road, guess who was waiting for me?"

You're kidding! They let him go again?

"Yep. He was screaming and carrying on even worse than before. When the light turned green he raced the bus from the sidewalk and when I stopped at the next light, the dude jumped into the street, in front of my bus. He actually dared me to run him over! Good freakin' grief with this guy! I locked it up and called for police. The THIRD time. They were there in seconds. By then, this dude was shirtless, screaming at everyone and blocking traffic on Burnside in all directions. After a few minutes they had him cuffed again so the intersection was clear of this freak and the cop came back to get into his car next to my bus.

"I said 'I thought you had him back there!' and he said 'You told us not to arrest him!'

"I gotta ask that cop when the hell it became my job to tell him how to do his? I mean this guy could have attacked me, and this cop is acting like this was all my fault! Dude coulda killed me for crying out loud!"

Our session over, he was still visibly shaken two days after the incident. He said he hadn't slept well, and worries what might happen if the guy gets on his bus again. He had driven a different line the day after the incident, but it still affected him. I was moved by what he said next, because his thoughts were about what had been interrupted.

"I feel terrible about my regular passengers. I mean I had to leave them standing, late at night, waiting for me to give them a ride and I didn't show

up. They're good folks and didn't deserve this, but at the same time I owe them a safe ride. I hope they got home okay."

Mercifully, the Station Agent allowed him to wait out the rest of his time in the bullpen. He wasn't forced to drive in a diminished condition, which is best for everyone. Instead of allowing him a day off to recover however, he would have had to take sick leave. This would have been time loss, which ironically counts against his accumulation of safe driving hours for our recognition program. If you take too much sick leave, your 'clock' starts over from zero and you lose however many safe driving hours you've accumulated. In theory, you could have a safe driving record for years without being recognized as a Master Operator by our district, simply for using sick leave. Instead of risking time loss, he chose to drive the next day when he should have been recovering at home.

This is often what happens to many operators. You don't hear about all the verbal assaults we endure. Many border on violent, are brutally vile, and don't make the news. His wasn't an isolated experience, nor did it end violently. It has however, for other operators.

When Pamela Thompson was attacked a few years ago, her assailant's attorney whined to the court about what a horrible time the accused had experienced prior to his horrible crime. Poor thing. I'm sorry, but I don't give a damn. We all have a rough time at points in our lives, and we persevere. It's no excuse for punching a helpless civil servant several times in the face over a lousy couple of bucks. Imagine Pamela's distress, fear and pain. Did that matter? Her assailant was given a year's probation and exclusion from riding local transit for a year. He was also ordered to pay Pamela's medical bills including her broken glasses. Big deal. Slap on the wrist. He should have spent a year in prison and been thrown out of town. Records say he apologized and Pamela forgave him. She's a sweet, decent lady and he's a lucky jerk.

Transit management bleats operator safety while turning the other cheek when faced with our daily reality. Until a few years ago, we had fare inspectors ride our buses, checking fares and creating a deterrent for bad behavior. It was a reminder that people could face a hefty fine for not paying. Nowadays, the fare inspector is all but a thing of the past. Management made fare inspection another duty of road supervisors who are already stretched to the limit. Our warnings to fare evaders they can ride at the mercy of an inspector boarding are met with "Yeah, whatever." Unruly passengers are even more brazen now, and we're increasingly vulnerable.

When you're in the driver seat, range of motion is extremely limited. If confronted with danger, we're still expected to "remain in the seat" or face discipline. This makes us easy targets, and sometimes afraid for our lives. Our Standard Operating Procedures are extremely vague, saying only that we may employ "reasonable self-defense" when attacked. I'm sorry, but when somebody attacks me while doing my job of driving a 40,000-pound vehicle full of people, or even on a break outside the bus, I would expect the district to have my backside rather than kicking it when my body screams "fight or die." We're not even allowed to carry pepper spray.

Until state legislatures declare that violence against any civil servant is subject to severe penalties, we'll continue to be the public's punching bag. Especially in the corporate press when contract negotiations begin.

We hear about how they want to retrofit buses with 'protective cages' around the driver seat. That's not encouraging for those of us who are claustrophobic, and insulting to the many passengers who actually enjoy friendly interaction with their driver. It won't stop the violence though; we have to get out of the cage eventually.

Our district won't truly protect us, it seems, until one of us (God forbid) dies from an attack. Makes us wonder, would they still blame the operator?

Deke's People

"Deke," a reader told me the other day, "you're getting crabby. Why don't you write something about your good passengers?"

"Well," I stammered, "I reckon I could write about you and a few other folks. Y'all are always nice to me, and it makes my day to give you a ride."

So yeah, okay. I have been a bit more ornery than usual. After helping one operator write a speech he delivered to the board of directors and stressing over the epidemic of assaults on operators, I have been a bit cranky. Downright angry, even. But I don't like to be. It's not my nature to be a snarling beast. Even my beloved has noticed I've been particularly cranky the past few months. My apologies. I'll try to invert my literary frown.

One of my favorites is Lady D. I've been driving her home for almost five months, most afternoons during the work week. She gets on downtown and I give her a courtesy stop near the end of the line. Lady D and I have had some fun conversations. She reads this blog and we talk about the things operators face on daily basis. Most people who ride just show me their pass and take a seat, but Lady D is a bright star shiner. I'm bummed when she doesn't ride. She's one I watch for if she's late to the stop. I'll even burn time to make sure she doesn't miss the bus. People who make an extra effort to catch my bus usually find I'm one of the operators who will wait for them. If they're rude when they board however, they won't be so lucky the next time.

I've always been a people person, usually able to ascertain whether I like someone within seconds of meeting them. If somebody throws off a weird vibe, it's hello, sit down and shut up. But once I've decided they are "cool," we're usually friends for years afterward. Just ask my best buddy Henry; we've been close since the first day of high school, and that was over four decades ago.

Nice weather is helping improve people's moods lately. Folks are smiling more. Teenagers are actually smiling back and thanking me when they leave instead of snarling. They put seats up in the Priority Seating area when people using mobility devices board, and put them down again when they exit. They're more light-hearted and easy going. More motorists have been letting me merge back into traffic.

The other day I came upon a favorite passenger I haven't seen in months. Featured a few posts earlier, Johnny Stingray made a surprise appearance on my bus. Having him onboard made my day. I would introduce him to my own kids. He said his shift had changed so he usually catches the bus right after mine and that's why I haven't seen him. We had a good chat, and I was so glad to hear he's doing even better than the last time we met.

Then there are the regulars who surprise me. This past week, a little kid boarded with his grandpa. Every other day for the past few months, he'd walk right past me without a word and sit silently until they got off the bus. But this time, he burst on the bus proclaiming "Today's my birthday!"

"Wow buddy," I said, "that's cool! How old are you now, 10?" I always add a few years on to how old I think kids are because it makes them feel special.

"No silly," he laughed, "I'm SIX!" His grandpa, just a bit less dour than usual and sporting a rare smile, ambled on after him.

"Okay everyone," I announced on the PA system. "We have a special rider today, and it's his SIXTH birthday! So please folks, join me in wishing him a VERY happy birthday!"

To my delight and the lad's, the bus cheered and what had been a rather quiet, subdued group sang this beaming child the happy birthday song. The rest of the trip was filled with friendly banter and laughter. Adding the beautiful Portland spring weather and the day became a grand masterpiece.

Soon, the summer signup begins. My routes and days off will change. New faces will appear, and I look forward to finding the shine in others. I will miss the folks I've come to know. It's the part of the job I truly enjoy the most, meeting new people. It's hard to leave regulars behind.

There you have it. A nice post, full of smileys. Aw hell, I was almost as sweet as Mr. Rogers this time. I'm going back to writing my book. It's where my mind has been lately. I hope you all buy a copy when it comes out. Then you can say "I knew Deke before he was rich and famous." If I'm lucky, you'll slap me upside the head if I get too big for my britches. A deacon needs to be humbled from time to time.

Now That's Entertainment!

When we reach the end point of our shifts, it's rather comical how many people think we should continue giving rides. Our overhead sign reads "Garage," yet they still don't understand: we're done and headed home.

Only a few routes go past either of our three garages, unless the buses are deadheading outbound to the starting point of a run. People don't realize we actually have to drive to wherever the route begins. Buses don't magically appear there. They don't drive themselves. In 2016 that is. Maybe someday into the far beyond they will, but I hope not.

Because I road-relief my bus, I finish every night with a deadhead back to the garage. It's amusing to see the antics of people who are waiting for a bus as I go by. It's apparent these people expect me to stop and pick them up anyway. As if I'm their special chauffeur. It doesn't occur to them that perhaps I'm finishing up a 10-hour day, and the last thing I want to do at that point is give anybody a ride. Well, except for other drivers... every uniform is a bus stop to me (thanks Lyn!).

Behaviors displayed as deadheading buses cruise past people can be amusing. There's one I call the "LORD, STOP THIS BUS!" maneuver, where the person throws both hands skyward, followed by major stink-eye as my dark ride rolls past. Then there's the "HOPPER," where they wave their hands and jump out into the road. This evolves into what I've termed the "POOCH," because one night a girl with a pink pompadour hairstyle was so enraged I didn't stop, she looked like a pissed-off poodle who's just learned she lost the top prize at the dog show to a mangy old blue tick hound. Of course, this was followed by a heartily-screamed expletive and two raised birds. Impressive show lass, but alas, still no ride. Sorry.

Some maneuvers are passive. This one I call the "THINKER." These riders understand the drill. As I approach a stop, the person will look up from their phone, start to raise their hand, then actually READ the overhead and put their hand down. Or, in an attempt to either be friendly or to avoid looking silly, they'll wave as I go by. I usually return the gesture. One night a lady did this, and since I was stopped at a traffic light anyway, I opened the door and let her know an in-service bus was only two minutes behind me. She was very grateful and thanked me for the information. She also wished me a nice evening and thanked me for being a driver. It was extremely rare but greatly appreciated. The next time I did this, the wanna-be passenger offered to perform a sexual act on me if I'd ferry her down the road. She didn't appreciate my slamming the door in her face.

Next comes the "RUNNER." They see the bus in the distance, but are too far away for them to read our destination sign. They race to the stop like a hungry lion chasing its prey. Usually this is accompanied by a frantic waving of the arms and the occasional glance over the shoulder to check distance. It's fun sometimes to slow down just a bit, giving them a glimmer of hope, only to zip past as they reach the stop and turn to see you pass them by. A typical response is a stomp of the foot followed by a hearty flip off. This is a mean trick though, and I will only admit to doing it one time, after a particularly hard day dealing with horribly rude people. Karmic payback isn't a dog to mess with.

Someone is bound to give me a hard time about this post. We're often portrayed by the public as heartless, uncaring dirtbags. However, when you consider the source of this unfair description is usually a degenerate slacker, it's a wash.

I've started rating the Deadhead Routines on a 1-10 scale. So far most have scored in the 5-7 range. Nothing truly remarkable yet. But I'm waiting for a perfect 10. It's great entertainment, and I have the best seat in the house.

It's My Anniversary!

▣ DEKE'S NOTE: *By the time the third anniversary of From the Driver Side rolled around, I was at a creative crossroads. My alter ego was becoming more difficult to keep separate from my true self. The two personalities were inching closer to one entity. The Deke had more exposure, but the writer I've always been was jealous. I write two blogs which have the same author using two names. FTDS blossomed with hits, while the other languished with a hit counter resembling a drunkard's comatose slow drool. Some of my best writing lurks in the shadows under my real name. Now "Deke" is poised to publish this book, which is a dream I've had since childhood. The logical solution to this strange dilemma would be to just blow off the pen name and stand up for who I truly am. Am I simply embracing the notoriety attained while writing beneath its shroud, in fear that if I shed the cloak I would lose not only my job, but the very (humble) success Deke has earned?*

My life has been a constant uphill struggle for survival. After several careers, careening about like a rubber ball from one profession to the next, my writing has always been there. Begging me to begin again. I'm a writer who now drives a bus. An idiot savant? Perhaps. FTDS has been fun practice, and dust no longer coats my keyboard. The illusion of writer's block blew into infinite directions with my first clumsily-composed posts. I've published several hundred posts between the two blogs, continued the novel I began two decades ago, finished this book and started a new Young Adult story. It's ludicrous to keep this **nom de guerre** *charade. It can't continue if I expect to succeed. I'm one who has many things to share. I might not be a classic composer, but you and I have a connection. When you read what I write, it somehow resonates. A truly egotistical statement, I'm afraid. However, what if your favorite artist doubted him/herself and never let the magic flow? Hesitated rather than leapt? Your memories wouldn't be intertwined with their art, but* *they would surely be with another's. That "other" would be the one who threw doubt out with the broken eggshells and moldy cheese and said "why not me?"*

I would say it's my birthday, but I fooled ya! It "bloggles" my mind to realize I've been writing this for three years now.

Within a week or so FTDS will achieve its 60,000th hit. Once again, I thank everyone who has helped make this humble tome a success. Al Margulies (Rantings of a Former Bus Driver) started publicizing and linking to it from its earliest stages, has always been supportive, and for this I am deeply appreciative. The Rampant Lion also took notice and has been great helping me keep facts straight. Many other drivers have had my back, reading posts and offering encouragement.

A close friend of mine is working on a cartoon drawing of the Deke; a radio personality from Nova Scotia invited me to give an interview; fellow operators often approach me with great blog ideas. The past three years have truly been wonderful, and I'm eager to see what awaits my next anniversary. It may not be the best driver blog out there, but it sure is a fun ride.

It's really cool to see people from all over the world reading my words. I met Ken from Scotland on "holiday" at the beach, and has become a regular. Ellen in Minnesota is the mother of a friend, and her two cents are always worth a buck. Operators chime in from Denver, Tucson, Philadelphia, Dallas, Canada, Australia and other locales around the world. I only dreamed this would happen, and I'm overjoyed to see it come true. Hopefully my book of these posts will earn success as well, but just being read by these wonderful people is reward enough.

Oh, and speaking of the book, I need to get back to it. I only have a few hours each night before the eyelids droop too low to see the words. One night I actually woke up with my head on the keyboard. One look in the mirror revealed an almost perfect 'QWERTYUIOP' dent in my face. Luckily, I didn't drool into the keyboard.

HIT COUNTER: 60,000 (MAY 2016)

The Wave

Bus and rail operators wave at each other. Usually. It's a sign of recognition and respect. I first noticed this as a passenger, when I rode the bus to school and work, and thought it was cool that operators had such a tradition. Like a club's secret handshake, the wave has subtle nuances.

We're accustomed to not being recognized by other motorists for our efforts to keep them safe. When we pass by another transit employee, it's customary to give a friendly wave. Unless we're busy, most operators and other transit workers observe this time-honored tradition. I'll even give a "thank you" wave to motorists who stop on my Yield signal and allow me to merge back into traffic. It beats the obscene gesture the unwashed few usually flash me.

Lady operators have the most creative waves. There's what I call the "beauty queen" wave, where they pivot their hand at the wrist and add a sweet smile. Some reserve this for folks they know, opting to use the common "swath in front of the wheel" for others. Ladies who recognize close friends will add the "kiss blow" to their own patented version.

Another one of my favorites is the "big wave out the window." If you don't know the driver, you wonder if it's a desperate plea to "come drive this thing for me willya I need a break!" The most common I see is the nonchalant "hiya brother" half-salute. Or the barely discernible wrist-pivot from the steering wheel that means either "whatever, dude" or "oh yeah hello to you too, I guess."

Then there are those who see you wave, but look right through you as if you don't exist. No wave there. If they're close enough you sometimes see a subtle eye roll. It's rather disheartening. But then again, not everyone who drives a transit vehicle is having the best of days. I give them a pass, because usually the next time you see them they at least give you a half-hearted hello. If they never wave at all, so be it.

Sometimes I'm guilty of failure to wave. If I'm having a truly rotten day, it's hard to even acknowledge my passengers as they board. Seeing a sad puppy dog face from a waver to whom I fail to return the gesture is usually enough to snap me out of it. They don't deserve the bad vibes I'm feeling. On the return trip, I'll be sure to at least single out those I ignored with an exaggerated makeup wave.

Oftentimes my beloved will catch me waving at bus operators when I'm driving our car. "Roopsie, long day," I say. "But I know that gal!" She'll remind me they can't see me driving on the down low.

One driver I know gave me a puzzled look when I asked him why he didn't wave back one day. "I didn't know it mattered all that much," he said. Later that afternoon as I drove by him downtown as he waited to do his road relief, he gave me an exaggerated double wave with his customary dry-wit sardonic half smile. It was hilarious, but also a signal to me: it's no biggie, get over it.

A few drivers out there are so green they are more focused on scanning and being careful than waving. That's okay. I'd rather they get a feel for safely driving with two hands than acknowledging me. They have to successfully pass probation without a scratch or a dent, and I'm past that.

I appreciate all my brothers and sisters out there. When I wave at them, I'm showing respect. To my more senior brothers and sisters, I sometimes shoot them a salute. It's not mandatory or expected. It is however, a nice tradition.

Bloody Wednesday

It was another busy day. Full load every trip, wise guys and nut jobs, the usual regulars. Then I had a surprise.

On my layover I was walking to my bus and saw what appeared to be... BLOOD! It was splashed on the bottom of the front door. My blood pressure raised a few hundred points. Did I flatten Fido? Squish a squirrel? Pulverize a possum? Thunk a skunk? No smell, no memory of any disturbing squishy noise. Nothing out of the ordinary had happened; I shrugged it off. Then I shuddered back to reality.

Next, I called Lady Dispatch and explained the situation. She was calm, asked where the "blood" was located, and didn't sound the least concerned. She said to tell the spotter the bus needed a bath. "1730," she signed off in military time. Perplexed, I hung up. Shrugged. I had done my due diligence. No NCIS van would be sent to test the substance, no news crews (thank God), no management scrutinizing me, no report to write. Whew!

As I pulled into the spotter's shack, I asked him to look at it and closed the door. He frowned, bent down and studied it. When I opened the door again, he sported a smile.

"What is it?" I asked.

"It's just the grease they use on the doors," he replied with a grin. "Kinda looks like blood, but it isn't. And I'm not gonna taste it."

Mystery solved. I'm such a goober.

They Stole Our Bus!

Two 15-year-olds are accused of recently stealing a bus out of the Center Garage. Hard to believe? Perhaps, if you don't work for our transit agency.

I have walked the tracks of buses, thinking how easy it would be for some fool to take off in one. When it happened, I was amazed the perps didn't get hurt. Instead of immediately reacting to this with a blog post, I wanted to see how it would play out over a few weeks. I'm glad I waited, but irritated with the outcome.

Management has blamed operators as being the main cause for this dangerous joy ride, which is insulting. Not a word from them about their own role, except they are "investigating" and studying how to keep it from happening again. Oh, come on folks. Without going into detail, let's just say the blame is on the wrong foot. People trip when they wear their shoes incorrectly, and in this case, our management has also tied them together.

Frankly, there are many ways our management fails to secure our assets. My blog purposefully doesn't inform the public how to do drive a bus, but management loves to teach people (and brag about it on media outlets) how to do so. As another blogger has stated, there are videos online which give detailed instruction on the basics. However, I cannot stress enough how foolish these kids were to try such a stunt.

I learned how to drive when I was 10, watching my father. He only let me get behind the wheel on remote dirt roads. Granted, I didn't possess the critical problem-solving skills to drive safely, but the basics are fairly simple. A teenager watching a bus driver would quickly figure some things out on their own. The finer points require months of training by professionals and years of experience to master.

Considering a 15-year-old is hardly capable of driving a standard vehicle, it's amazing they had the balls to steal a bus. Of course, they smashed it up a bit trying to drive it out of the yard, but they actually made it five miles down the road before police could stop them. It's amazing they didn't kill somebody. Of course, they'll brag about it for a lifetime, but someday they'll realize the folly of this foolish stunt.

What I'm worried about is that it will happen again and somebody will be hurt or killed. Management has a bad habit of blaming its operators for everything from its own financial blunders to its lack of security. It should accept responsibility rather than throwing the blame on the worker bees. Sure, we could all do better keeping our properties secure. But it takes proper framework, organization, and leadership. An honorable response to this fiasco would include a resignation of an embarrassed party; instead operators were treated to a memo blaming us for "training" those responsible.

It's obvious somebody tripped here, but it wasn't us. We know which shoe fits on each foot, but someone tried to lodge *his* in our collective derrières. Sorry pal, you missed.

A Toast for Willie

Passing by the "rookie table" in the bullpen these days, I often chuckle at the stories they tell. While the adventures described are amazing to them, it's easy to remember being greenhorns.

Newbies congregate far away from the Extra Board table, as if veterans are intimidating. When you're new to something you tend to cling to comforting familiarity. It's intimidating to venture away from those with whom you were trained. As the miles click by, you meet operators who are kind and helpful. Some aren't much senior than you, and your circle begins to widen. Eventually you feel more at ease around your fellow operators. Then you come across a hardened old-timer who won't even acknowledge you. There are some who don't speak to trainees or newbies or even those they have never met. Reality bites in every vocation, especially in a seniority-driven career.

Occasionally, you meet a veteran who goes out of his/her way to help, extending a friendly hand when you're feeling isolated. One of my favorite veterans here is Willie Jack. He's earned so many Safe Driving Awards they keep having to create new levels to honor his excellence. For almost 40 years he's graced this city with his unique and personable service. A true gentleman, part of a family known for exemplary community service, he's humble and prefers to downplay his accomplishments.

When I first met Willie, my Line Trainer introduced him as "our finest, most decorated operator." Willie's reaction? "Come on now Steve, I'm not that good!" Yet, he *is* that good.

About six months ago, a local television station featured him in a news story when he locked up his bus and ran out to help a blind elderly lady cross a busy street. This attention embarrassed him, most likely because being kind is simply his nature. Back then, our transit agency had created "Gold Master Operator" just for him, but he recently became our first "Platinum."

His daughter is a good friend of mine, but I didn't immediately make the connection. I should have, because she's a lot like him (a bit more ornery, but a sweet lady nonetheless). Jenelle was just a few classes ahead of me, and for a few signups I unknowingly picked her old routes. She gave me great pointers and let me know who the regular riders were. As is her father, she is eager to help.

As others who are intelligent, kind and truly caring, Willie is soft-spoken. While I'm sure he's a force to be reckoned with when somebody acts up on his bus, he's also one of the most beloved operators we have. Passengers who know him sing his praises. Fellow operators admire and respect him. I don't know him as well as I'd like to. Every time I've been invited to join a family gathering, work or other obligations have intervened. Someday soon, I look forward to sitting down and getting to know this truly decent gentleman.

All good things come to pass, and this summer is Willie's last as a bus operator. He's retiring, leaving behind a family of fellow operators who will aspire to honor his legacy.

Roll easy, Mr. Jack. We're sorry to see you go, but you've earned a long and happy retirement. Congratulations, kudos and may the Lord always bless you and yours with the best life has to offer.

I Don't Need to Be a Jerk

Ever known a guy who initially annoyed you, yet your conscience insisted that patience was the key to working with him? I have such a passenger this signup.

Nearly every day, this guy boards my bus around 3:30 in the afternoon. He asks if he'll be able to catch a bus that will get him to the east side of town by 7:00. After a few days of this, instead of being irritated at having to answer his daily query, I realized he must have a memory issue. He's usually disheveled and reminds me of a scared kid. At first, I was impatient. I groaned when I saw him shuffling toward the bus with a frantic wave. He always has his pass, but he has to dig for it. Sighing impatiently, I'd tap my foot. After three days of this, my impatience turned inward. Is this what I've become? The snarling driver people always complain about? After my run this evening, I just sat in my car, head hung low, as I realized how horribly I've treated this poor fellow. Shame sunk in, along with the painful fact that I'm not as kind as I should be.

He's always apologetic, polite and grateful. Compared to many, he's the type of passenger I should look forward to helping. Lately, I've had some real bozos ride my lines, and it's been hard to be kind and gentle. My temper has recently been tested on several occasions. It has been very difficult to remain calm. I would hate for another to be as impatient with me as I have been with him. He's somebody's family member. What if someone treated my brother, born with Down's Syndrome, the way I treat him? Deke, why are you such a jerk?

Beginning today, I resolved to be the person he doesn't need to fear. I've nicknamed him "Frank," after a dear friend of mine who was as ornery as I, had a heart of gold and the patience of a saint. I miss my friend, and by giving this poor soul his name, I'm going to turn myself around.

While Frank dug through his wallet this afternoon, I told him, "I know you always have your pass sir, it's okay. Please have a seat."

"Thank you," he said quietly, then added "but do you think we'll make it to the transit center in time for me to get to Powell by 7:00?"

"Yes sir," I replied, smiling. "It's only 3:30, so you'll have plenty of time. Now go ahead and sit down, and I'll get you there with time to spare!"

He half-smiled, trembling, his eyes betraying a remaining trace of fear. "Thank you, yes I'll sit. Thank you, sir. Thank you so much."

As I continued down the road, he rose and came up to me. "Are you sure I'll make it on time?"

"Yes. It's gonna be okay," I reassured him, knowing this same scene will play out again every day. If I work on it, maybe he'll lose some fear. Perhaps I won't become the type of driver I said I'd never be.

When he exited at the transit center, he turned back around as always, waited for people to board. He thanked me twice. Then he asked if the next bus would pick him up at that stop. I assured him with a smile and a nod. He thanked me yet again.

He seemed slightly more at ease.

Of all the people we transport daily, there's no real way of knowing how many are scared to death, fighting illness or inner demons. It's hard sometimes to remember patience. It is, after all, part of my mantra to be kind, thoughtful and patient. We're often treated to a large ration of rude, and it's hard to avoid people fatigue. But I'm ashamed of myself for allowing it to happen. Life is full of bad news, hard times and mean people. Why must I be one of them? There's no excuse, but there is redemption.

That old song, "What the World Needs Now, Is Love Sweet Love" comes to mind. Not just for some, but for everyone, it says. I also remind myself that we are judged by how we treat those with the least, and I have so much to be thankful for.

I'm sorry, Frank. You deserve better from me. From now on, you'll have it.

I'm a Dork... Again

It's easy to become distracted when you are constantly welcoming or dropping off passengers. Sometimes my mind doesn't match what my mouth says.

I doubt that I'm reaching senility at this cool age of 50-something. However, I begin to wonder sometimes. Here's why.

I try to greet even the grumpiest-looking folks as they leave the bus, as well as acknowledge the many thank-you's and "have a nice day" folks, I get a bit tongue twisty.

One lady de-boarded through the front door as I was printing fares for those boarding at a busy downtown stop.

"Thank you," the nice lady said as she exited.

"Hi," I replied.

To the new passenger I printed the fare for: "Have a nice day, thanks for riding."

Hmm... I seem to be stepping backwards on my tongue.

With Liberty and Justice for Whom?

Our society faces a growing lack of common decency.
There's talk of "making America great again," but I don't hear any intelligent plans to do so. All I see is a dangerous amount of disrespect and an absence of true political debate. This country, the entire planet in fact, is in danger of imploding. Yet, all we hear is which American party is to blame. We're so self-involved we fail to acknowledge our country is overrun by a bunch of juveniles. It's terrifying that the world's most powerful country has descended into a state where ignorance is celebrated, propaganda is glorified, and the truth is anybody's guess.

This is evident in the smallest town councils, across every state and up to the highest levels of our, I repeat (what is supposed to be) OUR federal government. A country founded on the principle that *"all men (and women) are created equal, that they are endowed by their Creator with certain unalienable rights, that among these are life, liberty and the pursuit of happiness,"* is now mired in a ridiculous debate over what this statement, written in the simplest language, actually means.

Let's begin with all of us being equal. Are we? Evidently not. If you're gay, some say you're not deserving. I don't care who you're having sex with or who you love. It's not my business. Neither are my sexual habits any of yours. Come from another country (like ALL of our ancestors), you need to just go back there? Really? Good grief! What color is your skin? Is your God the same as mine, or whatever one collective says is the TRUE God? My God surely looks entirely different than yours, but does that mean my interpretation of The Creator is wrong? It bears arguing that there could only be one, yet there are at least seven billion (and counting) visions of the "Father" of humankind. People point to the one religious text they believe is the "true word," yet the most popular were written long before we understood the most basic principles of the universe. Science had not begun to explain how life even exists. The Earth was flat and water was just wet stuff rather than a combination of two hydrogen particles mixed with one oxygen. If we're equal, why do we often belittle those different from ourselves? Why is it so hard to learn from each other?

Our judicial system is unjustly weighted. The most severe punishment is meted upon those who have the least; those with the most truly get away with murder. Wages remain woefully behind each increase to our cost of living, yet we elect people whose main goal is to keep us wanting more. We vilify those who cannot "keep up." Instead of helping soldiers recover from the horrors we send them into, we spend the money on military excursions into civilizations at war for millennia. It's likely these conflicts will continue in spite of our interference. There always seems to be enough money for the rich to remain so, while we make do with less. Yet when we argue for our own cause, we're blamed for creating "class warfare." Isn't this ironic? Especially when those within our own class are fighting for those above us.

In any economy, equality is non-existent. There are those who have, and others who do not. There is a growing void in between. We are worker bees slaving for whichever queen rules the hive. Our lives are a constant struggle, even though we convince ourselves "happiness" exists in precious slivers of time. This is not to say we cannot be happy, but that which is good and lovely seems in short supply for many. Amazingly, if one professes to be joyful, their reasons are scrutinized, criticized and often scorned. For this reason, I prefer to jealously guard my happiness. It is spontaneous, and I choose to savor it like a first taste of fine wine. Nobody can taste it as I do. Your taste buds aren't the same as mine. We're individually unique, save for our strangely similar DNA.

If my desire to be happy includes the ingestion of certain naturally-occurring substances, shouldn't it be my right to do so? If it doesn't interfere with the peaceful existence of another, put them in danger, or alter our collective homeostasis, what business is it of government to prohibit it? I believe in your right to believe as you do, without any interference or argument from me. Why then, is it so important to you that I conform to your belief system? Isn't this denying my freedom? Must we always believe we're right even in the absence of supporting logic?

Politics is a nasty game. I have dear friends with whom I heartily disagree politically. However, we respect our differences. Our similarities work concurrently to draw us closer. Over the past decade, I've learned it's not important to be right; it's more so to be true. Sure, I've lost some friends over politics, but those with whom I disagree have taught me great lessons. My respect and fondness for those who love me in spite of myself is immeasurable. You might not agree with every post I write, but your presence here honors me.

While certain differences separate us, we share commonalities and aspire to find peace within. Underneath our skin, we're the same color. Within our souls lies the ability to love or hate. Philosophers have long argued origin and causality of these two similar emotions, yet the former seems less evident than the latter. Whenever I've had so much anger as to feel hatred, it has devastated me. When I let go of the anger, a feeling of peace returns. In this moment, I've had to drop the stone, for I too have been guilty of causing the rift; if I throw this stone in anger it could easily boomerang back towards me in atonement for my own sins.

Perhaps I'm still seeing life through the optimistic eyes of a child. Companionship and fun are infinitely more preferable to arguments and defensive behavior. I still believe we have the power to be kind to one another. If I ever lose my love for people, this main staple of my being, it will be said I died of foolish pride.

Humanity's greatest moments were conceived through compromise and humility. If we don't reclaim these traits soon, our failures will overshadow our achievements. And that would truly suck.

HIT COUNTER: 75,000 (JULY, 2016)

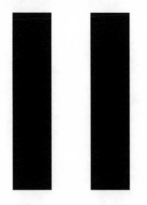

EPILOGUE

– 2017 –

A Journey Complete?

This book has taken a year and a half to complete. Since I began putting it together, I've written another 85 posts and an additional 100,000 hits have been registered on FTDS.

Always the perfectionist, I've worked very hard to present an accurate story for you, from new driver to hardened mid-level seniority operator. Reading each post I had written, editing and choosing which ones to include, adding them into one file, took nearly five months. Then I began a serious editing project which took a few more months. I also wrote a Glossary of Transit Terms.

Next, I sent the book out to trusted friends and family for their perusal and honest opinions. Three of them responded with hard-hitting suggestions to make it better. I went through the book again, chopping and editing, making sure to retain the blog's original flavor while eliminating unnecessary passages and frivolous verbiage. As I write this, within me grows a great sense of accomplishment and relief.

Since I've been quite prolific this year and I don't plan a sequel to this book, I felt it necessary to add a few more posts from 2017. There are now over 165,000 hits. A few months ago, the blog registered 15,000 hits, its best month ever. It's been a banner year for FTDS, so I leave you with a few more tidbits from 2017.

Hopefully, I'll still have a job as Deke the Bus Operator after this book is published. Regardless, here are this year's most popular pieces.

A Divine Intervention

It was hard to get in the mood to drive a bus that Friday. My body ached, as did my soul. All week I had read many discouraging reports about my brothers and sisters being slandered, insulted and assaulted. Not just in Portland, but everywhere.

While thankfully I've narrowly escaped a few dicey situations without a scratch, I've had my share of insulting and rude passengers. On this day, I was asked by a passenger if I'd allow him to get out on the near side of an intersection. The bus stop was far side, and my light was about to turn green. Although I normally would allow this if the light was going to remain red and conditions were safe enough, I knew it was a short cycle. I politely told him no, just as the light turned green. After I crossed with the light and smoothly came to a stop, I started to explain why I denied his request.

"It just doesn't matter," he snapped. "I don't need to hear an explanation that won't make sense anyway."

At least he didn't spit on me, or curse me out. "Have a nice day," I managed to say. To my abused driver's window, I quietly muttered a curse and let it slide off my shoulders. Realizing he wouldn't have been very appreciative had I missed my light and granted his request, I shrugged and moved on.

Later, my mood improved dramatically because of a sweet lady who boarded with a baby stroller. Assuming the stroller contained logical cargo, I asked her to remove the baby from the stroller, as per agency policy. She chuckled and explained "there's no baby, it's just an easy way to transport my stuff." Since she had such a kind voice and manner, and also because I knew this run wasn't bound to involve a full complement of passengers, I didn't ask her to fold up the stroller. We exchanged a few pleasantries, and I answered a question or two. My Friday was progressing without too many problems, and it was refreshing to have her on board.

A short time later, I noticed her writing something down. She looked up and saw me glance at her in the mirror. *Oh boy*, I thought, *I must have annoyed her somehow and she's going to complain.* It didn't seem likely, given our pleasant interaction up to that point. I took a chance as I waited for the signal to change.

"Is there anything I can help you with ma'am?" I asked in a gentle tone.

"Yes," she answered, "what time did we leave?"

Ruh-roh, I thought. I'd lolly-gagged a bit on my break, texting with my beloved, and had left a bit late. It's usually not a problem, as this route generously allows "bubbles" in the paddle and I can usually burn off any late time before reaching the next transit center.

"We're scheduled to leave there at 4:45 p.m., but I may have left a minute or so late," I said in a cautious tone. "Why, is anything wrong? Do you need to make a connection to another bus line?"

"Oh no, nothing's wrong," she said, waving her hand and laughing. "I'm just writing down a few things to make sure I get them right when I call in and say how gracious and kind a driver you are."

Man, did I feel like a dork. I didn't think I had been gracious *or* kind, but rather suspiciously trying to recover from some unknown *faux pas.*

"Why thank you," I said, smiling. "That makes my day, my *week* even!"

"It's no problem, really. You drivers don't get nearly the credit you deserve."

Then she told me a moving story about one of our retirees.

About 20 years earlier, she began, a message came that her father was dying. Since she lived on the opposite side of town and her soon-to-be ex-husband refused to let her use their car, she and her young son raced to a bus stop and caught a ride. Extremely distraught, she explained the situation to the operator.

"Not only did he do his best to get me to my connecting bus," she explained, "but he radioed Dispatch and explained my situation, asking they hold the bus we needed to catch until I arrived."

After nearly two hours of anxious travel, she reached her father's side just in time to say goodbye. "He passed away 20 minutes after we arrived," she said. "I was so grateful, I wanted to call in and let them know that if he hadn't made that call, I wouldn't have been able to say goodbye to my dad. Unfortunately, in my rush to get there, I failed to write down his name, and I couldn't even remember the route. I had no information on this man, and I felt so bad I couldn't thank him for what he had done."

It's normal to hear about complaints, but people aren't as quick to show appreciation. You would expect this passenger would have just let it go. She could not.

"I looked for this driver for *five years*," she continued. "But he must have switched routes. I'd watch drivers downtown, looking for this one guy who had done so much for me. I just wanted to thank him personally. If not for him, Dad would have died before we got there."

Then one day, she spotted the operator and boarded his bus. She asked if he remembered the incident, but he didn't. She thanked him and let him know just how important his actions were not only to her, but also to her young son who had accompanied her that day. Then, he said something truly astonishing.

"That driver just shook his head and smiled. He said, 'Thank you for telling me this, because I'm retiring today.' "

I shook my head in amazement. What a wonderful story to hear, just when I needed it most. Before I rolled to her stop, on time as I had promised, she gave me another gift.

"That's why I write down your bus and route numbers," she told me in a soft voice. "You people do a wonderful job, and I try to let the agency know. In 30 years of riding, I've only complained five times. Thank you for doing what you do."

Nearly moved to tears, I thanked her for telling her wonderful tale. Fate is an amazing thing. Not only did she *find* this kind-hearted bus operator, but she did so *just in time*. It makes one wonder if there was some divine intervention at work here. It sure helped me smile the rest of my day. It will again, every time I remember this story.

End of the Line

This job is dangerous. We lost a brother transit operator in Winnipeg this past week. He was stabbed while on the job, and died from his wounds. I'm sure my words echo the feelings of bus operators worldwide. Our deepest condolences and truly heartfelt prayers go out to his family and fellow operators. When one of us is killed in the line of duty, we *all* feel it.

We deal with every kind of human there is. Sometimes we are faced with such danger we're unable to think rationally, or do the right thing. When threatened, our bodies automatically prepare for fight or flight. There's no luxury of sitting in a comfy chair with a video of what's about to happen. There's no pause button so we can deliberate our options while sitting at a table with a group of fellow professionals.

It's a purely biological question, not mental. In fact, when presented with a life-threatening situation, only those who are trained to deal with this actually know how to respond. People in the military are far more equipped to repel attackers than bus operators. When they're attacked, they're expected to employ deadly force. If a bus operator were to use force in self-defense, the Monday Morning Quarterback team of lawsuit-repellant managers would frantically search for anything we did wrong in the heat of the moment. The attacker isn't their problem, it's ours. Problem is, they don't bother to train us to properly deal with threatening situations. They simply insist we "stay in the seat" and employ de-escalation tactics. Just sit there and be beaten to death, then we won't be fired.

Imagine we were given self-defense courses which prepare us for being attacked in the driver seat. If we used force that resulted in our attacker being seriously injured or killed, would they defend our actions? It's doubtful.

I've heard of operators being suspended because the Hindsight Committee deemed their defensive movements to be "aggressive." If an aggressor threatens your safety, are you supposed to kiss them on the cheek and read them a cute story? No. Human biology dictates that our body will prepare itself to fight back. We're supposed to have the supreme ability to overcome millions of evolutionary years? This would require a complete reversal of our physiological makeup. I don't know anybody who could take a punch, a stab or a slap without at least putting a hand up to prevent further abuse. Yet we face discipline for doing so. I'm shaking my head so damned violently at this I'm dizzy.

Which leads me to Mr. Irvine Fraser of Winnipeg, Manitoba Canada. It's reported that he was stabbed when the last passenger refused to exit his bus, and an argument ensued. I don't know Winnipeg Transit's procedure, but if passengers here refuse to leave the bus, we call for help. Sometimes it arrives quickly, but sometimes resources are thin. We're left to deal with situations until the cavalry comes charging in. Those few minutes can be deadly. Sadly for Mr. Fraser, help didn't come quickly enough.

This could happen in Portland. After 55 assaults on transit workers here last year and 67 so far in 2017, we're all nervous. If it did happen to one of us, would management blame the corpse? The way we're treated when assaulted makes us wary of their soft and fuzzy yet toothless "safety" messages. They say we're a "family," but it sure feels like a dysfunctional one.

If it does happen, I think we should take an old bus and paint it black. Put black lace curtains on the windows. It should serve as a hearse. The funeral procession should have a full police and transit escort. Transit should be suspended out of respect for the fallen.

We're public servants, and there's no guarantee we'll make it home safe each day. Our jobs put us in touch with violent criminals. Many people ride the bus who are armed with guns, knives or both. It's a crap-shoot, our safety is. I pray we never have to mourn a Portland bus operator lost to a violent "customer" as Winnipeg did this week.

RIP, Mr. Fraser. We're all devastated by your untimely death while simply doing your job. Rest in peace, it's the end of the line.

A Riddle and a Frog

The sun came out to play on Thursday. How refreshing to know spring is near! I finally had the chance to test my new eyeglasses, and thankfully they darken inside the bus too. It was quite a challenge when the rainy streets were ablaze in sunlight and my old specs didn't filter the glare. Either way, I hope this is a glimpse of more to come.

With the bright rays came a lighter mood. I was jovial, opposed to the previous five months of steady rain dampening my spirits. Plus, that happened to be St. Patrick's Day so people were playful. When thinking of bloggable subjects, I came up with this bus operator's riddle:

This shade of green beckons from afar,
Shining below an amber star.
But if you try to reach it too quickly,
The result could render some sickly.

I doubt this will fool most of you,
Today it's framed by a shade of blue
We Nor'westerners rarely can see;
Oh what then, my dears, could it be?

A sweet lass boarded my bus on a layover one recent rainy evening. Her hands were cupped protectively in front of her, around something I couldn't see.

Noticing my curious glance, she asked "Want to see my frog?"

Instantly, I wondered if this was acceptable behavior. She had ridden before, and had always been sweet and respectful. What came out of my mouth next was a surprise to us both.

"Oh," I said, "is that your service frog?"

After we both laughed at my clumsy humor, she explained.

"I'm bringing it to my friend because you see, I broke his terrarium earlier and I feel bad. I wanted to give him something to make up for it."

I was simultaneously amused and perplexed. What if little Freddy escaped his bondage and jumped up some lady's skirt? Might somebody's work boot accidentally prove fatal to this juvenile amphibian?

Stepping off the bus to contemplate amidst a satisfying cloud of nicotine vapor, I was flummoxed. Knowing the Standard Operating Procedures require pets to be in an enclosure, it worried me she didn't have one.

Luckily, a friend picked her up a few minutes later. My worries were no longer valid.

Service frog, indeed.

HIT COUNTER: 175,000 (October, 2017)

GLOSSARY OF TERMS

Battery Reset — When something mechanical goes haywire, you shut off the bus, then turn the battery off for a few minutes. This is like a computer reboot, and often fixes a myriad of problems. It's also one of an operator's favorite jokes. One time as I sat on the side of the road, flat tire on the curb side, another operator rolled up. "Didya reset the batteries?" he asked with a wink.

Bike Rack — A folding contraption on the front of the bus to transport up to two bicycles. Some municipalities' buses have racks which hold three or more. Passengers are asked to signal bus operator before they load, and again prior to unloading, their bikes. If an operator isn't aware somebody is about to walk in front of their bus as they leave a stop, they can become quite upset with the guilty party. Luckily for those who commit this transit faux pas, an operator usually scans in front of the bus before moving it; otherwise, their fancy bike jersey could be stained forever red.

Break — The time where, at the end of a bus route, the schedule has "recovery time" built in. During this interval, a driver is allowed to decompress, use the restroom, stretch, eat and enjoy some quiet time before continuing the route. It's not always the best time to ask a them a question; if you see a driver on their bus with the doors closed, consider it to have a huge "DO NOT DISTURB" sign displayed.

Bullpen — The inner sanctum of a bus garage, where operators gather before, in between and after their runs. This is where drivers pick up their pouches, learn information regarding driving conditions, pick up mail, play a friendly game of pool, take a nap or enjoy some television. It's kind of like a clubhouse, in which only bus drivers and their co-workers gather.

Bus — A large vehicle designed to convey passengers via motorized transport. Usually powered by a diesel engine, this vehicle has a capacity of approximately 60 plus the driver. Normally weighing up to 20 tons, a standard full-sized bus is 40 feet long, 11 feet high and nearly 10 feet wide (including mirrors). It requires strength, gross and fine motor control, intuition and split-second decision making to operate. At this time, these qualities are only found in humans. However, there are prototypes which allow for driverless operation. If this were to become an acceptable practice, thousands of transit operators worldwide would be replaced by machines; additionally, if this were allowed, many occupations would be eliminated and humans would eventually become obsolete.

Bus Shelter — A tiny structure commuters use to try and avoid wet weather while waiting for a bus to arrive. Usually they're too small to accommodate more than a few people, and too poorly designed to offer protection from the elements. Often mistaken for a "bus stop." Other names for this are Smoking Lounge, Transient Motel, Happy Hour Tower, and others. Supposed to be for transit use only, but this rule is often ignored.

Bus Stop — Marked by a pole with the route number displayed upon it, found just past the shelter on most routes. This is the point where an operator aims to place the front of the bus to board passengers. Their placement is measured to account for safe opening of the rear doors; this annoys passengers who wait at the shelter expecting the bus to stop there instead. A bus stop is located within a Bus Zone, an area reserved for boarding passengers where auto parking is usually illegal. It's also the best place to use a flashing beacon of light alerting bus operators you are at the stop. A cell phone, cigarette lighter or a small flashlight is usually enough to signal a driver who may not see you standing there in the dark. Always wear bright, colorful clothing; reflective materials are a plus. Want to actually ride that bus? Make sure the operator sees you before he goes flying by.

Contrary to public belief, we do not possess superhero vision that can pinpoint bodies hiding behind a pole or shelter.

CAD — Acronym for Computer Assisted Dispatch, the communications console for a bus. Dispatch messages are sent to and from this device. Fare tickets are dispensed from here as well. Old timers used to refer to it as "The Control Head."

CDL — Commercial Driver's License. A special driving license issued to those who drive special vehicles for a living, including passenger-hauling vehicles and interstate tractor-trailer drivers. They must successfully complete a certified training program, pass a driving test/vehicle inspection exam and a written exam. CDL holders must be regularly re-certified as medically capable of performing the duties of professional driving. We are also subject to regular and random drug testing, and must submit to an alcohol/drug screen whenever involved in any type of collision.

Commendation — When a passenger or another citizen calls in a compliment about an operator who does something "over and above" expectations. We hear too many negative comments on situations over which we have little or no control. Passengers are quick to condemn, even when they don't understand a situation, yet usually reluctant to commend transit workers. We love to see positive affirmations, as do people in other professions; it reinforces our commitment to be, as my friend the Rampant Lion says, "shepherds of the public's safety and general well-being."

Creep Seat — The seat directly behind the driver's compartment, which is nearly impossible for the driver to see. On older buses, side-facing seats extended past the wheel well up to the Yellow Line, so the one closest to the front was almost directly across from the operator and immediately adjacent to the front stairwell. A common spot for The Talker, who would drone on and on about any and every subject imaginable for the duration of their ride. This is usually the spot where someone is sitting when a driver thinks he's all alone and bursts into a finely-honed rendition of a favorite tune, or leans over in his seat to relieve abdominal pressure.

Deadhead — The distance traveled from the transit garage to starting point of route, or back after the shift is finished. When a bus is deadheading, it doesn't stop to pick up passengers unless they're wearing a transit uniform. The exterior overhead sign will display GARAGE, which confuses many people at bus stops along the deadhead route. Contrary to public belief, jumping up and down waving one's arms at a deadheading bus will not convince the operator to pull over and give you a ride.

Dispatch/Control — The command center of a transit agency. Dispatchers are like conductors of a symphony, directing hundreds of buses throughout the service day. They communicate with front line workers, emergency services, and management. The first to respond when anything goes wrong, they have the ability to see and listen to what's happening on a bus or train when necessary. Our lifeline on the road, Dispatch/Control can help keep us calm while directing emergency services to our exact location.

End of the Line — The final point of a route, where operators take their break. Perhaps, if the operator arrives at this "recovery point" on time they might have a few minutes to decompress, make/take water, eat a bite or two, and take a deep breath before turning around and starting the next trip.

Extra Board — An assignment in which an operator reports daily as directed by the Station Agents, either to their assigned garage or to a run left vacant for any number of reasons. When given a report time, the operator waits in the bullpen until they are "up." At this time, they watch the sign-in sheets to make sure each run is covered by an operator. If a run "goes over," meaning its regular operator doesn't sign the sheet by the assigned start time for the run, the EB operator signs the run and does this work for its duration or as directed by the SA. Any operator who shows up even one second late can lose not only their assigned run, but may also be sent home without that day's pay. EB operators can sit on report an entire day and not drive at all, or drive up to four runs in 12 hours. An EB operator must be prepared to drive any of the transit agency's runs with as little as 10 minutes notice. They are required to call the SA each day for the next day's assignment, and their schedule can change daily. Often, those who transition from part- to full-time are assigned to the Extra Board especially if they are promoted in the middle of a signup period. It's also an option for a driver to "sign the Extra Board," and there are many operators who prefer this to regular run assignments.

Extra Service — An Extra Board operator assigned this duty is given a radio and a pouch with route maps for each of the agency's runs. Directed by Dispatch, they fill runs which are taken out of service, trade buses for operators whose bus is having mechanical problems, perform shuttle services when light rail goes down. They also can be directed to fill in on a line that is having on-time performance issues to assist those operators so they can salvage a break at the end of their line. Noobs sometimes refer to this as "Extra Nervous," because they haven't driven many runs yet and are expected to drive any of the district's routes at a moment's notice.

Fare — The fee charged for a passenger to ride a transit vehicle. There are a variety of options at our transit agency. Adult, Honored Citizen (people over 65, or those with disabilities), and Youth fares are either paid for a 2.5-hour ticket or an All Day Pass. We accept cash, pre-paid passes, tickets purchased via cellphone transit app, and a tap card on which money is deducted from their balance each time they "tap" the card as they board. Those who ride without proper fare face citation, a court appearance and a stiff fine. Long gone are the days when an operator could make change for the hapless rider who accidentally puts a $20 bill in for a $5 ride; an operator here in Portland was recently assaulted because he couldn't provide a passenger with $0.50 change.

Fare Evader — One who rides transit without paying a fare, who lies or cheats the system, or whose ticket to ride has expired. It's considered a theft of public services. In Portland, it is unlawful to ride transit without proof of proper fare.

Fare Inspector — Any peace officer, inspector, vehicle operator, or District Rail Controller is empowered to enforce transit code with relation to passenger fares. When they board a bus to check passengers' fares, they have the authority to cite fare evaders.

FTDS — FromTheDriverSide.blogspot.com, a blog I write about being a bus operator in Portland, Oregon. It pays tribute to the many people I work with, and chronicles the everyday thoughts and feelings associated with the job. This book is a direct product of the blog.

Garage — Once referred to as "The Barn," its origin is from when trolleys were horse-drawn in the late 19th and early 20th centuries; before cable cars or electrified catenary wires; and, long before diesel-powered buses put trolley systems out of business in the 1940's. A facility where buses or light rail vehicles (LRV's) are stored and maintained, and also where some operators report for duty. An agency can have several garages within its district. It's also where operators, supervisors, Station Agents and management conduct business with each other. It can be a starting point for a run, and the point where evening and night runs end.

Holiday Schedule — Most transit agencies operate every day of the year. Because ridership is usually lower on a holiday, runs are often less frequent. Operators usually sign different runs on holidays if they volunteer or are too low in seniority to automatically have the day off.

Hours of Service (HOS) — Our transit agency mandates that bus drivers have more time to rest. Regular operators must have 10 hours off between shifts, while Extra Board Operators can report again after nine hours. Also under this agreement, we cannot work more than 70 hours in any one-week period nor can any operator work more than 13 consecutive days.

Jerry Springer Run — A line on which troublesome issues occur on a regular basis.

Jump Light Signal — A special traffic signal to allow buses priority to proceed from a bus stop at an intersection. Usually placed where a bus stop is at the front position of a turn lane, it is programmed to turn green a few seconds before the signal for adjacent lanes. Very helpful in rush hour periods when motorists usually refuse to yield the right-of-way to buses trying to re-enter traffic after servicing a stop during a red light.

Layover — A spot, or point in time, where a bus is temporarily out of service while the operator takes a break.

Light Rail Transit/Train (LRT) — The form of mass transit that involves vehicles which operate on tracks.

Light Rail Vehicle (LRV) — A commuter train. In Portland, they are powered by electricity provided by overhead catenary wires. The operator controls the vehicle from a secure cabin in the front. At the end of a line, the operator moves to the cabin at the opposite end of the vehicle.

Line — The geographic route over which a bus regularly travels, usually identified by a number. It is also given a "train," a term unrelated to Light Rail Vehicles, which is the identifier of a specific run on that route. For example, Line 33, Train One, is identified as 3301 and has a different schedule than 3302, etcetera.

Mini Run — Usually a commuter run, assigned to part-time operators. Many operators choose to remain part-time. They have the option of a "split," consisting of morning and afternoon shifts, or if their seniority is high enough, they can sign a "straight" mini run which averages about six hours in length.

Not in Service — A vehicle that is between routes (an "interline trip"), deadheading to a start or end point, or not mechanically able to continue in revenue service. An operator can also be taken out of service if they are sick, involved in a traffic accident, assaulted or incapable of operating for any number of reasons determined by a supervisor or dispatcher.

Offline Run — A route that changes once or several times during a shift. An operator could, for example, begin his day on one line and change to a different one for the rest of his shift.

Oversleep — When an operator is even one second late, or a "no-show," requiring another operator to drive their run, they are assessed this penalty. Since transit is a schedule-driven service, operators are expected to be punctual. A time-honored saying is that "if you're not 15 minutes early for work, you're late." An operator who is late for an assigned run is assessed an Oversleep by the Station Agent. The SA might assign different work to the operator, or send them home without pay. Operators with too many oversleeps during a specified period are often severely disciplined, up to and including termination.

Paddle — Device used to punish naughty operators. Not really. Actually, it's the portion of the published schedule or timetable which pertains specifically to the assigned block, or run. It tells an operator where a run begins, gives deadheading directions, lists recovery times and durations, and lists widely publicized, scheduled time points for the run. The time points operators see on their paddle correspond with the published schedules the general public uses to plan their trips on transit vehicles.

Parking Brake — Locks wheels in place so vehicle cannot move. Except, however, when the vehicle is on an icy road with minimal grade pointing up or down hill. Then, all bets are off. Whenever a bus stops at a layover point, an operator deploys the parking brake and puts the transmission in neutral before shutting off the engine. The parking brake is also used when passengers access the bike rack on the front of a bus, or when the ramp is deployed to board a person using a mobility device.

Passenger (or Rider) — Any person who chooses to travel on a transit agency vehicle. They are subject to all agency rules and regulations, and are compelled to cooperate with the Operator as directed. The Operator is the officer/agent representing the transit system in the field. We are entrusted to represent the district, its rules and laws. While responsible for ensuring the safety of everyone in or around our vehicle, Operators also have the official and legal authority to inspect, inform, and enforce the district's rules and procedures. Contrary to a widely-held yet incorrect belief, it is a privilege to ride transit, not a right. Privileges can be revoked; rights are inherent.

Pick — The routes a driver chooses to drive in a signup period. Each operator is assigned a seniority number based on the amount of time they have been employed in their current position. Operators choose their runs in order of their seniority; the most senior drivers get to pick first, and the remainder follow.

Pouch — Just as it sounds, but it's filled with all the goodies an operator needs for their route. Except for Ibuprofen, Imodium, porta-potty and pepper spray. It actually contains a route map, paddle, re-route info, extra roll of ticket paper, punch tickets if the printer quits working, standard operating procedures, schedule book and various forms. Each driver on a route has this vital item, and if they accidentally leave it on their bus when they return to the yard, they must do the Walk of Shame to retrieve it (walking against the "flow" of bus drivers heading home after a day of service, who actually remembered their own pouches).

Priority Seating — The front area of the bus normally reserved for seniors and people with disabilities. Sometimes, it is occupied by young people who have to be told to vacate the seats when qualified passengers board. An operator has the authority by law to assign proper seating.

Radio — Each bus is equipped with a two-way radio tuned to a frequency used by Dispatch for communication with front line workers. Extra Service operators, supervisors and maintenance personnel carry portables. Field Operations uses numerous radio frequencies to facilitate clear communications for supervisors, transit police, LIFT operations, LRT & Bus frequencies, transit security, not to mention recorded telephone lines. All these means of communication are available for public review, and several channels are monitored by citizens who advocate for accountable public transportation.

Ramp — Once upon a recent time, buses were equipped with a lift which extended out from the front door, then lowered to the curb for people in mobility devices to board; once the passenger was on the lift, it was raised over the steps to allow boarding. Today's low-floor buses have a ramp which deploys onto the ground to allow them to roll on/off the bus. This type of ramp is much easier, and less time-consuming to use; they are arguably safer in most cases.

Road Relief — When one operator relieves another while the bus remains in revenue service, at a certain time point on the route. The new operator takes over driving the route, and the previous driver is either done for the day or off to drive a different run.

If an Operator who is scheduled to relieve another fails to do so, they are assessed an Oversleep at the very least. A truly different scenario from "Relieving Myself," one of the posts featured in this book.

Road Supervisor (RS) — An extremely vital transit job. Road Supervisors are our equal partners, there to help us all deliver a consistently safe, efficient, and sustainable service to the public. First agency personnel to respond to an operator-involved accident, they assess the situation and work to calm the operator. They're often the first to behold grisly accident scenes. A RS is responsible for documenting the progression of an accident scene, investigation of possible causes, and conveying such reports to the accident review committee. When an operator needs assistance outside of Dispatch, these supervisors respond. Clearing jammed fare boxes, handling minor repair jobs, or assessing any number of sticky situations, the RS must be prepared for any eventuality. They aid and calm operators who have been assaulted. The RS is the next highest "authority" in the field. When there is a disruption in service due to an unruly passenger, the RS is dispatched to the scene to assist in whatever way helps return a vehicle to regular service. I've even seen some handing out cold water on hot summer days to overheated operators. During icy winter storms, they offer aid to operators maneuvering through treacherous situations. Giving advice in all matters of revenue service operation, they respond to operators in need of assistance, and help us return to service on the Line. They direct traffic around disabled buses, while also helping passengers transfer to the next in-service bus. Their primary function is to "observe and report" transit information. I can't say enough about their job because I still haven't seen all they do. Truly our brothers and sisters in the trenches.

Rock & Roll — Also known as "Bob & Weave" or "Walkin' the Butt Cheeks." How an operator moves in the driver's seat in order to see around vision barriers in front of and to the sides of a bus. Operators may vary in their technique with time, but this is the only way to see pedestrians obscured by the A-frame side window on a newer bus.

Route — A specific bus line defined by the course it takes. Some are called "short lines" when they stop before the end of the line, or only run in one direction during rush hours. Still others could be Express Lines, having the same route as another but only servicing a few specific stops rather than all.

Running Hot — Being early instead of exactly on time. Operators who consistently run hot are unpopular with regular passengers who may miss their bus if it glides by their stop earlier than it is scheduled to. Conversely, an operator is "Running Down" if they are more than a few minutes late.

Scan — The constant eye, head and body movements an operator employs to view a 180-degree-plus view of the scene in front of and around their bus. A vigilant operator's eyes are never fixated in one direction for more than two seconds, or they lose valuable peripheral vision. (We are taught the "Five Points of the Smith System for Defensive Driving," which are: aim high in turning; get the big picture; keep your eyes moving; make yourself seen by others, and leave yourself an exit strategy.) This highlights the importance of passengers ensuring we see them at night. One brief flash of light may not be seen by an operator who is constantly scanning, so persistence by intending passengers in alerting a driver to their presence in the dark is vital to avoid being passed up.

Service Animal — An animal which is professionally trained to assist a person with disabilities. These are usually dogs, but can include other animals. Unfortunately, many passengers tend to dishonestly portray their pets as "service animals." Pets are usually allowed to ride, but only if confined to portable cages;

this rule is to help ensure the safety of other passengers as well as true service animals.

Service Brake — The air brake system regularly used by an operator of a bus, situated next to the accelerator. The only thing preventing 40,000 lbs. of machinery from flattening a cyclist removing their bicycle from the rack is the operator's right foot, covering the service brake. Pneumatic pressure applied on the pedal is variable, so it's very important to tell the operator before stepping in front of a bus so s/he can deploy the parking brake as an extra and crucial safety measure.

Shagger — A transit employee who moves a bus in the yard to and from the fuel line, wash rack or maintenance bay among other duties involving vehicle storage and care.

Signup — An event where operators, station agents and other transit employees choose their work for the upcoming three-month period, in order of their seniority. Those with the highest seniority choose earliest and have the advantage of picking the best runs available.

SIP (Service Improvement Program) — A negative complaint on an operator's record lodged by a passenger to the transit agency's "customer service" department. In theory, these become suggestions on how to improve our overall performance. Conversely, passengers also call in compliments about operator performance, which are a welcome addition to our personnel file. (See "Commendation.")

Spotter — Anyone who assists an operator in backing up a bus; also the person who checks a bus in after a run and instructs the driver where to park it.

Station Agent — Supervisors who direct daily operations of a transit garage, an operator's first line of communication. SA's directly supervise extra board operators, assign special duties, oversee time off requests, monitor operator hours-of-service requirements, update and distribute route pouches, facilitate time off requests, receive phone calls from operators reporting sick time or requesting extra board assignments, as well as many other duties. They work with Dispatch to coordinate added bus or light rail lines, and instruct operators on transit rules and protocol as requested or necessary. Extremely vital to transit, SA's coordinate transit operations with Dispatch.

Stop Request Cord — A yellow-colored cord running the length of either side of a bus, which when pulled, activates a bell and/or a light which alerts the operator of a passenger's stop request. There is also a yellow tape or button located beside each mobility device position, attached to the underside of the jump seat; it alerts the Operator of a request to deploy the ramp at the next stop. It is useful to have a distinguishing stop request signal/ tone/light to prompt the operator in advance that the next stop will need to have plenty extra space on the sidewalk to deploy the ramp or lift. We must properly position the bus to allow our passengers with mobility aids to safely disembark without running into danger after leaving the end of the ramp. Contrary to public belief, this cord doesn't magically halt the bus on a dime when a cellphone-entranced passenger rings the bell as the bus is sailing past their stop.

TDA (Turn Down Assignment) — When an operator asks to be relieved of the day's work for whatever reason. This results in a loss of pay for the hours not worked, but if they've already worked eight hours prior to the TDA, they incur no chargeable time loss.

Time Loss — When an operator is not performing the work he/ she is assigned due to illness or other absence. Even though bus operators accrue sick leave, they can be penalized for missing too much work.

Time Point — A specific location on a route from where an operator must never arrive "early" (more than 59 seconds). If they reach it and are running late, they are not required to stop unless passengers want to board or exit; an exception to this exists on the transit mall where bus operators are expected to service specific stops.

Track — A specific lane in the bus yard where buses are parked.

Train —NOT of the freight variety. This is the identifier of a run. A bus operator is driving a Line (Route Number) with a specific number which differentiates it from another driver's run on the same line. For example, Ollie Operator is on Line 12 Train 01 (1201), while Olive may be driving 1204 when they pass each other from opposite directions.

Trainer — A supervisor who instructs employees how to operate a bus or light rail vehicle. They usually have many years of in-service experience, giving them the knowledge necessary to instruct people how to function responsibly as an operator. They also write training curriculum and course syllabi, produce media presentations for classes, and provide instruction on any new equipment. Trainers also conduct "Ride-Alongs" to periodically check on the performance of regular operators well after that operator has long-since advanced past any probationary period. Trainers can be dispatched to observe the practices of regular operators when there is cause for some concern. They conduct routine re-training and re-certification of regular operators, both for annual requirements as well as after an operator has been away from regular service for an extended period due to illness or injury.

Transit Operator — A highly trained, licensed, and regularly certified professional who operates a bus or LRV, and holds a valid Commercial Driver's License and current medical certificate.

Transfer — Usually a piece of paper, with pertinent time and date information, purchased by a passenger which serves as their receipt and ticket to ride. It can be used on several modes of transit agency vehicles as long as it is valid. Usually non-transferable, meaning exiting passengers cannot legally give it to another passenger to save them from paying their own fare.

Transit — A system supported by a municipality and its citizens to provide safe, reliable transportation. A transit district may not necessarily be an agency of government, but in fact may be a government in its own right, thus a municipal corporation. Some transit agencies have their own district attorney and police force. They're comparable to a massive rogue, totalitarian government with no accountability or cause for transparency because they are not governed by elected officers.

Transit App — A smartphone application which allows people to track transit vehicle arrival/departure times, buy fare, and get updates on transit-related issues.

Transit Police — The "code" enforcement authority of the transit district, resourced by sworn officers of adjacent police forces and charged with keeping order in transit-related situations.

Transitway — A dedicated right-of-way lane of traffic solely reserved for transit vehicles. Most often found on a city's downtown transit mall, it is intended to keep auto traffic separate from transit vehicles to ensure safe operation and eliminate gridlock. Usually a favorite lane for impatient motorists who want to take an illegal shortcut to bypass heavy traffic in regular traffic lanes. A sore point with Portland transit operators is our city's refusal to enforce traffic code violations in this area, thereby creating countless dangerous situations.

Turn & Burn — When an operator reaches the end of the line so late the recovery time has passed, they commence the next run without a break. This can create a dangerous work environment because operators need sufficient break time to use the restroom, remain mentally alert and stretch sore muscle groups prior to continuing a run.

Union Rep — An operator (or mechanic, etc.) who volunteers and is usually elected to a position in which they represent a section of union members from an agency location or garage. In disputes with management, operators are allowed representation in hearings and review boards, where their union rep lobbies on their behalf. Union members are lawfully guaranteed the right to have representation present as a safeguard against unfair or unsafe labor practices. Non-union employees do not have this protection, nor do they have this advantage in negotiating wage and benefit agreements.

WORK — A four-letter word ending in "k."

WRDO — Work Regular Day Off — When an operator needs a few extra bucks above a normal paycheck, they volunteer to work on their day(s) off. Operators are allowed to work overtime if they don't violate Hours of Service rules. An operator employed by our transit agency can only work 13 straight days, or no more than 70 hours in a one-week period before they are required to have at least one day off. These regulations ensure operators have enough rest time to allow for safe operation of their vehicles while in service.

Yard — The area at each garage where buses are stored between runs, with each lane defined by track numbers.

Yellow Line — A colored line painted on the floor of a bus, located in the front section directly behind the operator's seat. Passengers who cross beyond this line into the prohibited area while a bus is in service are violating Federal Motor Carrier Safety Administration regulations.

Yield Signal — A flashing red triangle on the rear of the bus with the word "YIELD" prominently displayed within. Oregon state law prohibits vehicles from passing a transit vehicle merging into traffic after servicing a stop. Most motorists don't care about this unenforced law, as evidenced by showing me their driving test score as they fly by it.

Kudos and Appreciation

Without the love and support of so many, I would never have imagined myself at this point, thanking them for helping me realize this lifelong dream. Beginning with the powerful love and guidance of my cherished parents, to the unwavering support from my beloved wife and children, and my one grandchild, I am truly blessed. Add them to a treasure chest of brothers, in-laws, aunts and uncles, cousins and nephews, teachers and classmates, allies and adversaries, and I am luckier than most.

To those of you who have read my blog, words cannot give justice to the gratitude I feel for your support. Without you, these words would ring hollow in the enormous blogosphere.

From the Beginning...

Throughout my life, I've been graced by the enduring friendship of many. They have all contributed to my life in many ways, and I am eternally grateful for them. By listing some of them here, I offer my deepest gratitude and love. Katie Montaño, Roger Kelley, Hans Wang, Robert Booker, John DiMarco, Mark Felix, John Armas, Joel and Debbie Nuttall, Wayne Kyle, Lenny Smith, Craig and Joan Bull, Miss Pat, Nina and Rod, Louis Hyde, Dan and Linda Carlson, Tobi Perham, Oma Guard, Terry and JoAnne Gilmer, Rita Garcia, Bob Scoville, Ray and Sarah Woyak, Edie Brown, Dave Turton, Al & Allee

Steinberg, Mike and Wendy Watson, Don Steinberg, Joe Padilla, Edie Brown, Irene Daniels, David and Nancy Haase, Marilyn Buckelew, David English, John Sowers, Andy and Racquel Arenz, Mike Sauceda; Kay McVicker-Rippere, Kathy Berlyn, Telena Phillips, the Lizaragga Family, Sandra Owens, Walt Rodriguez, Michelle Wahlmeier, and many others, especially including my entire family, who have always supported me.

From My Portland Fellows...

To think I didn't know a soul when we arrived in 2002, it amazes me how many people here have become tremendously vital to my happiness. Here are some of the most endearing, sweet and supportive friends I've had the honor of enjoying valuable fun with: Mark and Celest Elmer, Angelique and Carlos Ramirez, Liz Halperin, Tom Patterson, Walt and Carol LaChappelle, Jodi Neelin, Tracy Varnell Family, James Pepe, Pat Oles, Roger Kofler, and scores of others who may be unnamed here but hold a dear place in my heart.

... to My Brothers and Sisters of the Road:

I cannot begin to name the hundreds of brothers and sisters I have the honor of working with, but I couldn't publish this without thanking those who constantly amaze me with their love and support. Instead of naming you all, and possibly forgetting someone or putting you in the unfortunate and uncomfortable position due to my insistence upon anonymity, I beg your pardon for this blanket note of appreciation.

Many of you have been with me since this bloggery began. You kept me level-headed and focused on what's important to all of us. This initially shy voice grew from a whisper in the wilderness to a raucous roar from a busy overpass, thanks to your encouragement. You slapped me down when I became too big for my britches, then helped me up again.

My fellow operators both here in Portland and across the globe are my true inspiration. Your bravery in the face of the increasingly-violent society through which we weave keeps me dedicated to speaking up for all we face "out there." Without us, those in management would be stuck in some dreary corporate nowhere. We make economies roll; our wheels are huge cogs in the machinery of progress. Thanks for all you've done for me, but most important, for doing what we do with integrity, efficiency, and grit. You all contribute to improving my life, and your friendships strengthen me. May your lives be filled with love and peace, and may you always keep all six on the road.

Those Who Give Me Creative Inspiration:

Abraham Lincoln, Robert Frost, Mark Twain, Charles Dickens, Emily Dickinson, Maya Angelou, Tom Petty, Edward Abbey, James Michener, George Carlin, Stephen King, Will Rogers, Louis Armstrong, George Burns, Martin Luther King Jr., Theodore Roosevelt, Harry Truman, John F. Kennedy, James Taylor and Chuck Maultsby.

And Last but Not Necessarily Least:

I truly appreciate the support of all my Amalgamated Transit Union 757 brothers and sisters, along with all chapters worldwide, for without your solidarity we'd have little hope for a better future. Although I can't name all my fellow operators who support my writing, I would be remiss for not giving kudos to Tom Horton and Sam Bryan, who have encouraged me from the beginning. Many thanks to fellow bloggers Al Margulies, Mr. "Roll Easy" Dan Christensen, and Robert at BusTropical.org for advice and encouragement. Their writing offers people more unique views about life in and around the transit world.

Thank you to my employer as well, for even though we don't always agree on vital issues, you allow me the honor to serve Portland as a bus operator. When I've written posts critical of management, it is with hopes that my words strike a chord that resonates in a manner that affords us an opportunity to improve relations and foster constructive dialog. If we can once again work together, Portland's transit will once again be the world's finest.

To those who bought this book, you honor me with your patronage. I hope it gave you a realistic view of what it's like to drive a bus. If I did it right, perhaps you had more than a few chuckles, shed an occasional tear, and learned how we can peacefully co-exist on Portland's busy streets and achieve safe travels.

Thank you all for believing in me when self-doubt threatened, giving me artistic inspiration, and finding the good in me even when I scowl and growl or make some stupid gaffe "out there." I am forever grateful, and eternally honored to know you all.

61732547R00184

Made in the USA
Middletown, DE
14 January 2018